RECALIBRATION ON   IMPRECISION AND INFIDELITY

RECALIBRATION: on imprecision and infidelity

Proceedings Catalog of the 38th Annual Conference of the Association for Computer Aided Design in Architecture (ACADIA)

Editors

Phillip Anzalone, Marcella Del Signore + Andrew John Wit

Copy Editing

Pascal Massinon + Mary O'Malley

Graphic Identity

Emilio Pérez

Layout + Design

Marcella Del Signore + Andrew John Wit

Printer

IngramSpark

Publication Editors

Phillip Anzalone, Marcella Del Signore + Andrew John Wit

Cover Image

Emilio Pérez

Conference hosted by the Universidad Iberoamericana, Mexico City

ISBN 978-0-692-17729-7

PROJECTS CATALOG

RECALIBRATION
O   N IMPR   ECISION
AND IN   FID ELITY

Projects Catalog of the 38th Annual Conference of the
Association for Computer Aided Design in Architecture

UNIVERSIDAD IBEROAMERICANA, MEXICO CITY

Editors
Phillip Anzalone, Marcella Del Signore + Andrew John Wit

acadia   IBERO

CONTENTS

Introduction
"LITTLE INFIDELITIES"

Pablo Kobayashi, Chair
Universidad Iberoamericana
Founding Partner, Protocolos

Brian Slocum, Co-Chair
Universidad Iberoamericana
Principal, Diverse Projects

The task we have set forth for ourselves with this year's ACADIA conference is to focus the discussion on our influence on processes of material expression and behavior. We see computation, fabrication, design agency, and the truths we encounter (or deny) in data as potential means by which we shape these processes. This gathering provides an opportunity to expand the discourse through the recognition that contemporary architectural production must inevitably result from the mediation between an "ideal" precision/accuracy obtainable through digital methodologies, and the imprecision and infidelity of the physical/material world around us, simultaneously acknowledging the interrelated importance of both analog and digital processes, and privileging neither one over the other.

In these Peer-Reviewed Projects, we consider the physical products of research—the material manifestations of the computational strategies employed—barometers for the present discussion and therefore useful instruments for the rhetorical emphasis of the conference. Of the many lines of investigation selected for publication, perhaps the only characteristic that we may employ to connect them is that they are ostensibly driven by rigorous methodologies: the testing of a set of hypotheses through the implementation of defined protocols, iteration, and the repeatability and analysis of the results. In this analysis, the degree of success or failure (if indeed any failure is acknowledged) is judged by a set of criteria determined prior to the execution of the experiment, and these in turn are conditioned by a theoretical framework, a set of paradigms within which we operate, whether consciously or unconsciously.

Throughout these processes, we are confronted with many little infidelities—instances of low fidelity in the system—that have the power to enrich or cloud the investigation. An infidelity is an act of deception, in this case a material or method that delivers not just an unexpected or surprising result, but one that runs contrary to an expected or desired behavior, whether that expectation was explicit or implicit in the postulate. When faced with these material dissimulations, two options are available: discard the outcome as an outlier, or incorporate it as a natural byproduct of the investigation. In either scenario, it is incumbent upon the investigator to arrive at an understanding of the causes of this infidelity, on one hand to confirm its eccentricity and to avoid future glitches in the system, or on the other to predict similar performance in future iterations, thereby enabling the potential exploitation of the behavior.

Whether we suffer from or merely tolerate these little aberrations, there is also the threat of another more insidious form of infidelity, more egregious yet more easily overlooked. This is when preconceptions lead to misinterpretation or outright circumvention of results. To begin, the use of the word "project" situates us in the midst of a contradiction. This could be dismissed as a semantic distinction, if not for the manner in which we are/were all educated as architects. To project is to impose; it implies forethought about consequences—desired outcomes—rather than the establishment of protocols that make a certain hypothesized result possible, even likely, but never foregone. We project ourselves in the project. And since perfect objectivity is impossible, this is inevitable, and therefore all the more critical that we recognize its role in the process. Since our ostensible aim is to investigate, we must ultimately suspend disbelief, abandon all pretense of control, and let the investigation run its course in all its messy imprecision.

Either directly or obliquely, the Projects included here all undoubtedly deal with these imperfections and deviations. It is our hope that this year's conference provides a forum for addressing them head-on as the product rather than the residue of the research. Framing the entire discussion is not simply the understanding of, but also a call to rejoice in the faults and eccentricities in the system, situating ourselves within and celebrating the history of an epistemics of uncertainty, from Norbert Wiener's "negative feedback" in Cybernetics, to chaos theory, and more recently to the reaction to this uncertainty in architectural practice described as a "surplus of precision" in Francesca Hughes's *The Architecture of Error*. This requires a constant questioning of the validity of the paradigms that condition our work within these contexts: how we view the problem at hand (indeed whether or not we even perceive a problem), formulate hypotheses, and later evaluate the fitness of the solutions. In the face of indeterminacy, uncertainty, and unpredictability, this year's ACADIA "recalibration" aims to understand the inherent infidelities of systems in which we have been working, and then to embrace them as a means to new tactics and increased knowledge, rather than attempt to reinvest in mechanisms of control.

Recalibrating
Computational Processes, Materials + Production Systems

Phillip Anzalone, *Technical Chair*
New York City College of Technology
Principal, aa64

Marcella Del Signore, *Technical Chair*
New York Institute of Technology
Principal, X-Topia

Andrew John Wit, *Technical Chair*
Temple University
wito* *"Laboratory for Intelligent Environments"*

Over ACADIA's long history, this community has continued to push the boundaries of architecture though the development and integration of novel research in the areas of computation, production, and design. Although this research creates novel avenues and solutions for explorations in design and practice, there often remains a disconnect from the larger architectural community. ACADIA's Project Catalog acts to link academic and professional communities, where cutting-edge research centered around computation and production is exemplified and made accessible through the display of built projects created by the ACADIA community, both inside and outside of academia. Bridging multiple scales and disciplines, these built projects act as a catalyst for the reimagining of traditional methods of design and production for the design community at large.

Recently though, this connection has begun to fade, as architectural research centered around computation, digital fabrication, and robotics has begun to over-embrace, and possibly feel dependent upon the production of artifacts and environments that are predictable, precise, optimized, and repeatable, utilizing tools that typically place these unique processes out of the research of the larger design community. Although novel in their pursuits, these projects can feel sterile, tending to focus on the tools and processes rather than the design of artifacts and environments, potentially minimizing their impact on the larger community. In contrast, the current conference highlights a shift towards the embracing of uncertainty as a productive design tool, where processes, materials, tools, and production methodologies are constantly recalibrated, potentially allowing for the emergence of alternate modes of design and production. The continuous tension between predictability/unpredictability, precision/imprecision, certainty/uncertainty allows for the emergence of design processes that reposition our vantage point towards recalibrated computational approaches and imprecise modes of production. This apparent duality, deployed

both as productive and generative, fosters novel forms of interdependency that rely less on deterministic, standard machine-driven approaches and more on recalibrated, refocused and renegotiated sets of boundaries. In this simultaneous mediation, the relationship among computation, tools, techniques, and production is embraced through the lens of error, inaccuracy, and imprecision in design, computation, materials, and production. In this framework, the role of the designer becomes less dependent on accurate registration and predictive protocols; on the contrary, the designer embraces the unstable/unsettled means of control that allow for the emergence of unexpected outcomes.

The Project Catalog for the ACADIA 2018 Conference presents a body of work that exists within the recalibrated, exposing some of the new fringe boundaries and emerging opportunities for the implementation of computational applied research in architecture and design. In this volume, multiple design trajectories are offered as means to fully embrace the "controlled" and the "uncontrolled," not as a binary dichotomy of exclusion, but rather as a process of reconciliation. The presented work aims to uncover and celebrate these recalibrated processes of design/production within the current discourse of computation in design. The volume is organized in distinct sections— Award Winners and Keynote Speakers, Exhibition Projects, and Peer-Reviewed Projects—which are not conceived as separated entities, but rather as codependent registrations of recalibrated forms of applied research in architectural practice.

The Award Winners and Keynote Speakers' contribution reflects on the current impact of computational theory/design/production in practice, education, and pedagogy. These works are presented as individual research trajectories and contextualized within this year's conference theme. The Exhibition Projects are grounded in the architectural context of Mexico City and the Universidad Iberoamericana, as ACADIA 2018 host city and institution. They aim to investigate the rich sociocultural context and technologically driven communities within which experimentations exist, and they aim to foster a lens for applied research that attempts to transcend the known borders of design through the merging of context and technology. The Peer-Reviewed Projects present design and applied research framed through a range of scales, processes, tools, and protocols manifested as built/unbuilt, physical/digital artifacts and environments. The projects are contextualized within two main categories that reflect critically on the notion of recalibration in computationally driven processes and in material and production systems.

"RECALIBRATION in Computational Processes"

expands on the potential of imprecision, error, and unpredictability in design and computation through the deployment of recalibrated tools, scales, and processes that are inherently codependent and interrelated— whether manifested as AI, AR/VR, adaptive systems or nonstandard machines. The projects presented in this section interrogate the possibilities of recalibrated computational processes that integrate multiple streams of applied research to delineate, amplify, and transgress normative computational protocols. Through these built projects several threads emerge to highlight current trends in computational processes, which seek to render themselves as less autonomous and favor the increase of relational complexity. Whether they take the form of artifacts or environments, the projects offer an array of explorations that open up to unpredictable recombinatory computational protocols among robotics, virtual and augmented reality, sensors, responsive environments, machine learning, AI, data-driven processes, and simulations. The recombinatory nature of these categories allows us to reflect once again on the meaning of "idealized" precision achieved in computational processes and the "apparent" control of the machine

and the designer over accuracy of the process itself. The varied nature of the projects presented in this section privileges design responses that challenge these notions in favor of an emergent ground where the continuous negotiation between a high and low degree of control and fidelity extends and amplifies tools and methodologies for computational design.

"RECALIBRATION in Material + Production Systems"

reflects on material and production practices that test, explore, and reframe margins of uncertainty and infidelities in matter, fabrication, robotics, manufacturing techniques, and hybrid systems. The projects presented in this section ask us to reconsider the limits of precision over processes that privilege inaccuracy and infidelity as generative design variables in material and manufacturing practices. Material- and fabrication-based procedures inherently embed in their processes the evaluation of tolerance, incongruencies, and infidelity to facilitate and transcend the gap between conception and construction. This gap intrinsically embraces variance, discrepancy, and infidelity to enable the production of variables and a richer array of design possibilities. The projects presented reveal and celebrate a body of applied research that pushes the limits of what we consider precise in material and manufacturing practices, allowing for unpredictable behaviors that exists in the physical world to be seen both as constraints and opportunities for accurate/ inaccurate, controlled/uncontrolled, digital/analog hybrid artifacts and environments. The constant duality between these protocols open up to a plethora of variables and outputs driven by nonlinear processes enacted by design methodologies that take into account low-res/process-variation tolerances that are perhaps less reliant on the direct translation of expected outputs, but have more potential to embody forms of design inquiry on the varied nature of recalibrated material and production systems in computational design.

RECALIBRATION: on imprecision and infidelity
KEYNOTES & AWARDS

Philippe Block

KEYNOTE

Prof. Dr. Philippe Block is Professor of Architecture and Structure at the Institute of Technology in Architecture (ITA) in the Department of Architecture at ETH Zürich, where he directs the Block Research Group (BRG) together with Dr. Tom Van Mele. A member of the faculty since 2009, Prof. Block was promoted to full professor in 2017 and also became Director of the Swiss National Centre of Competence in Research (NCCR) Digital Fabrication and Deputy Head of ITA.

Trained in architecture and structural engineering at the Vrije Universiteit Brussel (VUB) in Brussels, Belgium (MSc 2003). and at the Massachusetts Institute of Technology (MIT) in Cambridge, MA, USA (SMArchS 2005, PhD 2009), his research and teaching are located at the interface of both fields. For his PhD in Building Technology at MIT (2009), under the guidance of Prof. John Ochsendorf, he developed "thrust network analysis," an innovative approach for assessing the safety of historic vaulted structures with unreinforced masonry and for designing funicular (compression-only) three-dimensional structures.

Prof. Block's multidisciplinary research interests span graphical design and analysis techniques, computational form finding and optimization, structural and architectural geometry, digital fabrication and appropriate construction. With the BRG, and as a founding partner of Ochsendorf DeJong & Block (ODB Engineering), Prof. Block applies these interests into practice for the structural analysis of historic vaulted masonry with complex geometry and the design and engineering of compression structures pushing innovation in unreinforced masonry. Projects range from unique signature vaults in cut stone, such as the MIT Collier Memorial in Cambridge, MA, USA, or the Armadillo Vault at the 2016 Venice Architecture Biennale, to sustainable construction solutions for developing countries, such as 2009s "world building of the year," the Mapungubwe Interpretation Centre in Limpopo, South Africa, or the Droneport project with the Norman Foster Foundation for Rwanda. More recent ventures have focused on the use of recycled or grown materials, as in the vault made from bricks of compressed, shredded Tetra Pak for the Ideas City Festival in New York City in 2015 or the MycoTree, a naturally grown mycelium structure for the Seoul Biennale for Architecture and Urbanism 2017, both made in collaboration with Prof. Dirk Hebel of the Karlsruhe Institute of Technology. Finally, the NEST HiLo Unit, to be built in Dübendorf, Switzerland, in 2019 in collaboration with the Chair of Architecture and Building Systems, Prof. Dr. Arno Schlüter of ETH Zürich, is a flagship project that unites several research streams. It has already resulted in floor system demonstrators that show how the methods allow for drastic reductions in material use, and a full-scale, 1:1 prototype of the roof shell, built using a uniquely innovative cable-net and fabric formwork system.

Prof. Block has received numerous awards and recognitions for his research, including the Hangai Prize (2007) and the Tsuboi Award (2010) from the International Association of Shell and Spatial Structures (IASS) for innovative contributions to the field, the Edoardo Benvenuto prize (2012) for "scientific research on the history of Structural Mechanics and Art of Building," the Berlin Art Prize for Architecture (2018), given by the Academy of Arts,

1 MycoTree - Load-bearing mycelium tree structure. "Beyond Mining – Urban Growth", Seoul Biennale of Architecture and Urbanism, 2017. (Photo © Carlina Teteris).

2   KnitCrete - Knitted textile formwork for complex concrete structures, 2017. (Photo © Block Research Group, ETH Zurich / Mariana Popescu).

3   ETH Waste Pavilion, Ideas City Festival NYC, 2015. (Photo © Albert Veserka).

and most recently the Rössler Prize (2018) for most promising young professor at ETH Zürich. He was also awarded the Golden Owl from the Department of Architecture at ETH Zürich for engagement and excellence in teaching (2010). His work was exhibited at the Design Triennial 2009 in NYC, USA, and at the 2012 and 2016 editions of the Venice Architecture Biennale.

He serves on the editorial boards of the International Journal of Space Structures and the Journal of the IASS and is on the academic committee of the LafargeHolcim Foundation for Sustainable Construction. An active member of the IASS, he is a member of the executive council and co-leads the working groups on concrete shells and graphical statics. In addition to numerous peer-reviewed publications, he is also co-author of the book *Faustformel Tragwerksentwurf* (2013, 2015), co-editor of Shell *Structures for Architecture: Form Finding and Optimization* (2014), and co-author of *Beyond Bending: Reimagining Compression Shells* (2017).

4   3D-printed funicular floor, 2016. (Photo © Block Research Group, ETH Zurich / Matthias Rippmann).

5   Armadillo Vault, "Beyond Bending", 15th International Architecture Exhibition - La Biennale di Venezia, 2016. (Photo © Iwan Baan).

6   Droneport prototype, 15th International Architecture Exhibition - La Biennale di Venezia, 2016. (Photo © Norman Foster Foundation / Nigel Young).

7   HiLo roof prototype, Robotic Fabrication Lab, ETH Zurich, 2017. (Photo © ETH Zurich / Michael Lyrenmann).

RECALIBRATION ON IMPRECISION AND INFIDELITY

Francesca Hughes

KEYNOTE

Some Indiscrete Notes on the Universal Discrete Machine

The *histoire longue durée* of computation is above all a testament to our desire to house in the machine the automated correction of our own errors. If to err is human, to design corrective systems is all the more so. Ramon Llull's thirteenth-century paper machines were to correct our faith; Ivan Sutherland's Sketchpad algorithms, to curtail our sloppy drafting. In what was the beginning of predictive programming, errors would be eliminated before they could ever be made by simply never registering within the system. The prehistory of corrective algorithms, from their medieval origins to the 1800s, or what Thomas Khun calls the Second Scientific Revolution, charts a now newly familiar course from qualitative to quantitative reasoning, powered by the measure of all. Data feeds logic; logic generates new "truths." This is all predicated on the vagaries of precision—what and how we measure in the first place. The eighteenth-century project for a Universal Language, which through its extreme reduction could then be universally rolled out to rewrite (and implicitly redesign) all, led to the formulation of discrete inputs that secured computation's ultimately binary rule, and the exclusion of that which could not—or would not—be measured. As Leibniz had anticipated, calculation became the new "truth" and the unmeasurable was exiled to a domain outside of this axiomatic paradigm.

Friedrich Kittler describes the binary paradigm as the logical product of the zero-sum game of warfare: you win or you lose. Nothing else counts in its eternal present. In 1967 Turing's "manic cutter," as Kittler named it, became IBM's city-designing computer, Man and Computer, which claimed it could "calculate the desires of all of its residents." This was itself a startling prefiguration of the "manic cutting" behind the operations of parametricism's highly reductive architectural "truths" that followed a few decades later. Each are a direct legacy of the reterritorialization of thought by the Enlightenment project to render everything in discrete terms. Implicit in the question of ACADIA's "Recalibration" this year is a desire to interrogate the costs of the discrete and readmit the undeniable exactitude of analogue analytic models, of the non-discrete. That is, to question how any maximally deterministic system can ever possibly reconcile its eclipsing of the never fully knowable property of material life, not to mention the compelling authority of the random.

Architecture's very particular relations to this historical trajectory are uniquely acute. Suffice to say our engagement with precision is congenitally imprecise. The various mantras that organize the historiography of architecture's twentieth century, as we recite them ad nauseum ("materials got more honest," "ornament was removed," "solid became ephemeral," "linearity delivered the uniformity of mass production," etc.), all quietly saw to a rise in precision whose ever-fattening margins of excess were, like all excess, symptomatic of a pathology: our special fear of material error. As with all pathologies, normal logic does not apply—the more we cornered error, the more we feared it; similarly the more we armored our methodologies with precision-enforcing regimes, the more exquisite the errors they produced. Within this, precision—itself historically (ironically) a most imprecise term—aided and abetted by its metaphoric promiscuity within our discourses, quietly

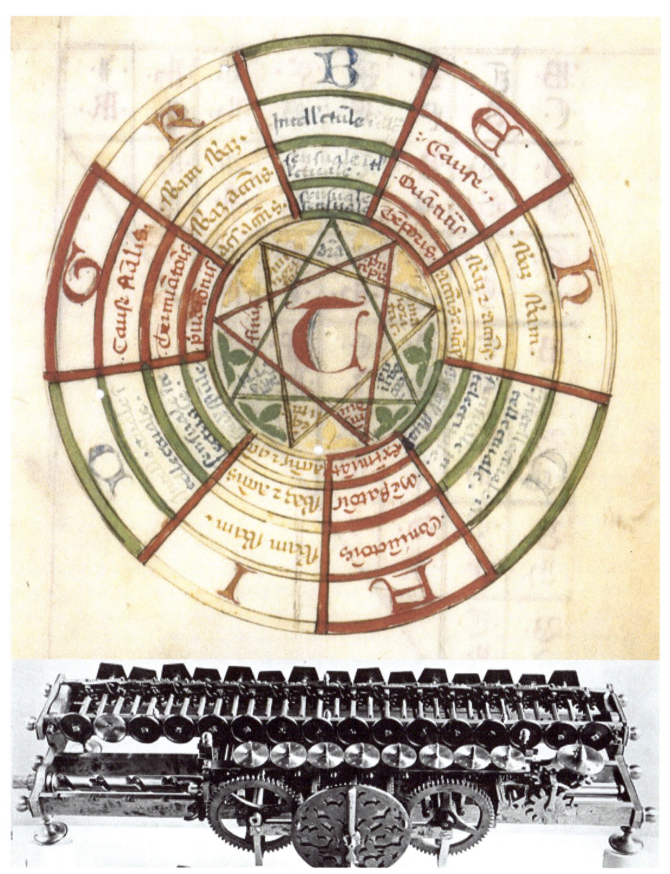

1   Top: Ramon Lull, Seconda Figura mnemonic wheel. Johannes Bulons, *Commentary on Ramon Lull Ars Generalis et Ultima*, Venice, 1438. Bodleian Libraries, Oxford. Bottom: Gottfried Wilhelm Leibniz, Stepped Reckoner without the cover, 1694. *Encyklopädie der Mathematischen Wissenschaften mit Einschluss ihrer Anwendungen*, Vol. 2 Arithmetic und Algebra, Druck und Verlag von E. G. Teubner, Leipzig, 1904.

RECALIBRATION ON IMPRECISION AND INFIDELITY

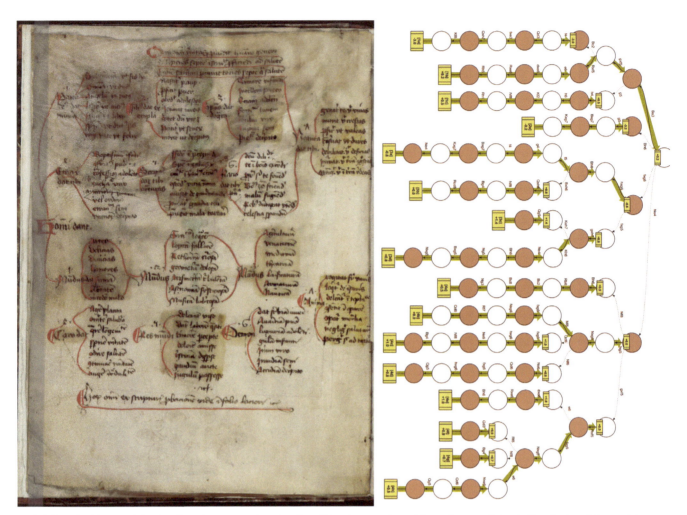

2   Left: Flowchart from early fourteenth-century mnemonic system from Cistercian monastery of Kamp, Germany; Beinecke Rare Book and Manuscript Library, Yale University. Right: Chess decision tree, Kevin Binz, 2015.

cleaved from its contract with veracity. A greater degree of precision no longer necessarily yields a more exact (truer) measure. The saturation resolution of military grade satellite images, duly combined with the authority of mechanical objectivity, both arch signatures of veracity, now promises "truth" itself. And yet we find in their highly mediated artifice, as with gaffs in image recognition software, that the testimony of the digital image too is in crisis. Like all highly refined systems of logic, they too are producing their own equally refined falsehoods.

Such are the pathologies at play in these relations that the convergence of architecture's fetishization of precision with the essentially corrective project of computation brought about not a rationalization of architecture's redundant precision, but a further elaboration of its now baroque capacities. When we draw brick walls to more decimal places than we can remember, any logic of appropriate approximation is long gone.

Modernism's fear of material error constituted a powerful

undertow in all its material relations. Articulated as the ideological division of materials that lie from materials that don't, the rejection of anisotropic materials in favor of the easy predictability of the isotropic laid the ground not only for faster (and ultimately, computed) truth to necessarily be better truth, but more crucially, for the predicted truth to necessarily be even better truth. Von Neumann's prophecy—"All stable processes we shall predict; all unstable processes we shall control"—came home to roost. Measurement of Kittler's eternal present was no longer enough. Measure of past events allowed the possibility to predict measures of future events via the temporal loop of induction, and then to ostensibly correct the future itself. Now David Hume's fallacy of induction, the Achilles heel of machine learning, haunts our every move: How will we know if we are simply over-fitting? Simply seeing patterns and hallucinating logics where none exist? As we measure the materials with which we build—their behavior and performance—they in turn also "measure" us back: not only our errors, but also our duplicity, our gullibility, our pathologies.

3 Left: Operative (possibly Timothy Johnson) using a light-pen to delete a line in Ivan Sutherland's Sketchpad program run on a TX2 Console at MIT in 1962. Courtesy of The MIT Museum. Right: Gest, a personalized gesture controlled wearable that allows sufficiently exact input to control a computer or mobile device. Apotact Labs, 2016.

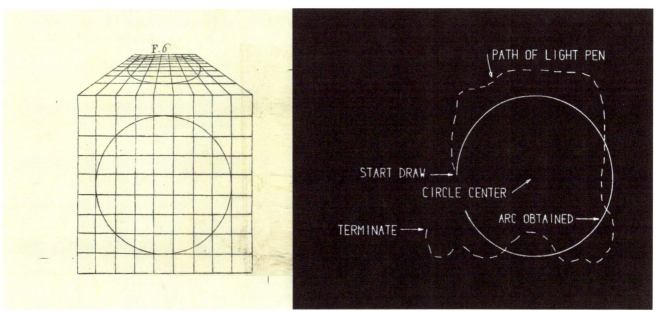

4 Left: Leon Battista Alberti. 1804. *Della Pittura e della Statua*. Milan: Società Tipografica de'Classici Italiani. Right: Illustration of the drawing of a circle in Sketchpad, showing how the program's constraint logic ignores the erratic radius, inputting only the degree of arc drawn; Ivan Edward Sutherland. 1963. "Sketchpad, A Man-Machine Graphical Communication System." PhD diss., MIT.

RECALIBRATION ON IMPRECISION AND INFIDELITY

Rafael Lozano-Hemmer

KEYNOTE

Rafael Lozano-Hemmer was born in Mexico City in 1967. In 1989 he received a B.Sc. in Physical Chemistry from Concordia University in Montréal, Canada.

An electronic artist, he develops interactive installations that are at the intersection of architecture and performance art. His main interest is in creating platforms for public participation by perverting technologies such as robotics, computerized surveillance, or telematic networks. Inspired by phantasmagoria, carnival, and animatronics, his light and shadow works are "antimonuments for alien agency".

His large-scale interactive installations have been commissioned for events such as the Millennium Celebrations in Mexico City (1999), the Cultural Capital of Europe in Rotterdam (2001), the UN World Summit of Cities in Lyon (2003), the opening of the YCAM Center in Japan (2003), the expansion of the European Union in Dublin (2004), the memorial for the Tlatelolco student massacre in Mexico City (2008), the Winter Olympics in Vancouver (2010), and the pre-opening exhibition of the Guggenheim in Abu Dhabi (2015).

Recently the subject of solo exhibitions at the San Francisco Museum of Modern Art, the MUAC Museum in Mexico City, and the Museum of Contemporary Art in Sydney, he was the first artist to officially represent Mexico at the Venice Biennale with a solo exhibition at Palazzo Soranzo Van Axel in 2007. He has also shown at Art Biennials and Triennials in Havana, Istanbul, Kochi, Liverpool, Montréal, Moscow, New Orleans, Seville, Seoul, Shanghai, Singapore, and Sydney. Collections holding his work include the MoMA in New York, Tate in London, AGO in Toronto, CIFO in Miami, Jumex in Mexico City, DAROS in Zürich, Borusan Contemporary in Istanbul, MUAC in Mexico City, 21st Century Museum of Art in Kanazawa, MAG in Manchester, MUSAC in Leon, MONA in Hobart, ZKM in Karlsruhe, MAC in Montréal, and SAM in Singapore, among others.

He has received two BAFTA British Academy Awards for Interactive Art in London, a Golden Nica at the Prix Ars Electronica in Austria, "Artist of the year" Rave Award from Wired Magazine, a Rockefeller fellowship, the Trophée des Lumières in Lyon, an International Bauhaus Award in Dessau, the title of Compagnon des arts et des lettres du Québec in Québec, and the Governor General's Award in Canada. He has lectured at Goldsmiths' College, the Bartlett School, Princeton, Harvard, UC Berkeley, Cooper Union, USC, MIT MediaLab, Guggenheim Museum, LA MOCA, Netherlands Architecture Institute, Cornell, UPenn, SCAD, Danish Architecture Cente, CCA in Montreal, ICA in London, and the Art Institute of Chicago.

1 Rafael Lozano-Hemmer, "Amodal Suspension, Relational Architecture 8," 2003. Yamaguchi Center for Art and Media, Yamaguchi, Japan. (© ArchiBiMing).

RECALIBRATION ON IMPRECISION AND INFIDELITY

2   Rafael Lozano-Hemmer, "Call On Water," 2016. Preabsence, Haus der Elektronischen Künste Basel, Basel, Switzerland, 2016. (Photo © Franz J. Wamhof).

3   Rafael Lozano-Hemmer, "Under Scan, Relational Architecture 11," 2005. Trafalgar Square, London, United Kingdom, 2008. (Photo © Antimodular Research).

4   Rafael Lozano-Hemmer, "Bilateral Timer Slicer," 2016. Untitled Art Fair, birtforms Gallery, Miami, Florida, United States. (Photo © Antimodular Research).

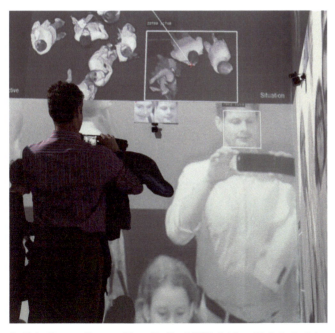

5   Rafael Lozano-Hemmer, "Zoom Pavilion," 2016. Art Basel Unlimited—Art Basel 47, Basel, Switzerland. (Photo © Antimodular Research).

6   Rafael Lozano-Hemmer, "Zoom Pavilion," 2016. Art Basel Unlimited—Art Basel 47, Basel, Switzerland. (Photo © Antimodular Research).

RECALIBRATION ON IMPRECISION AND INFIDELITY

Diego Ricalde

KEYNOTE

Diego Ricalde is Professor of Architecture and Urbanism at Universidad Iberoamericana in Mexico City, where he directs a diploma design studio focused on the urban and territorial complexities of Mexico City's basin and the development of architectural proposals that incorporate diverse digital tools, most importantly the assimilation and incorporation of composite thinking into the design process. Diego works as consultant for diverse practices in Mexico, and along with Jorge Arvizu, Ignacio del Rio, and Emmanuel Ramirez, is principal at Estudio MMX; a multifaceted architectural and urban design studio based in Mexico City.

Diego pursued a Bachelor of Architecture at the National Autonomous University (UNAM) and a Master of Architecture and Urbanism at the Design Research Lab (DRL) at the Architectural Association (2007–2009). During those years Diego's team, under the guidance of Yusuke Obuchi, developed a project called "Crackology," which focused on understanding how "space" is created when forces travel through a specific material system. Since then, his disciplinary interests have developed in different fields, which include urban strategies and design, architectural and computational design. He has been invited by diverse national and international institutions to critique, teach, and lecture about topics related to these interests and Estudio MMX's projects.

As part of IBERO and MMX, Diego has tested some of the ways in which the principles and techniques of digital design can be adequately tested and applied in Mexican circumstances, and how these intellectual and physical processes can begin to inform an alternative understanding of the architectural practice within a very strong modern Mexican architectural tradition. Whereas the academic results of this endeavor are in an early stage or are still to be fully developed, in the professional realm, MMX has found a particular niche through which to display these interests. A series of commissions that relate to temporary structures and interventions show the way in which these logics can be tested and expressed in a particular Mexican practice.

Projects of this series include the FNO Pavilion, a canvas made with 21,000 interlaced credit cards, built in late 2011 as part of a larger design exhibition in Mexico City, and the ECO Pavilion, a temporary intervention built in early 2011 in the courtyard of the Eco Experimental Museum in Mexico City. This project consisted of two interwoven systems of ropes that created a series of screens of varying densities to reconfigure the openness of the original space into a multiplicity of ambiences that could host the different programs of the institution. Moreover, the "No - precedents" exhibition and Pavilion at the Arnold and Sheila Aaronson galleries at the Parsons School for Design at The New School in New York City, was part of the Architectural League Prize for Young Architects + Designers 2012 awards. As a continuation of those explorations, Diego, along with Estudio MMX, developed the LIGA 12 Pavilion—a 561 m² intervention made with low-cost fabric and height-adjustable columns built with conventional scaffolding elements—in 2013 at the MUDE Museum for the Lisbon Architecture Triennale. In 2015, MMX accomplished the temporary venue for the Friend Cultures Fair in the city center of Mexico City: a temporary structure built

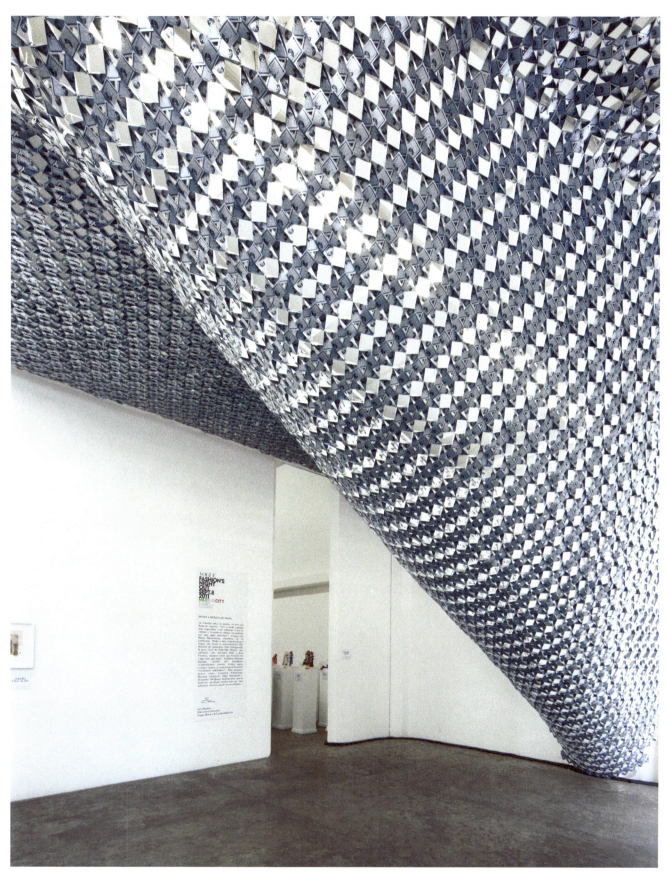

1 MMX: FNO Installation (Yoshihiro Koitani, CDMX, 2011)

RECALIBRATION ON IMPRECISION AND INFIDELITY

2   MMX: LIGA 12 (MMX, Lisbon, 2013)

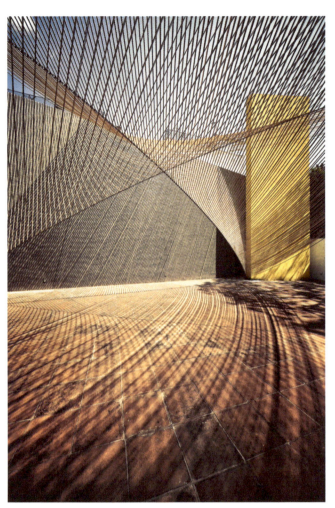

3   MMX: ECO Pavilion (Yoshihiro Koitani, CDMX, 2011)

with standard scaffolding and mesh fabric, covering a 6,000 m² space, spanning 24 m and assembled in three days.

Academically, Diego has received numerous awards, including the FONCA "Mexican Young Creators Award" and the Abraham Zabludovzky Prize in 2003; the Marcelo Zambrano CEMEX Grant for Architects in 2007; and along with Estudio MMX, The Architectural League Prize for Young Architects + Designers and the Design Vanguard Award from the Architectural Record in 2012 and the CEMEX National and International Award in 2013, along with numerous winning entries for urban and architectural competitions.

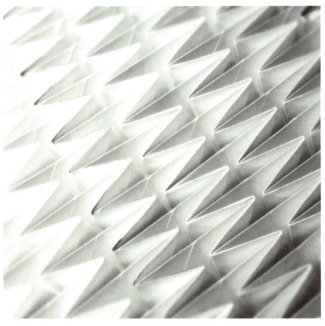

4   MMX: ENP Pavilion (MMX, New York, 2012)

5   MMX: ECO Pavilion (Yoshihiro Koitani, CDMX, 2011)

6   MMX: FCA Pavilion (Rafael Gamo, CDMX, 2015)

7   MMX: FCA Pavilion (Rafael Gamo, CDMX, 2015)

Mónica Ponce de León

ACADIA Teaching Award of Excellence

This year's ACADIA conference asks us to consider how architecture must "mediate between an 'ideal' precision/accuracy obtainable through digital methodologies, and the imprecision and infidelity of the physical/material world around us, simultaneously acknowledging the interrelated importance of both analog and digital processes, and privileging neither one over the other." This is a great topic, at the core of architecture, and one that has been the subject of much of my teaching and practice. However, this premise reinforces false dichotomies that privilege the myth of the digital as precise, while the analog is relegated as inaccurate. I would argue that a more productive dialogue may emerge if we move away from these stereotypes, acknowledging that all design and fabrication methodologies, whether digital or otherwise, have various degrees of imprecision (some built into the method itself, some due to error), and recognize that analog and digital have both historically strived for accuracy, with the exception of some deviant instances that rejoice in the messiness of the imprecise.

Two examples from the 19th century come to mind to illustrate my point, since Gideon's mechanization that "took command" during the industrial revolution was, after all, not machine-based. The assembly line, which aimed to increase accuracy, was in fact a line of workers laboring by hand. Conversely, the Arts and Crafts movement, which arose as a critique of industrialization and fetishized the hand-made, introduced "errors" to simulate the imprecision of the hand, even when using tools with a great degree of exactitude. This history, while seemingly outmoded for the analog/digital topic at hand, may help steer us clear of false stereotypes about making and refocus the conversation away from tools and techniques in themselves towards what they may mean in the context of architecture as a cultural practice.

These ideas have been at the heart of my teaching and professional practice, and at the core of my administrative roles as professor or dean at four institutions in the US (Harvard, Georgia Tech, the University of Michigan, and now Princeton). As a means of expanding the discourse of the discipline, I have focused on doing away with the boundaries between traditionally distinct categories—digital/analog, high-tech/low-tech—and by proxy, undermining the constructed dichotomy between academia and practice. My trajectory began very analog: working in a millwork shop while studying English as a second language. By the time I started teaching at Harvard in the early 1990s, through my experience in private practice, I realized that the building industry was moving very quickly into CNC technology, but architecture schools were not aware of the shift. At the time, academia was focused on software as design tools, but there was little conversation about the impact of the digital on the actual making of buildings.

Working across professional practice and the academy, my work has ultimately centered on a few interrelated disciplinary questions: First, a fascination with precision (or lack thereof) led me to projects such as Fabricating Coincidences for the Museum of Modern Art and more recently the U.S. Memorial in New Zealand, which examine the tension between the tolerances of the digital tool being deployed and a desire to create the effect

1 Banq restaurant, Boston, MA.

2 Georgia Institute of Technology Installation, Atlanta, GA.

3 Fabricating Coincidences, Museum of Modern Art (MoMA), New York, NY.

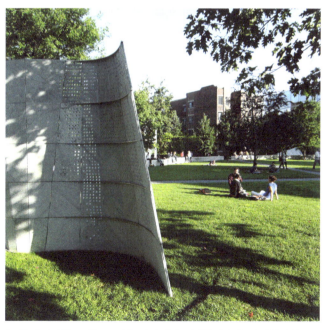

4 Surfacing Stone, Harvard Graduate School of Design, Cambridge, MA.

RECALIBRATION ON IMPRECISION AND INFIDELITY

5   Helios House, Los Angeles, CA.

6   Fleet Library at Rhode Island School of Design, Providence, RI.

of precision. Second, the capacity afforded by digital technology to fabricate variation economically led me to explore the design possibilities of mass customization in architecture. For instance, we no longer need to design for the average human body, but instead we could incorporate multiple bodies with varying degrees of abilities, as with the Library at the Rhode Island School of Design. Mass customization is also at the core of my constant re-examination of part to whole. If parts are no longer required to be identical, then each part can seamlessly take on multiple functions, such as structure, joinery, or scaffolding, to name a few. My workshop class on material experiments at Georgia Tech, followed by the construction of Banq, as well as Harvard's Surfacing Stone in collaboration with Bechthold and McGee, focus on this potential.

In the American context, to explore these topics required a rethinking of both teaching and practice. In the academy, I worked to develop what was then a new model of teaching and research where undergraduate and master students with little technological background could take a deep dive into the design potential of digital fabrication. At Harvard and as Ventulett Chair at Georgia Tech, I developed workshop courses where students experimented with the use of digital tools through assignments involving different materials and fabricated full-scale installations in and around campus. In an active feedback loop with my practice, these experiments allowed us to explore variation vs. repetition, hand assembly vs. machine construction, digital vs. analog. In architectural practice, I sought to break the distance between the architect and a building's construction. It is said that "architects do not build, they draw." An entire industry, reinforced by a large legal infrastructure, revolves around this division of labor. The built work required the invention of new delivery systems where the boundary between the work of architect and the fabricator was blurred for the sake of efficiency. Shop drawings and liability were redesigned.

While these strategies have been fruitful in my work, I have spent a big part of my career trying to understand whether it was possible to translate them into tactics that can

Ponce de León

7   Digital Fabrication Lab at Taubman College, University of Michigan.

impact the discipline at large. To that end, as a university administrator, I have sought to provide the infrastructure to encourage and enable experimentation across digital and analog, virtual and material. As director of the Digital Fabrication Lab at Harvard in the early 2000s, later as dean at Michigan (FABLab), and currently at Princeton (ECL), I have structured large digital fabrication laboratories, which unlike the European examples, are open to all students and all faculty regardless of the level of expertise. At Michigan, the lab was paired with a reinvention (or elimination) of faculty offices and the development of a large collaborative working space that we called the Liberty Annex. The intent was not only make available a myriad of tools—high tech/low tech, digital/analog—but also one of our most important commodities: space. The same concept of blurring categorical boundaries led me to test various funding mechanisms such as the Research Through Making program at Michigan. Erasing distinctions between research and creative practice, the program awards faculty with seed funding to work with students. Over the course of a decade, these research projects have developed advances in uses of materials, digital tools, and interactive designs.

I am honored to receive this year's ACADIA Teaching Award of Excellence and, in particular, to be receiving it this year, when the conference focuses on a topic that I think is central to the digital question. The work being done by the ACADIA community is pushing research in academia and practice in ways that are critical for the discipline to transform building practices.

RECALIBRATION ON IMPRECISION AND INFIDELITY

Oyler Wu Collaborative

ACADIA Digital Practice Award of Excellence

Bio

Dwayne Oyler and Jenny Wu established the architecture and design firm of Oyler Wu Collaborative in Los Angeles in 2004. The firm is recognized for its experimentation in design, material research, and fabrication, and was the winner of 2013 Design Vanguard Award from Architectural Record and 2017 The J. Irwin and Xenia S. Miller Prize recipient.

Their recent completed projects include the competition winning project, The Exchange, for Exhibit Columbus, a 3D-printing Culinary Lab in Los Angeles for 3D Systems, and The Monarch Tower, a 16 story residential high rise in Taipei, Taiwan. The office was recently selected by the City of Los Angeles to design a large-scale public project for the city, the LA River Bikeway and Greenway. The office has won numerous awards, including the 2013 Emerging Talent Award from AIA California Council, the 2012 Presidential Honor Award for Emerging Practice from AIA LA, Taiwan's ADA Award for Emerging Architect, and the 2011 Emerging Voices Award from the Architectural League in New York.

Their book *Pendulum Plane* was published in 2009 by the Los Angeles Forum for Architecture and Urban Design, and a recent book entitled *Trilogy: SCI-Arc Pavilions* was published by SCI-Arc Press. Both partners are members of the design faculty at the Southern California Institute of Architecture and Harvard GSD. They have previously taught at various other institutions such as Syracuse University and Columbia GSAPP.

Firm Philosophy

Our office is committed to the idea that architecture's full potential is born out of its ability to operate simultaneously at multiple scales as an art form, affecting human experience in nonlinear ways as it moves from large architectural strategies to intimate forms of engagement. We reject the increasingly pervasive idea of the architect's role as a simple coordinator of various interests, and we believe that we have an obligation to reclaim an expertise based in a deeper understanding of material effects, formal and spatial language, and their associated cultural meanings. Given this belief, our practice is focused on a constant exchange of ideas that move between large architectural proposals and small architectural installations.

Relocating from New York to Los Angeles in 2004, our office has utilized the last eleven years to establish a way of working that is committed to experimentation through a relentless hands-on approach to our work. Heavily invested in academia (currently both of us teach at SCI-Arc, the Southern California Institute of Architecture), we consider it our obligation as instructors and architects to not only put ideas forward, but to test their application. We believe that ideas find their greatest potency through the feedback of human experience, material resistance, and iterative processes.

1 Oyler Wu Collaborative, 3DS Culinary (photo by Scott Mayoral).

2 Oyler Wu Collaborative, The Exchange.

3 Oyler Wu Collaborative, 3DS Culinary (photo by Scott Mayoral).

Eager to test our ideas, and impatient in our desire to see the effects of our work, our office turned to our own love of building to transform small projects with modest budgets into a testing ground for our ideas. Los Angeles, SCI-Arc, and most recently Taipei have served as an invaluable test bed for our ambitions. Our work consists largely (although not entirely) of work that we have built ourselves. This way of working has grown out of necessity, an insistence on detail-driven work on small budgets, and out of the desire to allow the design process to continually respond to feedback provided by the fabrication process. The lack of conventional separation between the architectural and construction fields has allowed us to use the construction phase as an extension to the design process. It has also provided a more direct translation of ideas from digital form to reality while ensuring a level of articulation often difficult to achieve through a more conventional means of construction. It has been a period of material discovery, invention, and experimentation that comes only through the difficult, but profoundly rewarding task of realizing the work on a given site. Most importantly, that knowledge

brought with it a new concept for building that went beyond the material itself—one that is interested in extending the role of experimental work to better engage ideas of use and human engagement.

In the past 6 years, our office has expanded on the initial ideas to include larger and more robust projects. The office continues to rely on the constant exchange between design and making, often with small intense installations being built alongside the design of large-scale projects. We believe that this insistence on hands-on experimentation should remain one of our most fundamental philosophies and is the key to our continued growth and evolution.

4 Oyler Wu Collaborative, The Exchange.

5 Oyler Wu Collaborative, Monarch, Taipei (photo by Po Yao Shih).

6 Oyler Wu Collaborative, Monarch, Taipei (photo by Po Yao Shih).

RECALIBRATION ON IMPRECISION AND INFIDELITY

IAAC: Institute for Advanced Architecture of Catalonia

ACADIA Innovative Academic Program Award of Excellence

The digital revolution and current unforeseen environmental, social, and economic challenges have become the drivers of IAAC's academic body and research. Combining design with science and technology, IAAC's work seeks to envision the future habitat, materializing and building it in the present. IAAC's multidisciplinary programs include the Master in Advanced Architecture (founded in 2002), Master in City & Technology (2014), Master in Advanced Interaction (2015), Open Thesis Fabrication applied research program (2010) and the new additions of the Master in Advanced Ecological Buildings, Master in Design for Emergent Futures, and Master in Robotics and Advanced Construction (2018).

Through the different master programs at IAAC, students work closely with faculty and the industry to redefine architecture as a performative and self-sufficient organism, operating with the principles of ecology, biology, or artificial intelligence. They develop projects to redefine the city as a productive and circular metabolism that responds to real-time data flows, peer-to-peer empowerment, as well as distributed systems of resource transactions (energy, mobility, or economy). They finally redefine design and construction principles using digital technologies to allow a maximum degree of customization, human—machine interaction, and minimum environmental and economic impact, questioning the traditional principles of building, managing, and consuming.

The 9-month, 12-month and 18-month master programs run every year, with more than 150 students coming from approximately 40 different countries around the world, enhancing the international and diverse culture of the IAAC. The methodology and approach of the master programs is based on two crucial pillars: on the one hand the importance of acting on multiple scales, and on the other hand, the necessity to integrate multiple disciplines.

The IAAC incorporates teaching and project realization, from material nanoscale exploration to building design, from sensors and physical computing to the strategic development of master plans, from bits to geographies. Additionally, the educational programs run in close collaboration with specialists from diverse fields, from architects and designers to biologists and engineers, from anthropologists and sociologists to arborists and permaculturers, from programmers and manufacturers to economists and policy makers.

IAAC's educational model is based on learning out of making and on peer-to-peer learning. The goal of the institution is precisely to teach students how to learn, how the tools to learn can be found, and how distortions can be detected; how to recognize our kin, and for peers to learn from each other and interact—in short, to grow intellectually. IAAC educators pass from being content providers to connection sources, giving students the necessary background to learn how to create connections and to learn from and together with one another. On the one hand, peer-to-peer learning happens physically in IAAC's classrooms and Fab Labs, where learning is emerging through making. The access to fast prototyping, DIY technology, and multidisciplinary peer-to-peer exchange radically influences the way students think and make architecture: visionary design for positive change combined with

1 3D-printed building with raw earth. Credits: Open Thesis Fabrication, Studio Dubor & Cabay, Students: Graaf van Limburg, Refalian, Sevostianov, IAAC, 2018.

2   Adaptive kinetic structure with embedded lightweight distributed
     systems of actuation. Credits: Master in Advanced Architecture, Studio
     Markopoulou, Digital Matter Students: Won Jun, Alcover, Silverio. IAAC,
     2017.

3   Soft robots and graphene composites for responsive architec-
     tural membranes. Credits: Master in Advanced Architecture, Studio
     Markopoulou, Digital Matter Students: Temel, Alayeli, Jotanvic. IAAC & IIT
     Smart Materials Group, 2017.

fast prototyping and testing, creates a remarkable feed-back loop that expands ideas and brings them to reality. On the other hand, peer-to-peer learning happens in the virtual world of the Web, following the culture of open source, or collaborative and distributed making and learning.

Collaboration with public and private bodies in pilot projects in the city is a common methodology of IAAC's education and research. The city becomes the laboratory of experimentation and action, and students have the possibility to connect with industry and administrations, as well as participating in numerous European-funded research programs that can be evaluated in terms of social impact, economic feasibility, and cultural meaning.

IAAC recognizes the importance of using the latest technological means to develop novel solutions for the current social, economic, and environmental challenges. Rather than just exploring technologies to test their limits or potentials, IAAC students and faculty envision and materialize

solutions for the ever increasing challenges faced by society. Architecture becomes more collaborative and socially driven, and technology is the means to enhance architecture as a platform where different disciplines meet and which people can use to improve their quality of life. In the different master programs at IAAC, developing research and projects around social manifestos becomes more relevant than doing so around technological or design complexity manifestos, without, of course, one discarding the other.

The impact of technologies in the way we perceive, design, fund, and construct our spaces have manifested themselves in many different ways, but this means nothing without a shift in how we think and how we prepare the new thinkers and professionals to bring positive change to today's unprecedented challenges, beyond technology per se.

IAAC works in education, preparing our thinkers and

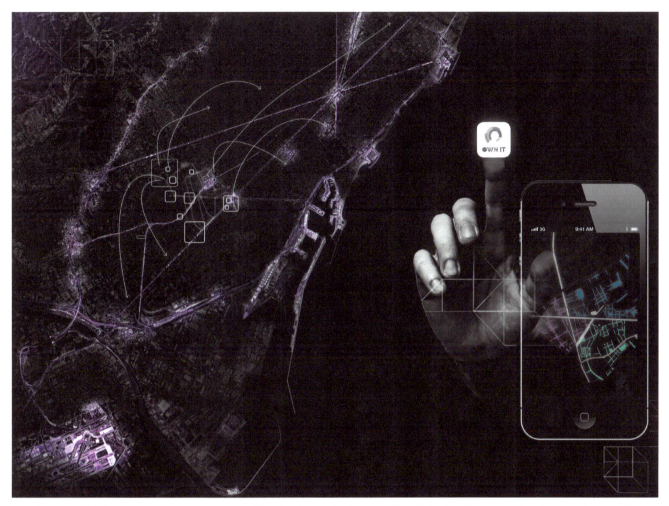

4   Urban app used in bottom-up processes for dynamic mobility planning. Credits: Master in City & Technology, Studio Designing with Fluxes Students: Ciccone, Marcovich. IAAC with MIC & Urban Standards, 2017.

change-makers for the experience age, the age of partic-ipation, where technology recedes into the background of our lives and is not just a catalyst, but the foundation for social interaction. Students work intensively on topics of open source culture, artificial intelligence, virtual and augmented reality, blockchain, robots, or smart and biosynthetic materials, developing completely new ways of defining what buildings, cities, and citizens are.

In this era of rapid innovation, IAAC highlights design that emerges as the constructive synthesis of thought and action, being open to include an architecture of systemic correlation among humans, technology, and nature, degrowth, climate justice, and new forms of social and political inclusion.

Areti Markopoulou, Academic Director

5   Industrial cable bot transformed into lightweight and mobile 3D printer for on-site construction. Credits: On Site Robotics, OTF, IAAC with Tecnalia, 2017.

Madeline Gannon

ACADIA Innovative Research Award of Excellence

Dr. Madeline Gannon is a multidisciplinary designer inventing better ways to communicate with machines. In her research, Gannon seeks to blend knowledge from design, robotics, and human–computer interaction to innovate at the intersections of art and technology. Her work has been internationally exhibited at leading cultural institutions, published at ACM conferences, and is widely covered by diverse media outlets across design, art, and technology communities. Her recent installation, Mimus, was awarded an Ars Electronica STARTS Prize Honorable Mention in 2017, and she was also named a 2017 World Economic Forum Cultural Leader. Gannon holds a PhD in Computational Design from Carnegie Mellon University, where she explored human-centered interfaces for autonomous fabrication machines. She also holds a Masters in Architecture from Florida International University.

Gannon advocates for an expanded definition of architecture; one that is not constrained by the disciplinary boundaries of today. She sees an architect's hypersensitivity to how people move through space as an invaluable asset to many different domains. She focuses her efforts on bringing these sensibilities into the fields of human–computer interaction and robotics. However, her training as an architect is foundational to the novel perspectives and technical innovations she contributes to these fields.

Through her research, Gannon creates human-centered interfaces that make machines more contextually aware and attentive to the people around them. The software she develops strives to foster shared understandings between a person, a machine, and an environment. She has built computational design tools for crafting intricate wearables around the body, and has invented interfaces that transform the body into an interactive canvas for digital design and fabrication. However, she is perhaps best known for her work taming giant industrial robots.

Her work with industrial robots illustrates a future where the tools of automation can be reconfigured to expand, augment, and enhance human capabilities, not replace them. To help seed novel experimentation, Gannon contributes open-source hardware and software for developing creative and atypical use cases for robotic arms. She uses these tools in her own research to develop interfaces and interaction design principles for safely cohabitating with these potentially dangerous machines. These techniques were recently tested in the public exhibition of Mimus, where Gannon transformed a 1,200 kg industrial robot into a living, breathing mechanical creature. Mimus lived at the Design Museum London for six months, and offered a first point of contact between museum goers and a creature of intelligent automation.

More recently, Gannon's research interests have shifted from robotic automation to autonomy. She sees these intelligent machines that are leaving the lab to live in the wild as increasingly relevant to architecture: not in what these robots will make, but for how they are joining us in the built environment. Through her research and writing, she hopes to inspire other designers and architects to become more actively involved in defining how these intelligent machines will coexist with us in our cities, streets, sidewalks, and skies.

1 Gannon's software system, Quipt is a gesture-based control software that facilitates new, more intuitive ways to communicate with industrial robots. Using wearable markers and a motion capture system, Quipt gives industrial robots basic spatial behaviors for interacting closely with people (© ATONATON / Autodesk, 2015).

RECALIBRATION ON IMPRECISION AND INFIDELITY

2   Quipt explores the possibilities of industrial robots moving out of the factory and into live, ever-changing environments. Wearable markers worn on the hand, around the neck, or elsewhere on the body let a robot see and respond to you in a shared space (© ATONATON / Autodesk, 2015).

3   Mimus is a giant industrial robot that's curious about the world around her. Unlike in traditional industrial robotics, Mimus has no pre-planned movements: she is programmed with the freedom to explore and roam about her enclosure (photographer: Luke Hayes, © ATONATON, 2016).

4   Using the robot's body language, posturing, and motor sounds to broadcast a spectrum of emotional states, Mimus' behaviour acts as a medium for culti-
vating empathy between her human visitors (video still from *Meet Mimus, The Curious Industrial Robot* © ATONATON / Autodesk, 2016).

5   The interaction design and physical design of Mimus is helps visitors forget they are looking at a machine, and instead let them see her as a living creature.
And like any zoo animal, Mimus has a limited attention span: if she finds you interesting, Mimus may come in for a closer look, but stay still for too long, and
she will get bored and seek out someone else. (video still from *Meet Mimus, The Curious Industrial Robot* © ATONATON / Autodesk, 2016).

RECALIBRATION ON IMPRECISION AND INFIDELITY

Sigrid Brell-Cokcan & Johannes Braumann

ACADIA Society Award for Leadership

Making Robots Accessible

Architects have always been inventors and technological trailblazers, finding inspiration in processes like the highly efficient production lines of the automotive industry. For the past 40 years, robotic arms have been the archetypical machines in that industry, seemingly autonomously assembling cars in perfect synchronicity. But less then 10 years ago, robots were still just a side note at architectural conferences, with only a few first trailblazers like ETH Zürich, in close collaboration with mathematicians and software developers, publishing research on robotic applications. When we acquired a KUKA robot at TU Vienna in 2007, we did not yet consider the full potential of robotic arms—instead, the decision to invest in a robot was based mostly on an accident, as the industrial robot turned out to be the cheapest robust 5+ axis CNC machine on the market at that time. However, by working with the robot we quickly realized that these machines are not as complicated as they appeared, and that "robot programming" is not such a mystery that architects could not solve it on their own—after all, robots have been designed with factory workers in mind, not mathematicians. The challenge was mostly the static programming in an industrial software environment, which prevented easy access to robots by novice users. So the initial idea was to streamline the data flow from our known design environment directly out of CAD to control the robot, and to be independent from further complicated and expensive CAM software.

This was the motivation for us to develop a set of tools within the visual programming environment Grasshopper, which was later published as KUKA|prc—parametric robot control. Our first workshop happened during the Advances in Architectural Geometry conference in 2010, where we were surprised by the level of interest in robotic processes from both the academic community as well as professionals. Shortly thereafter we founded the Association for Robots in Architecture, as we felt that it would be much easier to bring change and innovation as a large community, rather than as just two motivated individuals. Legally, every association has to have a specific purpose, so in our case we defined our goal in "making robots accessible for the creative industry"

We based this effort on two pillars. The first is the Association for Robots in Architecture, which acts as a network for "creative" robot users, both online as well as offline. On the internet, the Association is now at 11.000 followers on Facebook, 2.4 million views on Vimeo, and 141.000 downloads of our book series at SpringerLink. Our efforts beyond the internet focus on the Rob|Arch conference, which we first initiated in 2012 in Vienna and has since become a regular event taking place every two years at other international institutions: 2014 at the Taubman College of the University of Michigan, 2016 at the University of Sydney, and 2018 at ETH Zürich.

1   Large-scale additive processes using KUKA robots and KUKA|prc at Branch Technology.

          RECALIBRATION ON IMPRECISION AND INFIDELITY

2   Research into novel robotic processes by RiA: AROSU.

3   KUKA|prc in the browser via Autodesk FORGE and Microsoft Azure; Controlling KUKA robots in an accessible way through visual programming and KUKA|prc.

Becoming a sister organization of ACADIA, the homeland of all digital natives in architecture, has further nourished the growth in interest in robotics, especially in architectural research and education. We are very grateful to be part of this active community.

The second pillar is Robots in Architecture, a research institution that aims to develop tools that can not only be used for a single project, but are accessible and multifunctional, providing a value to the entire community. The notion of accessibility has been a driving factor in the development of KUKA|prc, coming in at over 15.000 downloads of the free version per year, and 150 members that support the continuing development through their membership fees.

The software has thus made great strides and is not only used by more than 100 universities today, but powers innovative efforts such as ultra-large-scale wood fabrication at Zublin Timber, high-end additive processes at Branch Technology, as well as start-ups like Print-a-Drink, Mobbot, and more. Together with KUKA, we have been able to bring

mxAutomation to CAD environments, which allows users to stream commands to KUKA robots without requiring a real-time-capable operating system. In the upcoming version, KUKA|prc will also be available on Autodesk Dynamo, with prototypes already running on platforms such as Unity, VVVV, and simply on the cloud.

Today, we notice that there are again less robot-specific sessions at conferences. We consider that to be the greatest confirmation of our work, as it means that robots are no longer the centerpiece of the research, but have become accessible, valuable tools—interfaces that allow researchers and professionals to turn their digital ideas into physical processes and to apply their expertise in materials and processes in new areas and domains.

Our next goal is to directly address machinery for the construction site. We are thus opening up new kinematics with intuitive software control. Our new focus is on robust platforms such as demolition robots and cranes. The new Center for Construction Robotics was recently opened at

Brell-Cokcan, Braumann

4 First Robots in Architecture workshop at AAG 2010, with participants from Snøhetta, Herzog & de Meuron, ETH, Sharjah University and University of Innsbruck.

the RWTH Aachen Campus, right in the middle of an engineering campus where the first electrical car in Europe has just been built.

The research of our community stands on the shoulders of engineers who have worked on robotic arms for decades. For us, the next evolutionary step for our community is therefore to open ourselves up to the greater robotics community and to develop bespoke machinic solutions for the challenges of the AEC community. We support this development through our involvement in the euRobotics network and the new Springer *Construction Robotics* journal.

Making robots accessible is therefore only the first step on a long journey to change the way we build today—we are looking forward to taking that step together with the ACADIA community.

About Us

The Association for Robots in Architecture was co-founded by Sigrid Brell-Cokcan and Johannes Braumann in 2010. Sigrid is the president of the Association, full professor at RWTH Aachen University, member of the euRobotics directorate, and coordinator of the new topic group on Construction Robotics. She has just opened the cross-disciplinary Center for Construction Robotics on the RWTH Aachen Campus, and is chief editor of the new *Construction Robotics* journal published by Springer. Johannes is the vice-president of Robots in Architecture and professor at UfG Linz. He heads the KUKA|prc development and is the director of the Association's commercial branch Robots in Architecture Research LLC.

RECALIBRATION ON IMPRECISION AND INFIDELITY

RECALIBRATION: on imprecision and infidelity
EXHIBITION PROJECTS

Digital Craft in Semi-peripheral Nations

Pablo Iriarte, *Exhibition Chair*

These curated projects and the accompanying exhibition explore the material and cultural possibilities of digital craft in semi-peripheral countries. Digital craft can be described as follows:

> "pragmatic delivery processes and material constraints [define] an emerging territory known as 'digital craft' where the exchange between the technology of the digitally conceived and the artisanry of the handmade is explored." (Huang 2013)

The selection of each of the curated projects was based on three main criteria: (1) the material system, (2) the embedded labor, and (3) the socio-political context.

1. Material Systems

Some of the innovative materials explored in the curated projects include: widely available natural fibers such as jute (Transmutations III); labor-intensive wood joinery (Ditebus Torus); wood shavings employed in combination with digital technologies (Tangible Formations); and repurposed objects with cultural meaning such as glazed ceramics (Milkywave). These material systems use locally available materials or cultural traditions in new ways. It is no surprise that concrete and brick repeatedly appear in the curated projects (DL1310, CGG, and CoBLOgo). One of the primary economic activities of semi-peripheral countries is minerals extraction. According to the 2017 Global Cement Directory, China, India, Vietnam, Brazil, Iran, and Mexico are among the top cement producers in the world. Additionally, brick, stone, and concrete are ancient, low-tech material systems which can be built with manual labor.

2. Labor Culture

Poured-in-place concrete is so prevalent in Mexico that over time it acquired cultural significance; "Día del colado" (pouring day) is considered a festive moment in the construction process of a building. In this way, the building acquires an emotional meaning not only as a final object but through the process of its construction. Buildings are always embedded within a specific labor culture and working conditions. In semi-peripheral countries, construction still relies heavily on manual labor. It is not a coincidence that these countries have a high carbohydrate-based diet, which provides the fuel for such work.

3. Socio-political Opportunities

The local social and political environment in developing countries tends to free of construction constraints. Codes are more loosely interpreted; this gives the opportunity to explore larger scales and take risks associated with experimentation. New forms may be explored through computational design, not only in the form of pavilions but also in large facade installations and building structures (DL1310 and CGG).

The curated projects in this exhibition reflect the values and opportunities in developing environments. They present an invitation to re-evaluate elemental modes of making with digital means of designing. By combining computational technologies with manual construction techniques, these projects embrace the interplay between digital perfection and human imprecision. The infidelities of the building become an expression of cultural values. Each project manifests the identity of the semi-periphery in its own unique way.

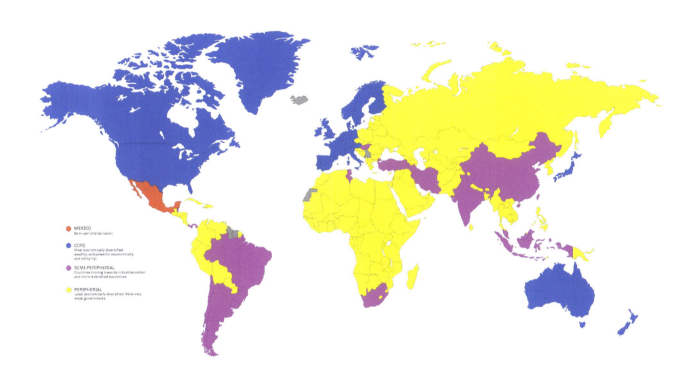

1　World map by trading status based on Babones (2005).

2　Poured-in-place concrete formwork, Buhairi Nawawi. Cairo 2017.

3　DL1310, Michan Architecture, Young & Ayata, Mexico City, 2018.

CGG Facade

1   Render of CGG House (Inicio Estudio, 2014).

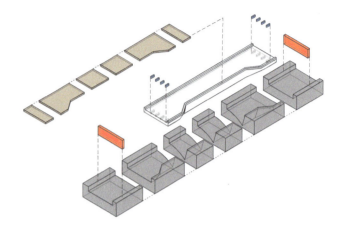

2   Components for concrete formwork (Alberto Lara, 2014).

3   Reconfigurable wood prototype (Alberto Lara, 2014).

4   Concrete formwork being rearranged (Alberto Lara, 2014).

Alberto Lara
ABLP

Collaboration:
Inicio Estudio

CGG facade is a prototype that explores mass-customization in prefabricated concrete facades. It introduces heterogeneity and variation to an established fabrication system, modifying it to make products that adapt better to specific contexts and conditions. This project operates within a low-tech context without escalating production costs and explores complex casting systems for construction and architectural purposes.

Wooden sheets are cut with CAM-CNC machines to match the specific curvature of the final surface. Perforations within the pieces allow the reconfiguration of the original sequence into new patterns without the need of fabricating additional pieces. In the second phase, negative concrete moulds are created from the wooden framework, providing robust pieces that can be used multiple times in the casting process, saving in material used prior to executing the final facade pieces. Final concrete pieces are the result of the specific combination of moulds and boundaries used; each piece can be adjusted to match the specific conditions where it will be mounted.

5   General view of installed facade (Inicio Estudio, 2014).

6   Detail of different window sizes for each concrete prefabricated piece (Inicio Estudio, 2014).

RECALIBRATION ON IMPRECISION AND INFIDELITY

Homo Faber Selection: CoBLOgó Factory and Office Annex

1   Exterior View (© SUBdV, 2014).

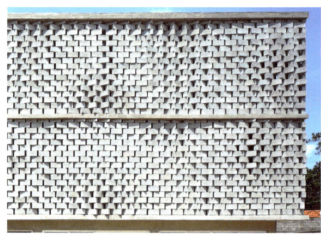

2   Exterior View, Elevation (© SUBdV, 2014).

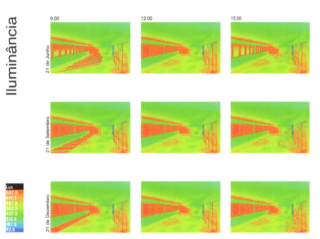

3   Environmental simulation (© SUBdV, 2014).

4   Interior View (© SUBdV, 2014).

Curator: David M. Sperling
Universidade de São Paulo

Co-Curator: Pablo C. Herrera
Universidad Peruana de
Ciencias Aplicadas

Homo Faber Exhibition
Digital Fabricatión in Latin
America. Sao Paulo, Brazil

Team:
Franklin Lee, Anne Save
de Beaurecueil, J. Swan,
V. Sardenberg, O. Campos,
R. Portelada and F. Gomes
(located in São Paulo)

SUBdV | Taboão da Serra, São Paulo, Brazil - 2014

CoBlOgo employs "high-low" fusion, where high-tech design strategies were combined with local low-tech construction methodologies, creating a "tropicalized" digital aesthetic. Parametric computation was used for generating geometric configurations, as well as to construct the façade itself. Scripts generated subtle gradation of rotating blocks, controlled by their distance from different "attraction points".

Different-sized openings and differently angled reflection planes were thus created and were tested using digital environmental simulations (Figure 3) to obtain the best combination of both shading and illuminance (Figure 4). To assemble the concrete blocks (Figure 5), a parametric script created comb-like "guides" to position the blocks, which were made by laser-cutting corrugated cardboard. Theses guides were placed on a movable wood stand and track system that was fabricated using the CNC router. The facade also illustrates the concept of "environmental ornamentation," where ornament is no longer perceived as merely decoration, creating a new type of "functional aesthetic".

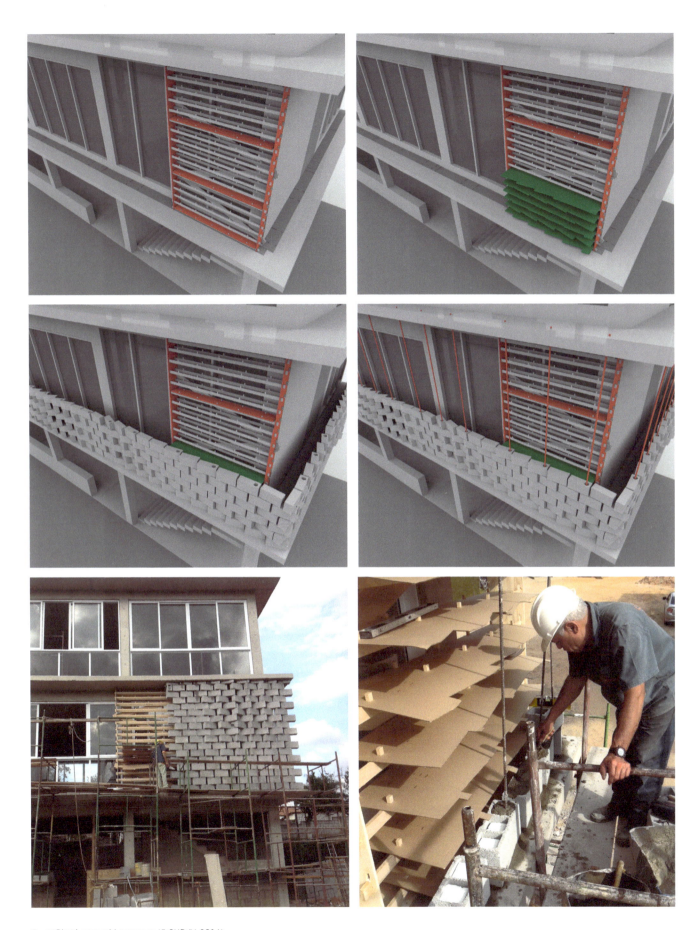

5   coBlogó, assembly process (© SUBdV, 2014).

RECALIBRATION ON IMPRECISION AND INFIDELITY

Ditebius Torus Pavilion

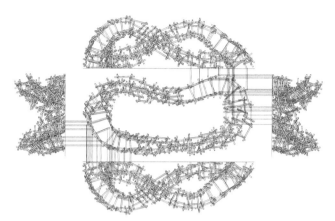

1   Plan and Views (© Digital Tectonics, UTDT Course).

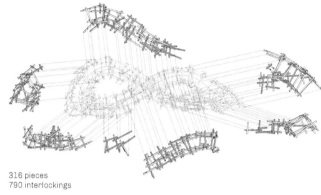

316 pieces
790 interlockings

2   Exploded Axon (© Digital Tectonics, UTDT Course).

3   Front View (© Digital Tectonics, UTDT Course).

4   Lateral View (© Digital Tectonics, UTDT Course).

School of Architecture and Urban Studies - Torcuato Di Tella University

Digital Tectonics

Professors

Matías Imbern,
Eugenio Tenaglia

Team:

Luciana García Campos, Felipe Ginevra, Agostina Giovo, Agustina González Morales, Gastón Hermida, Tomás Meneghetti, Victoria Nicolich Agustina Suar, Magdalena Viegener, Gabriela Zarwanitzer, Martín Zemma.

The system is developed from the investigation of reciprocal structures of wood, using square section elements and combined geometric patterns. The geometry begins with the development of a two-dimensional module, combining both horizontal and vertical lines forming a grid. Then, in order to generate thickness and inertia, two patterns are set in opposing faces, incorporating transverse pieces that sew both layers together, forming an adaptable module that is instantiated repeatedly in relation to the guiding coordinates of the generating surface (U, V, W). Once the pattern of the module is instantiated, it naturally rotates with the movement of the moebius torus.

The fabrication process combines digital manufacturing (CNC milling) with analog assembly, guided by a 1:1 drawing in the base and the internal geometry of the interlocks. A series of supports serve as jigs to control the height and rotation of some pieces of the pavilion, securing its geometric precision and its support while assembly moves forward, until the system is completed and the reciprocity begins to work.

5   Pavilion Close Up (© Digital Tectonics, UTDT Course).

RECALIBRATION ON IMPRECISION AND INFIDELITY

DL1310 Apartments

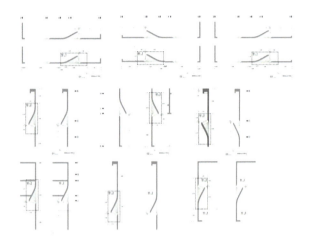

1   Window Module Typology (© Young & Ayata, Michan Architecture).

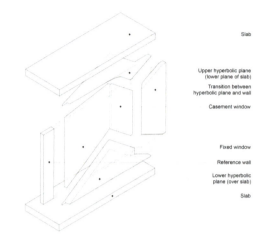

2   Exploded Facade Axon (© Young & Ayata, Michan Architecture).

3   Ruled surface, window to wall transition (© Young & Ayata, Michan Architecture).

4   Front door (© Young & Ayata, Michan Architecture).

Young & Ayata

Michan Architecture

The site strategy required rethinking the apertures as inverted bay windows to allow views and light from all sides. The rectangular windows are rotated into the building's facade, resulting in two ruled surfaces at the top and bottom, transforming the large apertures into trapezoidal windows. As the windows rotate in, the slabs appear to pull the head and sill into the building. This results in a facade that in one appearance is completely flat and at another creates a bas-relief of smooth shadows.

The design process was guided by iterative digital models testing the degrees of rotation that could be produced with the window geometry. When translated into the ruled-surface construction techniques and tested through a series of full-scale mock-ups, a series of material qualities appeared that weren't expected in the digital realm. This testing of construction techniques allowed us to develop a strategy for the cast in place ruled surfaces utilizing fiberglass molds to imprint a wooden formwork on the surfaces, heightening the perception of the wall to slab transformations.

5   Street view render (© Young & Ayata, Michan Architecture).

Landscape canopy

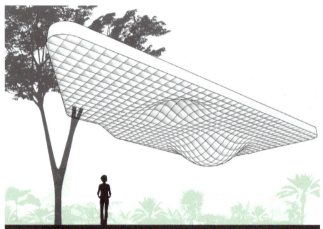

1   Conceptual proposal of canopy.

2   Canopy under construction.

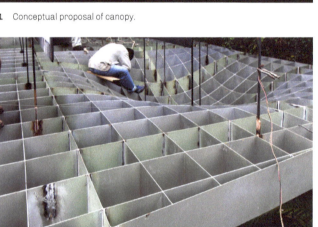

3   Canopy under construction.

4   View from below.

Paredes + Alemán Arquitectos

The 1000 square meter steel canopy covers a tropical landscape by cantilevering from the adjacent structure in order to avoid damaging any of the plants underneath or tree branches above. Due to the sensitivity of the site, the canopy was pre-assembled in approximately 25 square foot sections so they could be lifted up by hand using mechanical pulleys and conventional scaffolding. Once in place, these pre-painted sections were welded together leaving specific edges on the perimeter to be assembled on site section-by-section in order to weave around the tree branches. The welding points were then polished and retouched with polyester resin body filler before repainting the on-site welded areas. Handmade steel clips attached to tensor cables were then welded to hang the structure from a primary truss using the same finishing process. The canopy had to provide shade and privacy while also allowing sun-light, wind, and rain water through for the plants underneath. The open structural crate allows rain water to go through and also provides direct and indirect sun-light to the plants underneath at different times of the day. The structural crate surface of the canopy also responds to the geometry of the site, both in plan and section as its upper and lower synclastic curvatures avoid the tree branches.

5 Landscape canopy.

RECALIBRATION ON IMPRECISION AND INFIDELITY

Milkywave

A light installation made of repurposed ceramic yoghurt pots

1   The yoghurt ceramic pot turns into a light pendant (© AIDIA STUDIO).

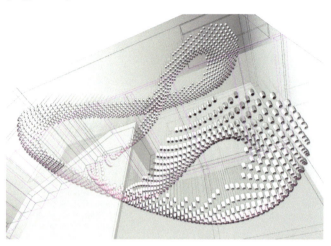

2   Design studies: a moebius strip of light clustering the pots (© AIDIA STUDIO).

3   Milkywave hangs on the stairwell of an old bicycle factory (© AIDIA STUDIO).

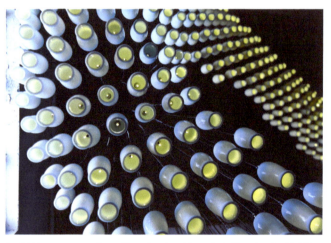

4   1664 pots were collected from local residents in Beijing (© AIDIA STUDIO).

Rolando Rodriguez-Leal
AIDIA Studio
Natalia Wrzask
AIDIA Studio

Milkywave reflects on the role of found objects and their associated narratives in a wider urban context. For this installation, we depart with a quintessential element of the *hutongs* (old city alleys) DNA—the ceramic yogurt jar. Native to the Beijing hutongs, millions of bottles circulate the streets uninterrupted meeting Beijingers on their corner shop and subway stall. We are drawn to the pot by its materiality, translucency, color, and unique shape, properties with the potential of becoming something more, and so we speculate with new forms of aggregation and clustering. The result is a collection of 1664 bottles reconstituted into a new construct. Repurposing is not just about recycling but about challenging perceptions and enabling new sensations; in *milkywave*, we are interested in triggering memories in the visitor and freeing the jar from its original function. It is also a way of celebrating the use of mass produced objects and promoting them as core components in the design of new systems and configurations. At a larger scale, *milkywave* is part on an ongoing research project focused on reading and re-thinking the city through the objects and situations that inhabit it, an attempt to unveil the narratives that speak of claims and conflict, not apparent at plain sight, but at the core of the dynamics that drive change in the city.

5   A moebius strip of light hangs on the stairwell of a former bicycle factory in the historic district of Dashilar in Beijing (© AIDIA STUDIO).

PREXPREN 2017

Exogenous Properties//Endogenous Protocols

1   PREXPREN 1.0 Pavilion, concrete/fabric/wood (B. Slocum, 2017).

2   PREXPREN 1.0 installation for Mextropoli 2017 (B. Slocum, 2017).

3   PREXPREN 2.0 final installation piece (D. Morgenstern, 2017).

4   Concrete/fabric/wood piece: Team Mesh/Cable Truss (B. Slocum, 2017).

Pablo Kobayashi
Adjunct Professor
Universidad Iberoamericana

Brian Slocum
Adjunct Professor
Universidad Iberoamericana

Alberto Vivar
Teaching Assistant
Universidad Iberoamericana

Studios PREXPREN 2017, Universidad Iberoamericana
PREXPREN is a vertical design studio in the undergraduate program at the Universidad Iberoamericana. The studio focuses on the use of active formwork in the construction of aggregations of self-supporting concrete components, employing both analog and digital tools with computational design strategies. The students work with applied design protocols in a process of form-finding whose results are directly affected by the physical properties of the materials with which they work. Additionally, the students are encouraged to explore evolutionary and generative design strategies, emphasizing design as research. #prexpren

5 Above, PREXPREN 1.0; below PREXPREN 2.0 (Various PREXPREN students/professors, 2017).

RECALIBRATION ON IMPRECISION AND INFIDELITY

PREXPREN 2018

Exogenous Properties//Endogenous Protocols

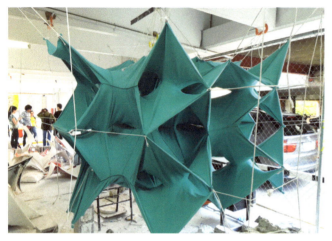

1   Team *Resistencia's* fabric formwork (B. Slocum, 2018).

2   Concrete/fabric pieces: Team *Arrugas y Verticalidad* (B. Slocum, 2018).

3   Concrete/fabric block: Cassandra Vargas (B. Slocum, 2018).

4   PREXPREN 4.0 final review (P. Kobayashi, 2018).

Pablo Kobayashi
Adjunct Professor
Universidad Iberoamericana

Brian Slocum
Adjunct Professor
Universidad Iberoamericana

Luis Carbonell
Adjunct Professor
Universidad Iberoamericana

Alberto Vivar
Teaching Assistant
Universidad Iberoamericana

Paolo Sarra
Teaching Assistant
Universidad Iberoamericana

Studios PREXPREN 2018, Universidad Iberoamericana

Studio PREXPREN is a workshop/design studio for material research in design at the University. The studio proposes a methodology that does not separate formal results from material qualities. Moving away from what Manuel DeLanda describes as "explicitly transcendental resources, eternal essences that define the geometric shapes imposed on materials," we focus on the combination of two materials and two completely different behaviors that, when combined, increase their capacities. On the one hand, concrete and on the other, textiles. Of importance is the approach to the understanding of these materials, their characteristics, qualities and behaviors. #prexpren

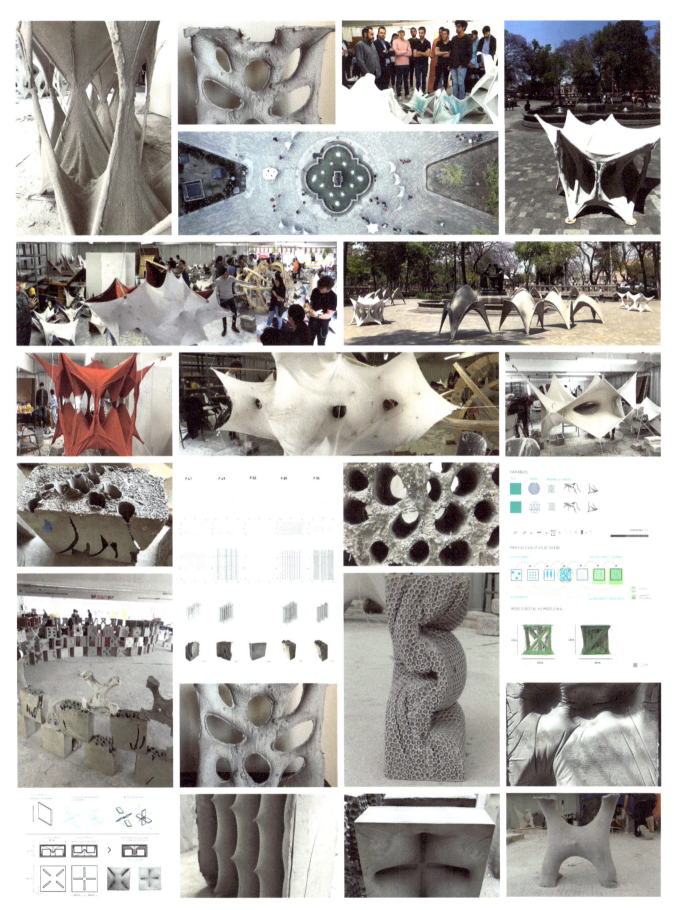

5   Above, PREXPREN 3.0; below PREXPREN 4.0 (Various PREXPREN students/professors, 2018).

Tangible Formations

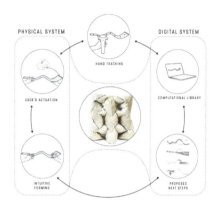

1   Design and fabrication process.

2   Physical prototype of an adaptive free form structure.

3   Digital recording process using VIVE handset.

4   Structure of the computational library.

Kyriaki Goti
ITECH/ University of Stuttgart

Shir Katz
ITECH/ University of Stuttgart

Ehsan Baharlou
ICD/ University of Stuttgart
UVA/ University of Virginia

Lauren Vasey
ICD/ University of Stuttgart

Achim Menges
ICD/ University of Stuttgart

Jan Knippers
ITKE/ University of Stuttgart

Towards Intuitive Design and Fabrication Process using Human-Computer Interaction

This project examines the potential of User Interfaces (UI) and sensor feedback to develop an intuitive design and fabrication process utilizing granular jamming. By taking advantage of the variable stiffness of granular jamming over time, an adaptive fabrication process is presented in which various structures are formed from individual jammed components which can weave or interlock in an overall system. A UI was developed as a design tool which would enable interactive design decisions and operations based on pre-designed formal and tectonic strategies. The project has four research trajectories that were developed in parallel: 1) material system research; 2) development of an ad hoc digital recording system; 3) creation of a computational library that stores users' iterations; 4) development of a User Interface that enables users' interaction with the computational library.

5   Assembly process for wall prototype using granular jamming.

RKFK_TRANSMUTATION PAVILION

1 Isometric.

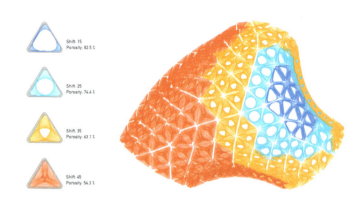

2 Different percentage of porosity according to the knitting.

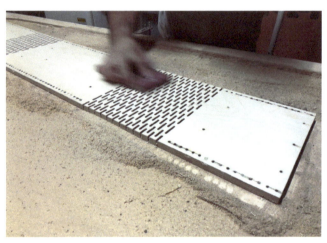

3 Sanding of a piece after cutting with CNC.

4 Prototypes with natural fibers weaving.

Michel Rojkind
Rojkind Arquitectos / RKFK

Yoshio Fukumori
RKFK

Transmutations III: Inform the digital process through craft techniques and vice versa

Ephemeral pavilion was developed using a process of computational design and local fabrication, to encourage social dynamics involving practice and teaching craft techniques. Traditions are preserved by practicing them. The idea is that this pavilion has to be built every 5 years to create a bond among the community, public space, craft techniques, and contemporary technologies.

The technological advance, focused on visualization and computational design, has transformed the way we create and communicate architecture. It has become increasingly easy to generate and conceive complex architectural concepts assisted by digital manufacturing, which can be done in a relatively practical way.

The practice of these technologies is common in economically developed contexts, where all the actors, the commodity chain, architects, engineers, and construction workers have proficiency in the use of these technologies, and the ability to communicate efficiently, resulting in a positive impact and creating innovation in this field.

5 Transmutation pavilion.

RECALIBRATION ON IMPRECISION AND INFIDELITY

RECALIBRATION: on imprecision and infidelity
PEER REVIEWED PROJECTS

RECALIBRATING
Computational Processes

Approximating Climatic Performance with ANNs

Zeynep Aksöz
University of Applied Arts
Vienna/Innochain

Kunaljit Chadha
IaaC/AAG

Alexandre Dubor
IaaC/AAG

Edouard Cabay
IaaC/AAG

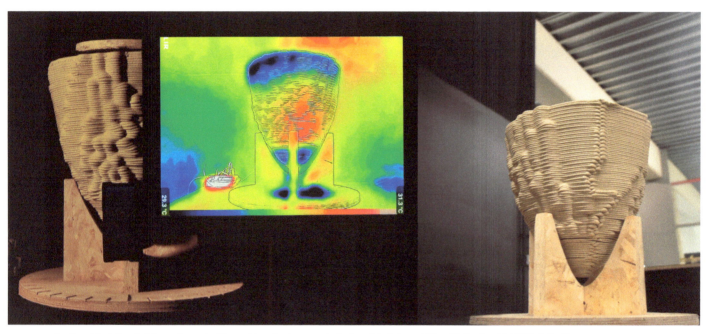

1   Acquiring climatic information using thermal imaging from a robotically printed clay pot (Kunaljit Chadha, 07/2018, © IAAC).

Integrating Artificial Neural Networks in Digital Prototyping for Learning from Physically Collected Climatic Data

The project investigates potentials for integrating artificial intelligence into a digital fabrication process to digitally approximate climatic performance for design evaluation before fabrication. The case study explores the evaporative cooling of robotically printed clay pots. Instead of building a simulation model, the project proposes to use artificial neural networks (ANNs) to learn from geometric features and their relation to physically recorded data. The trained ANN is then used to approximate the performance of the newly generated digital models. After testing the feasibility of such an approximation method, the goal is to expand the experiment to an architectural scale.

In a workshop at IaaC, students were asked to design "Zheer Pots," which are double layered systems containing two clay pots that are activated through the deposition of water into the sand layer between them. When the water starts to evaporate, the surface temperature of both pots decreases, which influences the temperature decrease in the inner pot. The indicators that influence this decrease are the morphologic properties of the clay pot—such as noise and thickness, as well as the properties of the physical environment, namely humidity, wind velocity, and high temperature—which accelerate the evaporation process. In the experiment, the environmental properties were monitored to test the relationship between morphology and the cooling performance. Students were asked to develop a design strategy that influences the cooling, making assumptions about

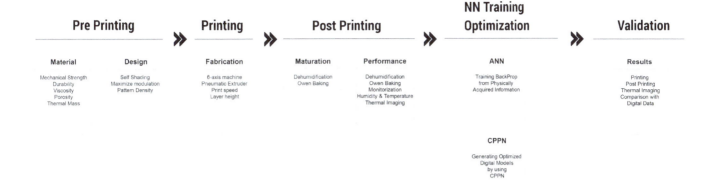

Pre Printing		Printing	Post Printing		NN Training Optimization	Validation
Material	**Design**	**Fabrication**	**Maturation**	**Performance**	**ANN**	**Results**
Mechanical Strength	Self Shading	6-axis machine	Dehumidification	Dehumidification	Training BackProp	Printing
Durability	Maximize modulation	Pneumatic Extruder	Owen Baking	Owen Baking	from Physically	Post Printing
Viscosity	Pattern Density	Print speed		Monitorization	Acquired Information	Thermal Imaging
Porosity		Layer height		Humidity & Temperature		Comparison with
Thermal Mass				Thermal Imaging		Digital Data

CPPN

Generating Optimized
Digital Models
by using
CPPN

2   Experiment Overview from pre production data input to post production data output to train the Neural Network and evaluation (© Kunaljit Chadha).

3   Some of the strategies developed by the students Ya-Chieh Chang and Quan Li during the workshop to increase the cooling performance (© IAAC).

4   Some of the strategies developed by the students during the workshop to increase the cooling performance (© IAAC).

the design-related indicators. These designs were then robotically printed to track their performance.

By deposition of the water in the system, robotically printed samples were activated, and their reactions were recorded. Through thermal imaging and temperature sensors, these reactions were tracked to generate a training set for an ANN. One of the limitations in working with physical samples and ANNs is the generation of a training set. If a single print would be taken as one training sample, a very large set of prints would have to be generated, which would require a long printing process. Therefore, a machine learning model was developed by subdividing a pot in a set of samples by representing it as a collection of mesh vertices to the ANN. Each mesh vertex was analyzed according to its geometric feature (e.g., the amount of convexity or concavity of a certain point in relation to its neighboring vertices) (Wilkinson 2014), the thickness of the print at that location, and its corresponding temperature performance recorded by thermal imaging. This information for each mesh vertex was represented to the ANN as one training sample. Such

a training model enabled the generation of a set of 2,000 samples from one single print, which ended up as a good approximation of the desired performance.

In a further step, an evolutionary learning method was used to generate new digital samples. Compositional pattern producing networks (CPPN) (Stanley 2007) were implemented as a parametrization method to learn from the successful local morphological features and generate new local features that generate noise patterns on the surface of the pot. Without having information on the global geometry, the CPPN generated features only by displacing the mesh points of an initially represented shape without any surface noise. The trained ANN approximated the performance of the generated local features to incrementally train the CPPN to generate good patterns. A different set of samples was inherited at the end of this process, which differed in the surface feature but shared a similar behavior in increasing the surface area. One of the best performing results according to approximation was printed and tested in the physical environment to validate the

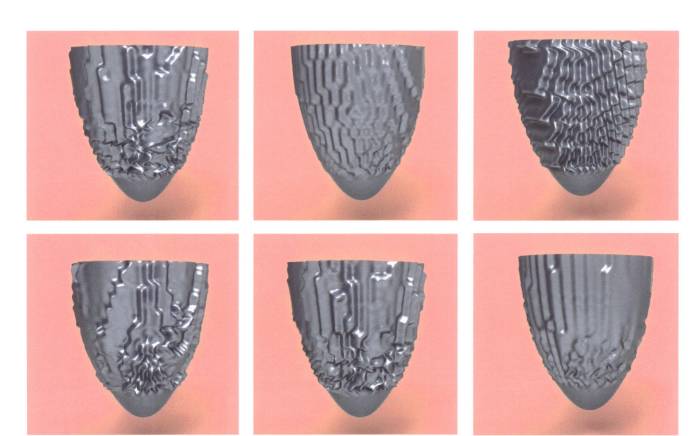

5   Set of generated noise patterns using compositional pattern producing networks. The CPPN was trained to extrapolate a rule of displacement along the surface normal at a given location on the pot to improve the cooling performance approximated by ANN on the certain location. (© Zeynep Aksöz).

6   Sample pot and one of the pots generated using CPPNs, which was robotically printed and tracked during the evaporative cooling process using thermal imaging to test the validity of developed prediction method (Kunaljit Chadha, 07/2018, © IaaC).

Approximating Climatic Performance with ANNs Aksöz, Chadha, Dubor, Cabay

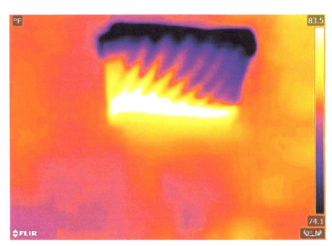

7   The physical data was acquired using thermal imaging and through heat and humidity sensors placed in the pot. (© IAAC).

8   This thermal image was taken during the cooling process, where darker color represents cooler areas. (© IAAC).

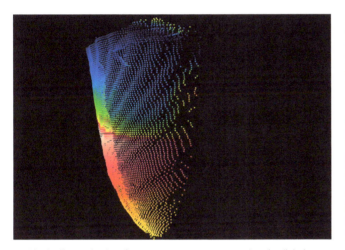

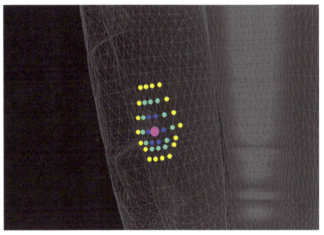

9   Physically acquired surface temperature was mapped on the digital model to prepare for the ANN training. (© Zeynep Aksöz).

10 Analysing local geometric feature (e.e., convexity or concavity of the mesh vertex relative to its neighboring vertices). (© Zeynep Aksöz).

feasibility of the developed process and the possibility of integrating such a process in larger-scale experiments.

ACKNOWLEDGMENTS

This project was developed within the framework of PhD research of ESR4 Zeynep Aksöz in Innochain* International Training Network through a collaboration between University of Applied Arts Vienna Institute of Architecture and IaaC, Institute for Advanced Architecture of Catalonia building upon experiments conducted in Open Thesis Fabrication in 2017:

IoA Faculty : Zeynep Aksöz, Klaus Bollinger, Anja Jonkhans

OTF Faculty: Alexandre Dubor, Edouard Cabay, Mathilde Marengo, Kunaljit Chadha, Sebastian Moreno.

Students: Ya-Chieh Chang, Daniele Fiore, Filipp Sevostianov, Gelder van Limburg Stirum,Quan li,Sheikh Rizvi Riaz, Dongliang Ye.

Collaborators : Windmill, La Salle, Nanosystems, ArtCon and SmartCitizen

*This project has received funding from the European Union's Horizon 2020 research and innovation programme under the Marie Sklodowska-Curie grant agreement No 642877"

www.openfields.eu   www.iaac.net   www.innochain.net

REFERENCES

Stanley, Kenneth O. 2007. "Compositional Pattern Producing Networks: A Novel Abstraction of Development." *Genetic Programming and Evolvable Machines* 8 (2): 131–62.

Wilkinson, Samuel, and Sean Hanna. 2014. "Approximating Computational Fluid Dynamics for Generative Tall Building Design." *International Journal of Architectural Computing* 12 (2): 155–78.

IMAGE CREDITS

Figure 3: © Ya-Chieh Chang, Qan Li, 09/2017

Figures 4, 6, 8, 9, 14: © IaaC 09/2017

All other drawings and images by the authors.

11 Training process overview: Physically acquired data is mapped on the digital model. The digital model is represented to the BackProp Neural Network as a set of mesh points and their geometric features. The mapped surface temperature on the certain mesh vertex is represented as output. (© Zeynep Aksöz).

12 Generative design process using CPPNs to learn to develop successful local geometric features based on the previously trained temperature approximation NN and evaluation of the optimized model by robotic printing and tracking with thermal imaging. (© Zeynep Aksöz).

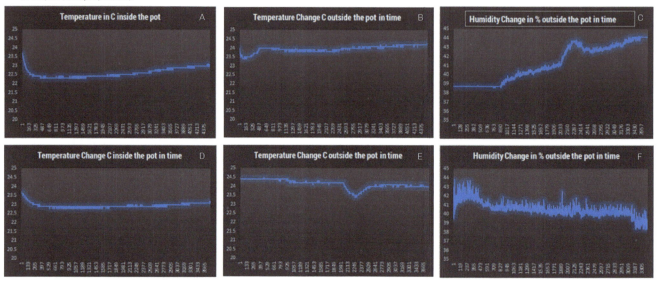

13 Diagrams A–F display a performance comparison between initial clay pots without any surface differentiation (A, B, and C) and the CPPN-optimized clay pot. Even though the final interior temperature in different pots is similar, over time the humidity outside the pot with surface differentiation drops drastically. Through the increased surface area, the evaporation is accelerated and the pot dries faster, whereas the pot with a lower surface area absorbs the water and remains humid.

Zeynep Aksöz is Partner in the design research studio Open Fields. She also is a Marie Curie Fellow, Research Associate, and PhD Candidate at the University of Applied Arts in Vienna. She received her master's degree in architecture at the Architectural Association from the Emergent Technologies and Design Program and a Master of Science Degree at the Technical University of Vienna. Currently, she is pursuing her research within the international training network InnoChain, where she is exploring generative design processes through the collaboration between human and machine intelligence, integrating systems based on machine learning techniques in an early design phase.

Kunaljit Chadha is an Indian architect and digital and robotic fabrication researcher. His early work experience at Menis Arquitectos (Canary Islands, Spain) helped him develop his curiosity towards materiality in architecture. To further investigate in this domain, he pursued his masters at the Institute for Advanced Architecture of Catalonia (IAAC) in Spain and he joined the IAAC R+D department in 2016.. His research interests involve the synthesis of material knowledge with fabrication techniques, and he has been involved with various research projects with biodegradable materials.

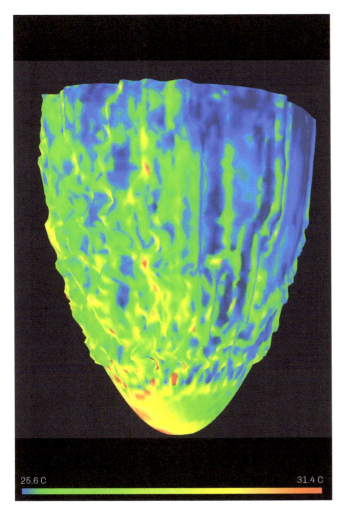

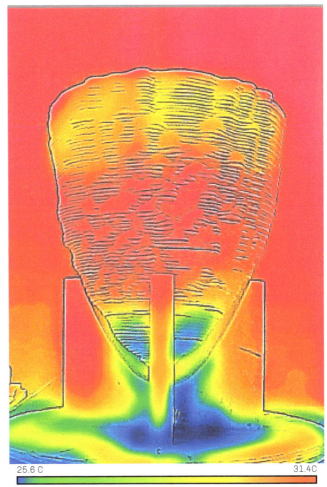

14 Surface temperature of the digitally generated pot, as approximated by ANN. (© Zeynep Aksöz)

15 Surface temperature extracted from robotically printed pot using thermal imaging. (© IAAC)

Alexandre Dubor is an architect expert in digital and robotic fabrication, currently working at IAAC as researcher, teacher, and project manager in R+D. He studied architecture and engineering (M.Arch. ENSAVT / ENPC, M.Arch. IAAC) and has worked in the past at Studio Libeskind, Atenastudio, iDonati, AREP, and Appareil. He's a multidisciplinary designer exploring the potential raised by digital tools and new materials for the improvement of the built environment. He is now leading the Open Thesis Fabrication program as well as the Master in Robotic and Advanced Construction at IAAC.

Edouard Cabay is an architect and educator. He founded and currently directs Appareil, an experimental architectural office in Barcelona. He teaches as senior faculty at the Institute for Advanced Architecture of Catalonia, where he also co-directs the Open Thesis Fabrication program. He has taught experimental design studios at the Architectural Association School of Architecture in London, at the Ecole Speciale d'Architecture in Paris, and at the Ecole Polytechnique Fédérale de Lausanne.

RECALIBRATION ON IMPRECISION AND INFIDELITY

Real Time Performing Architecture

Uwe Rieger
University of Auckland
arc/sec Lab

1   SINGULARITY Particle Space squence (Photo C.Brown, 2016).

SINGULARITY is a unique interdisciplinary architecture-dance-music-technology experience that shifts our understating of architecture as a static environment towards the
perception as a performative construction.

The project setup creates a mixed reality world. Large three-dimensional holographic
constructions appear interactively in space, visible without the need of any additional
viewing devices. The installation combines a live render programme (Unity) with a motion
tracking system (OptiTrack) and a triangular setup of laser projectors illuminating a volume
of haze particles. The core principle is a 1:1 calibration of input sensors and audio-visual
output devices that create a fusion of the virtual and physical environment. The outcome is
a 360 degrees haptic–digital volume, accurately defined in all dimensions, interactive and
inhabitable. The underlying programming allows for both: it reacts to body interaction and
it can autonomously generate architectural space.

The principle of projecting onto fog particles to create spatial effects is well known. It is
used in both spectacular entertainment shows and refined artistic projects. Examples
for this are the inhabitable architectural spaces projected in Anthony McCall's Solid Light
Works (2018) and the installation Parallels by Nonotak Studio (2015), creating the notion of
materialized light. Equally, there are multiple examples that combine dance and motion with
live responsive projections. Well known are the works by Adrien M & Clair B (n.d.), which
use interactive cave-type projections on multisided surfaces or on transparent gauze

PRODUCTION NOTES

Architect: arc/sec Lab &
             Carol Brown Dances
Client: Ars Electronica Festival
             Creative New Zealand
Status: active
Site Area: Indoor performance
Location: Linz, Austria
             Auckland, New Zealand
Date: 2017

2   SINGULARITY Breathing Space sequence (photo K. Simon, 2016).

RECALIBRATION ON IMPRECISION AND INFIDELITY

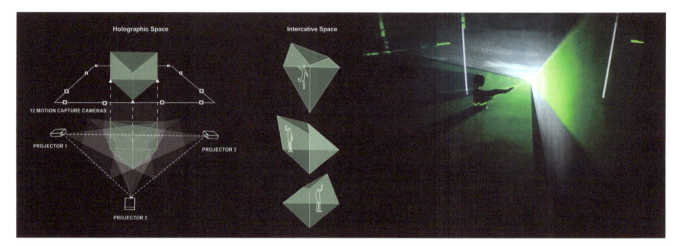

3 Holographic Volumers (graphic/photo Y.Liu, U.Rieger, 2016).

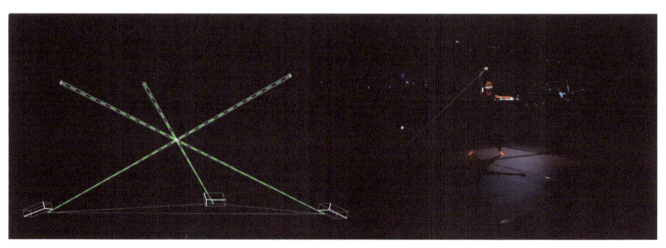

4 Triangulated point projection (graphic/photo Y.Liu, K.Simon, 2016).

screens to create immersive environments. What makes the SINGULARITY project distinct is that the projections are not based on two-dimensional representation, which creates a spatial effect. They are precisely calculated volumes generated through the triangular setup of three projectors. The logic of two-dimensional projection on fog particles is that a light point creates a beam, a line creates a wall and an outline shapes a tunnel-like enclosure. The intersections of these base shapes, produced by three projectors in the SINGULARITY setup, form volumes and inhabitable voids. The shaping, constructing and morphing of this holographic architecture is set in direct response to the user`s actions.

The technical principle was developed at the arc/sec Research Lab at the University of Auckland. Headed by Assoc. Prof. Uwe Rieger, the Lab investigates concepts for new buildings and urban conditions in which digital information is both connected with spatial appearance and linked to material properties. The approach focuses on the step beyond digital representation and digital

fabrication, working to the point where data is linked to immediate human interaction with the physical world. The Lab utilizes large-scale installations as the driving force for the exploration and communication of new dimensions in architectural space. Conducted in a cross disciplinary environment, the experiential investigations are aiming to make data tactile and to demonstrate new concepts on real-time responsive environments.

The performance SINGULARITY was developed with an international team, consisting of architects, a choreographer, a techno composer, and a sound artist. It is performed by three dancers and a band of three techno-operators, reminiscent of a live DJ set-up. Over a sixty minute period, the choreography transforms space, time, and energy to a compelling score of electronic music. On a 7 x 7 m centre stage, surrounded by the audience, the dancers' movements are tracked by 12 motion capture cameras. Reflective markers on hands, feet, and head provide the data of the performers' coordinates on the dance floor and are interlinked with the virtual architecture. Audience and

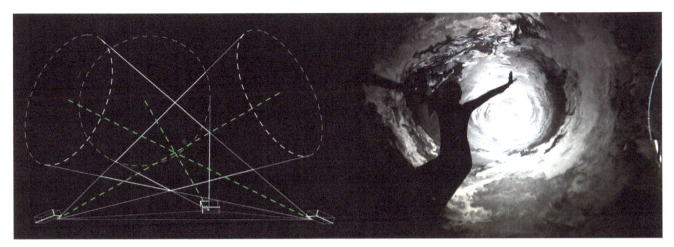

5   Piont to volume ((graphic/photo Y.Liu, U.Rieger, 2016).

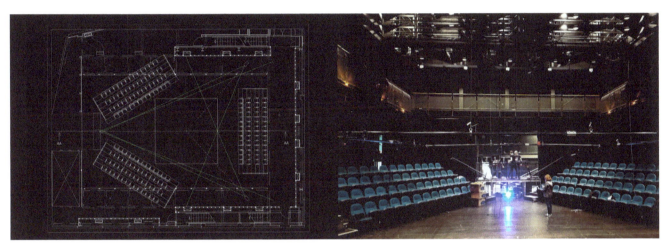

6   Triangular theatre setup (graphic/photo Y. Miao, U.Rieger, 2016).

performer experience an intermixing of physical movement and live-responding "holographic" structures , which
materialize as wormholes, watery walls, electrical volumes,
and magnetic particle streams. The dancers become the
experiential interface of dynamic spaces that house their
bodies and expand to integrate the audience

SINGULARITY can be described as a guided tour through
real-time Reactive Architecture. It was first performed at Q
Theatre in Auckland and re-designed as a two part version
for the Ars Electronica Festival in Linz in 2017. A video
summary is available under: www.arc-sec.com

ACKNOWLEDGMENTS

Creative Director Architecture : Uwe Rieger

Creative Director Choreography: Carol Brown

Interactive Architecture + Programming: Yinan Liu

Music: Jérome Soudan (Mimetic)

Spatial Graphics: Ying Miao

Sound Design: Russell Scoones

Performers: Zahra Killeen-Chance, Adam Naughton Solomon
Holly-Massey

Lighting Consultant: Margie Medlin

REFERENCES

Adrien M and Clair B. https://www.am-cb.net

McCall, Anthony. 2018. "Current and Upcoming." http://www.antho-
nymccall.com/

Nonotak Studio. 2015. "Parallels." http://www.nonotak.
com/_PARALLELS

7   SINGULARITY Drawing Space sequence (photo Ars Electronica, 2017).

IMAGE CREDITS

Figure 1: photo C. Brown, 2016

Figure 2: photo K. Simon, 2016

Figures 3 and 5: graphic/photo Y. Liu, U. Rieger, 2016

Figure 4: graphic/photo Y. Liu, K. Simon, 2016

Figure 6: graphic/photo Y. Miao, U. Rieger, 2016

Figure 7: photo Ars Electronica, 2017

Figures 8: photo Yan Li, 2017

Uwe Rieger studied physics and architecture in Germany. He was the co-founder of the interdisciplinary group kunst und technik e.V. and the architecture office XTH-berlin. His work on Reactive Architecture is based on mixed reality concepts. Since 2006 he is Associate Professor for Design and Design Technology at the School of Architecture and Planning at the University of Auckland, where he has established the arc/sec Lab for Digital Spatial Operations.

8   SINGULARITY Wormhole sequence (photo Y. Li, 2017).

RECALIBRATION ON IMPRECISION AND INFIDELITY

Cypher:
A Cyberphysical Architecture Machine

Güvenç Özel
Ozel Office Inc.
UCLA Department of
Architecture and Urban
Design, SUPRASTUDIO

1   Cypher 3D printed soft robotic helmet with Virtual Reality headset.

Cypher is an architectural installation that creates an interactive experience through robotics, virtual reality, sensor interaction, and machine learning. By combining a responsive soft robotic body with a virtual reality interface, Cypher establishes a bridge between the physical and digital worlds, collapsing them into the same experiential plane by synchronizing a virtual reality simulation with human–robot interaction.

Through an infrared sensor array and LIDAR (similar to technologies in autonomous vehicles), the sculpture has the ability to detect the proximity of the audience and change its shape accordingly. The virtual reality headset tethered to the sculpture teleports the user to its interior, radically shifting the scale of experience from object to space. While in VR, the user has the ability to change the shape of the simulation through natural hand gestures. As the user changes the shape of the VR simulation, the robot moves in real-time, aligning the physical and digital transformations. The relationship between VR and robotics is further negotiated through machine learning algorithms, allowing the sculpture to develop natural motions by learning to predict the way in which people are interacting with it. The AI component allows for the sculpture to get more "intelligent" the more it is exhibited, using the number of interactions it has with the audience to cumulatively shape its motion and behavior through time. Through the synthesis of these multiple technologies, Cypher challenges the notions of what is real vs. virtual, allowing the viewer to travel between multitudes of realities simultaneously.

PRODUCTION NOTES

Architect:	Ozel Office Inc.
Client:	Google Inc.
Status:	Completed
Date:	2018

2   Oblique view.

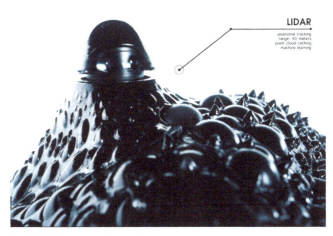

4   LIDAR detecting proximity of users.

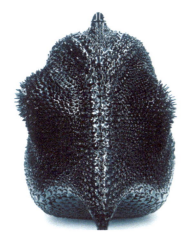

3   Back view.

5   Infrared sensors measuring close proximity of users.

Technical Assembly

Cypher is built through a combination of multiple digital fabrication techniques. Mounted to an aluminum t-slotted frame that is assembled through unique 3D-printed steel joints, there are 36 individual inflatable soft robotic clusters. Each cluster is attached to a computer-controlled solenoid valve. The lower part of the sculpture is made of carbon fiber–infused 3D-printed panels. Spanning between the soft robotic clusters and 3D-printed carbon fiber pieces are large scale silicone panels. These panels are actuated by 5 computer-controlled linear actuators to create an overall mass deformation. The computer and the air compressor are located at the center of the aluminum frame, as well as additional physical computing components. The computer is not only responsible for controlling all physical computing components such as relays, actuators, solenoids and additional IOs, but it also synchronizes the virtual reality content with the robotic components in real time.

Sensory Awareness

A LIDAR scanner attached to the top of Cypher detects the presence of any object or person up to a 40 meter range. Running on custom-made software, the LIDAR scanner collects and stores periodic point cloud data from its environment. The software not only uses this data to change the overall mass of Cypher based on the proximity of the people around it, but also has integrated machine learning so that Cypher can develop more natural motion patterns through time. In addition, the experimental machine learning application allows Cypher to "develop" motion patterns the more it gets exhibited, which eventually allows it to veer away from a typical finite-state machine. The same app is also used to "evolve" the geometry of the VR scenes. In addition, Cypher has 36 infrared sensors embedded in its silicone skin. These sensors have a range of 30 centimeters, and allow for a more intimate interaction with the sculpture. Each sensor directly controls a solenoid, which feeds air into the individual soft robotic silicone clusters, allowing the clusters to pulsate.

6   The VR helmet tethered to the sculpture teleports the user to the interior.

7   Actions taken in VR transforms the shape of the sculpture. Transformations triggered by sensor data also alter the geometry of VR scene in real time.

8   Interior view of VR scene with wireframe to 3D geometry.

9   Interior view of VR scene with interactive particle systems.

10 Initial fully retracted state of Cypher.

11 Proximity data from the LIDAR triggers the overall mass transformation.

12 Infrared sensors trigger pulsations on the silicone skin.

13 Entire mass of Cypher changes according to proximity of the user.

Virtual Reality

The helmet is made up of a combination of 3D-printed carbon fiber thermoplastic and silicone, fabricated through the same process as the sculpture. The helmet inflates and deflates due to the actions triggered by the user in the VR environment, fusing the user into the spectacular motion of the sculpture. A VR headset with inside-out tracking is integrated into the helmet that is tethered to the sculpture. This setup allows for the user to be "teleported" inside Cypher, radically shifting the scale of experience. Through this VR interface, Cypher blurs the boundaries between architecture, sculpture and fashion, allowing them to be experienced interchangeably.

Synchronizing VR and Robotics

The gaming engine Unity is used to synchronize all the VR, physical computing and additional custom software. This approach allows the computational system to develop behaviors. This method provides a platform to collapse physical and virtual actions into a streamlined interface, creating a continuity of experience between the digital and

physical worlds.

The experimental machine learning app allows for Cypher to process and make decisions on proximities of multiple users. Proximity and speed of the users are taken into consideration to smooth out reaction speeds and distances of linear actuators and inflations.

With this combination of multiple technological systems working seamlessly, Cypher exists simultaneously in the digital and the physical worlds. It has an ability to respond to changes in its environment both as simulation and as material. By merging the worlds of virtual reality and robotics, Cypher has an ability to translate concepts and experiences that are traditionally seen as opposite domains: architecture vs. sculpture, object vs. space, digital vs. physical, real vs. virtual, visual vs. tactile, machine vs. organism.

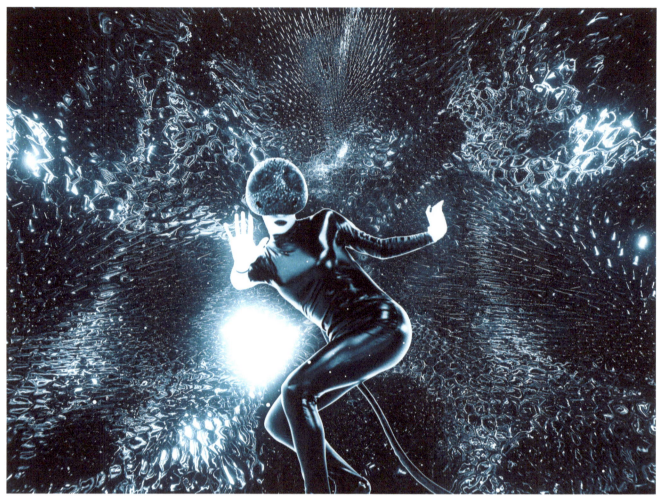

14 Interior view of the VR scene.

PROJECT CREDITS

designed by: Güvenç Özel, Benjamin Ennemoser

fabrication: Güvenç Özel, Tyson Phillips, Benjamin Ennemoser

programming: Benjamin Ennemoser, Tyson Phillips

virtual reality: Güvenç Özel, Benjamin Ennemoser

fabrication modeling: Güvenç Özel, Tyson Phillips, Zhe Liang, Nazli Tatar

special thanks to: UCLA A.UD IDEAS, Google Artists and Machine Intelligence

sponsored by Google. Inc.

IMAGE AND FILM CREDITS

produced by: Ozel Office Inc.

directed by: Güvenç Özel, Joseph Armario

art direction: Güvenç Özel

cinematography: Andy Chinn

edited by: Güvenç Özel, Joseph Armario

assistant camera: Toby Cueni, Jon Na

model: Barbie's Addiction

All Images Courtesy of Ozel Office Inc. All rights reserved.

15 Cypher is an experience machine that becomes architecture, sculpture and fashion simultaneously.

Güvenç Özel is an architect, artist, and technologist. He is a lead faculty member of IDEAS, a multidisciplinary research and development platform in UCLA A.UD, and the principal of Ozel Office, an interdisciplinary design practice located in Los Angeles. His work is at the intersection of architecture, technology and media. His projects and experimental installations were exhibited in museums and galleries in the USA and Europe such as Istanbul Museum of Modern Art and The Saatchi Gallery in London. His recent design and research on 3D printing was awarded one of the top prizes at NASA's 3D Printed Habitats Competition. At UCLA IDEAS, besides teaching his own masters design studio, he continues his research on virtual reality, robotics, interactive spaces and sensing interfaces with support from leading companies such as Autodesk, Microsoft, Oculus, and others.

MOSS REGIMES: Embedded Biomass in Porous Ceramics

Dana Cupkova
Carnegie Mellon School of
Architecture

Colleen Clifford
Carnegie Mellon School of
Architecture

1   Surface detail of porous ceramic tile, close-up photo.

Architecture is fundamentally a part of a larger planetary ecosystem. This project is an experiment conducted within a territory of material computation that argues for a fusion of natural and built environments. Moss Regimes is a prototype for a building façade system that operates as a tree trunk: a living, breathing, self-regulating system. The intention is to instrumentalize principles that exercise a wider range of design tactics in the choreography of thermal gradients between buildings and their environment. By integrating porous ceramics with embedded moss growth, the intention is to develop a vertical ceramic modular bio-facade by exploring variables such as material porosity, surface geometry, thermoregulation, material gradients, and moss species.

Moss Regimes investigates a shift from symbiotic, layered to embedded, multi-material systems (Figure 2). Current green facades are layered systems, operating as an assembly of different parts. Using inorganic building materials, geometry, and organic matter, our approach to integrating biomass into architectural envelopes involves creating morphological variation within the ceramic surface that enables moss rooting but prevents deeper root penetration. This experiment is focused on the relationship of overall tile geometry and control of the surface porosity to enable moss growth and hydration to occur organically over time.

Historically, architectural material engineering has focused on minimizing the effects of climatic processes and weathering on building cladding to ensure longevity and stable

2   Material Distribution diagram

3   [Top] Application of the moss substance onto the test tile with gradient surface porosity. [Bottom] Comparative image of test tile at the time of moss substrate application in June 2016 (left) and two years later in June 2018 (right), two years later, with minimal attention and no maintenance, the moss established itself loosely based on implemented porosity pattern.

performance over time. The role of the building envelope has been framed within the technological imperative supported by the engineering paradigm of materiality associated with a singular high-performing variable that produces assemblies made of serial layers with different parameters integrated into intelligent envelope systems. Many arguments have been made for the integration of biomass into architectural matter. Integration of plant matter into building facades, such as moss, offers a variety of benefits, including production of oxygen, absorption of CO_2, and absorption of pollutants such as nitrogen and air particulate matter (Safikhani et al. 2014). The designs focused on such integration have been mainly pursued from an engineering systems approach, rather than a biosynthetic one. This has been evidenced by the explosion of engineered green walls and roof systems that require

layered construction and high maintenance. However, the recent advances in synthetic biology, computational simulation, digital fabrication technology, and material science offer new ways of thinking about architectural materiality and performance. We believe that architectural materials need to be rethought within a biological paradigm as passive self-organizing systems.

Moss Regimes is a research project that takes on the multi-variable space of a ceramic cladding system to embed it directly with self-sustaining biomass. It dovetails on the previous investigation by the author (Cupkova, Yao, and Azel 2015; Cupkova and Promoppatum 2017) that looks at thermal mass performance actuated by geometric surface figuration properties due to convection. Taking advantage of the effects of complex geometry on the process of

4 Model of proposed tile geometry and water flow simulation using computational model based in mesh subdivision and recursive downhill flow interpolation. The simulation helps to identify the flow paths and drainage basins based on specific mesh topology. Here it is used to develop a porosity matrix to couple moss rooting and water capture.

5 Climate-specific plant research that outlines coupling of the moss species with localized microclimate of the façade surface geometry to support vertical plant growth.

6 Porosity Matrix: We explored porosity gradients in ceramics by mixing granulated perlite into the clay, developing a technique to build in different size of pores related to water capture as a nutrient source. Using three different diameters of granules this diagram shows a combination of the flow-pattern-to-porosity mapping to increase the concentration of the moss rooting based on specific surface topology.

4

MOSS	NAME	ZONES	HABITAT	SOIL pH	SOIL TYPES	MATURE SIZE	MOISTURE	MIN TEMP	GROWTH RATE
	Polytrichum Juniperinum "Juniper Haircap"	0-10	☀ to ☁	any, prefers acidic pH 3.4-5.0	mainly dry soils, also rocks, humus, peat, logs, clay	1" to 4"	💧 to 💧💧	arctic	very fast
	Polytrichum Commune "Common Haircap"	2-9	☀ to ⛅	any, prefers acidic	mainly moist soils, also rocks, gravel, bogs, logs, sand	2" to 6"	💧💧 to 💧💧💧 but drought tolerant	arctic	medium
	Polytrichum Piliferum "Bristly Haircap"	2-9	☀ to ⛅	any, prefers acidic	mainly dry soils, also rocks, sand, peat, grassland	0.4" - 2"	💧 to 💧	arctic	fast
	Dicranum Flagellare "Whip Fork Moss"	4-9	☀ to ☁	any, prefers acidic	rotting wood, trees, soils, humus, bogs, lime intolerant	0.4" - 2"	💧 to 💧💧💧 moist	arctic	medium

5

1.
Waterflow Engravings with Small Pores.

2.
Waterflow Engravings with Cutouts.

3.
Waterflow Outlines with Large Pores

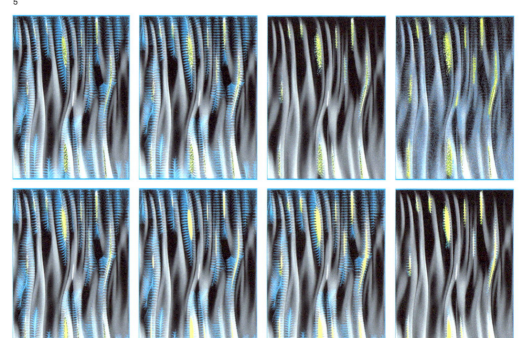
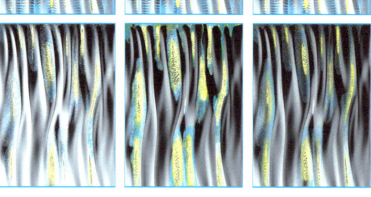

6

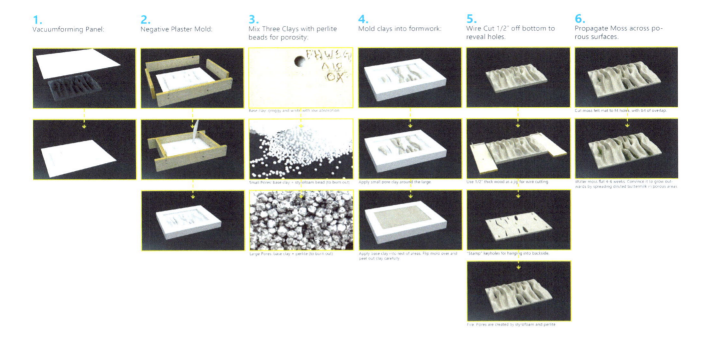

1. Vacuumforming Panel:

2. Negative Plaster Mold:

3. Mix Three Clays with perlite beads for porosity:

4. Mold clays into formwork:

5. Wire Cut 1/2" off bottom to reveal holes.

6. Propagate Moss across porous surfaces.

7   Fabrication process of the test tile: Ceramic mold-making process, casting, distributing of granulated pattern, and curing.

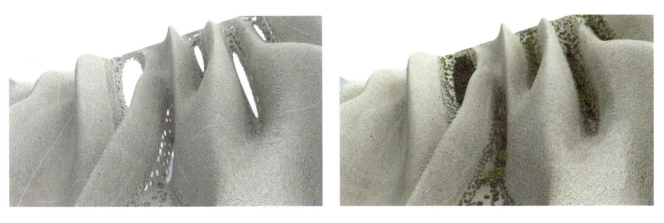

8   Rendering of ceramic tile geometry with pore size varaition (left) and distributed embedded moss growth (right) related to surface porosity change.

passive heat distribution in thermal mass systems and its simultaneous abilities to distribute and capture rainwater (Figure 4). Moss Regimes experiments with gradient materiality and surface geometry in two ways: by simulating the surface's ability to channel and capture water within its geometric configuration (Figure 6), and by coupling the material gradient between solid and porous ceramics for the purpose of enabling and disabling moss rooting within the surface (Figure 7).

Inspired by other works in moss ceramics, primarily coming from the arts where the objects coexist directly with the landscape (Mizuno 2009; Grozdanic 2013), we used contemporary research in material engineering and porous ceramics (Yang and Tsai 2008; Dreschel, Hall, and Foster 2004) to set up our prototyping and material testing.

The digital surface model of the ceramic tile geometry served as a basis for simulating water flow. Using a computational flow simulation (Cupkova, Azel, and Mondor 2015) that is based on mesh subdivision and recursive downhill flow interpolation, this project attempts to understand a pattern of water flow and its accumulation based on topological basin subdivision. The simulation helps to identify the flow paths and drainage basins based on specific mesh topology. Here it is used to develop a porosity matrix to couple moss rooting and water capture.

We used the expertise of the Carnegie Mellon ceramics department to create a matrix of clay types and porosity levels. Different types of clay inherently have more or less porosity; the amount of vitrification can be controlled through kiln temperature and measured by weighing the

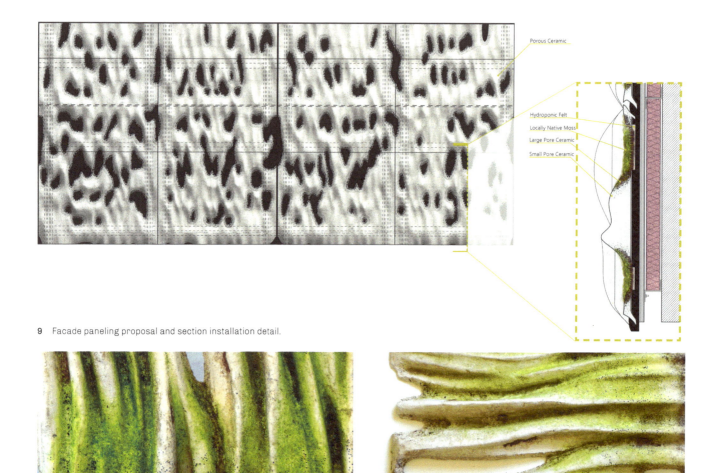

Porous Ceramic

Hydroponic Felt
Locally Native Moss
Large Pore Ceramic
Small Pore Ceramic

9 Facade paneling proposal and section installation detail.

10 Moss-porous ceramic tile surface details after two years of weathering period outdoors.

sample before and after firing. We also experimented with clay additives, such as grog, Styrofoam, and perlite, to enhance the porosity of the samples and provide various sized pores. We ended up controlling the porosity gradients in ceramics by mixing granulated perlite into the clay, mapping the territories with higher water capture directly onto the cast clay. This technique allowed us to build in different sizes of pores related to water capture as a nutrient source. Using three different diameters of granules, the diagram in Figure 5 shows a combination of the flow-pattern-to-porosity mapping intended to increase the concentration of the moss rooting based on specific surface topology. The final product of the experiment, as documented here, has been left weathering outside for two years.

ACKNOWLEDGMENTS

PI: Dana Cupkova, Research Assistant: Collen Clifford, Support Team: Sinan Goral, Thomas Sterling. This project was partially funded by PITA (Pennsylvania Infrastructure Technology Alliance) 2015 and supported by the ceramic studio of Prof. Joe Mannino, School of Art, CMU.

REFERENCES

Cupkova, Dana, and Patcharapit Promoppatum. 2017. "Modulating Thermal Mass Behavior through Surface Figuration." In *Disciplines & Disruption: Proceedings of the 37th Annual Conference of the Association for Computer Aided Design in Architecture*, edited by T. Nagakura, S. Tibbits, M. Ibanez, and C. Mueller, 202–11. Cambridge, MA: ACADIA.

Cupkova, Dana, Shi-Chune Yao, and Nicolas Azel. 2015. "Morphologically Controlled Thermal Rate of Ultra High Performance Concrete." In *MRS Proceedings* 1800. doi:10.1557/opl.2015.569.

Cupkova, Dana, Nicolas Azel, and Christine Mondor. 2015. "EPIFLOW: Adaptive Analytical Design Framework for Resilient Urban Water Systems." In *Modelling Behaviour: Design Modelling Symposium*, edited by M. R. Thomsen, M. Tamke, C. Gengnagel, F. Scheurer, and B. Faircloth, 419–31. Copenhagen: Springer. doi:10.1007/978-3-319-24208-8_35.

Dreschel, T. W., C. R. Hall and T. E. Foster. 2004. "Demonstration of the Porous Tube Hydroponic System to Control Plant Moisture and

11 Moss porous ceramic tile surface details after two years of weathering period outdoors.

Growth." *NASA Technical Memorandum* 2004-21 1533. Kennedy Space Center, FL: NASA.

Grozdanic, Lidija. 2013. "Mineo Mizuno Creates Living Sculptures From Ceramics and Moss." Inhabitat.com, May 17, 2013. https://inhabitat.com/mineo-mizuno-creates-intricate-living-sculptures-from-ceramics-and-moss/

Mizuno, Mineo. 2009. *Coexistence*. Solo Exhibition. Santa Monica, CA: Samuel Freeman Gallery

Safikhani, Tabassom, Aminatuzuhariah Abdullah, Dilshan Ossen, and Mohammad Baharvand. 2014. "A Review of Energy Characteristic of Vertical Greenery Systems." *Renewable and Sustainable Energy Reviews* 40 450–62.

Yang, Gordon C. C., and Chi-Ming Tsai. 2008. "Effects of Starch Addition on Characteristics of Tubular Porous Ceramic Membrane Substrates." *Desalination* 233 (1–3): 129–36.

IMAGE CREDITS

All drawings and images by the authors.

Dana Cupkova is a Design Director of EPIPHYTE Lab (Epiphyte-Lab.com), an interdisciplinary architectural design and research collaborative. She currently holds an Assistant Professorship at Carnegie Mellon School of Architecture, where she serves as the graduate program Track Chair for the Master of Science in Sustainable Design (MSSD) program. She has been a member of the ACADIA Board of Directors since 2014. Her design work engages the built environment at the intersection of ecology, computationally driven processes, and systems analysis.

Colleen Clifford is a recent graduate of Carnegie Mellon University, where she collaborated with Prof. Cupkova on range of architectural material research. Currently she is an Architectural Intern at Bora Architects. She utilizes Bora's supportive employee environment for tactile experimentation and research in soft architecture, parametric design, and sustainable materials. A unique experience in fashion design influences the tools and techniques she uses for architectural thinking. Dedicated to how architecture affects community, Colleen has participated in Design Week Portland and volunteered with Architecture in Schools: Portland.

Holo | Morph Redux

Gregory Thomas Spaw
American University of Sharjah

Lee-Su Huang
University of Florida

Jakob Marsico
Carnegie Mellon University

1   A student at the public showing of Holo | Morph Redux (Spaw, 2016, © SHO Architecture).

Holo|Morph Redux is composed of 168 identical base units connected with varying custom-ized locking inserts, each with unique angles generated computationally via parametric modelling.

Inspiration

The project was inspired by the planar-unitized subdivision of Ron Resch's folded tessel-lations and Buckminster Fuller's geodesic design. In spite of their geometric design and angles, Resch's folded tessellations allow for the generation of fluid surface curvature in 3D space. At the same time, Fuller's geodesic design, which is based on the durable strength of the triangle, allows for the use of lightweight material without compromising structural strength and stability. Holo|Morph Redux combines these design strategies and is made up of laser-cut folded triangular stainless steel units to generate a fluid surface curvature. Variation of the surface geometry is achieved only by varying the customized locking inserts.

Unit Design

The folding pattern of the base unit is a variation on Resch's famed Waterbomb, giving each unit its flexibility. When fully closed, it takes on structural and geometric properties similar to Buckminster Fuller's Fly Eye Dome. As a hybridization of the two, the unit prop-erties gradate as it transitions from open to closed, allowing for the construction of doubly curved surfaces without the need for mass customization or a large number of unique

PRODUCTION NOTES

Designers: SHO Architecture + Ultra
          Low Res Studio
Status: Completed
Site Area: 1,250 sq. ft.
Location: American University of
           Sharjah College of
           Architecture, Art and
           Design Gallery
Date: 2016

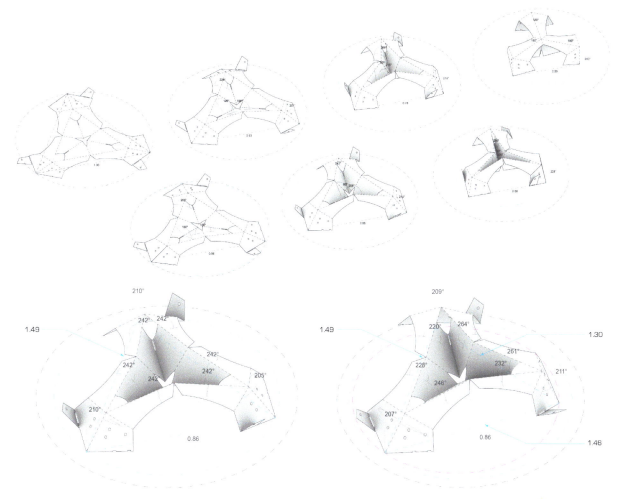

2   Series showing proportional flexibility of typical unit: (top) Comparison of equilateral unit configuration on left vs. scalene unit configuration on right (bottom) (2017, © SHO Architecture).

elements. This strategy enables the construction of various surface configurations while reusing 80% of the material; only the locking inserts need to be customized, while the base units are reusable.

Flexible Proliferation

The standard unit can populate any three dimensional surface through the latter's representation as a Delaunay triangulation. The surface subdivision is optimized using a mesh relaxation and equilateral triangle to generate a topologically advantageous configuration for unit population, with limits on triangle centroid to vertical length ratios of 1:1.724 (closed state vs. open state). Itemization of each mesh face in a field provides the anchor points for the parametric reverse-engineering of folds and angles within each unit.

Material & Assembly

Stainless steel provides tensile strength and enables lightweight tectonics and joining methods that require the folding of sheet cutouts. Metallic car paint provides a

3   A field of units awaiting assembly (Spaw, 2016, © SHO Architecture).

RECALIBRATION ON IMPRECISION AND INFIDELITY

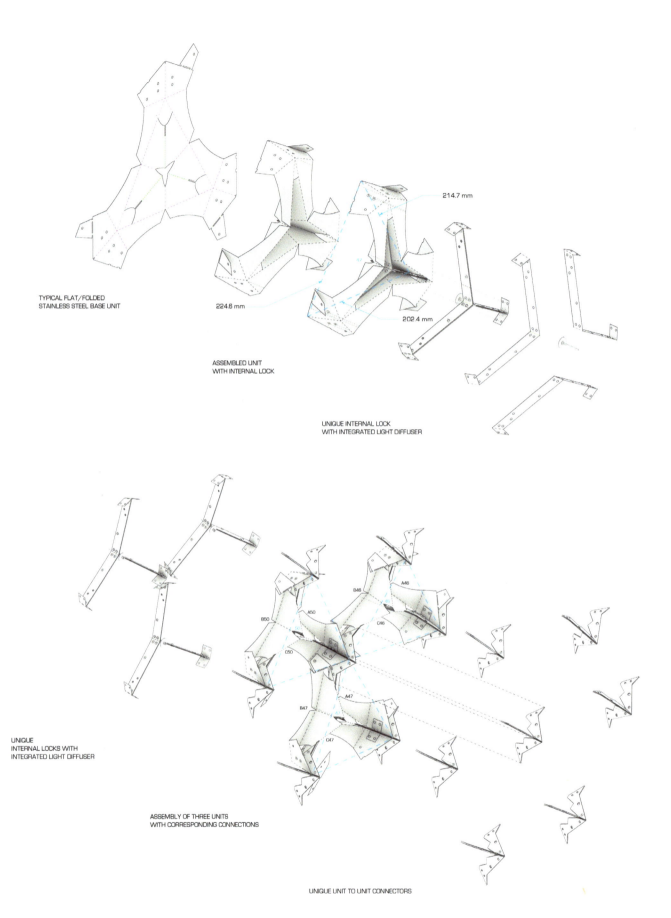

TYPICAL FLAT/FOLDED
STAINLESS STEEL BASE UNIT

224.8 mm

214.7 mm

202.4 mm

ASSEMBLED UNIT
WITH INTERNAL LOCK

UNIQUE INTERNAL LOCK
WITH INTEGRATED LIGHT DIFFUSER

UNIQUE
INTERNAL LOCKS WITH
INTEGRATED LIGHT DIFFUSER

B46   A46

B50   A50   C46

C50

B47   A47

C47

ASSEMBLY OF THREE UNITS
WITH CORRESPONDING CONNECTIONS

UNIQUE UNIT TO UNIT CONNECTORS

4   Typical folded base unit with unique parametrically generated internal lock: (top) Reverse vantage of three base units joined via unique generated unit to unit connectors (bottom) (2017, © SHO Architecture).

5   Seven unit test with both internal unit and unit to unit connectors: (top) Final installation assembly sequence (bottom) (Spaw, 2016, © SHO Architecture).

protective/ornamental coating. The units as fabricated and shipped are flat-packable—the angle lock units are unique and numbered for identification, while a simple hole and rivet system holds the units in place. Sequential assembly according to an indexed master model is required for proper construction.

Video of interactivity: www.sh-o.us/holo-morph-redux

ACKNOWLEDGMENTS

This project was supported by the Design-Build Initiative Faculty Skillset Development Grant, awarded by the American University of Sharjah's College of Architecture, Art, and Design. In addition we would also like to thank the AUS CAAD Lab staff and the CAAD IT staff for supporting and facilitating the creative inquiry.

Project Assistants: Piotr Pasierbiński and Ewa Sroczynska

AUS Student Assistants: Basil Al Taher, Mark Shehata, Saad Boujan, Mariam Elashwal, Adomas Ramzi Zeineldin, Abdukarim Umarov

REFERENCES

Burry, Jane, and Mark Burry. 2010. *The New Mathematics of Architecture*. New York: Thames and Hudson.

Fuller, Richard Buckminster. Geodesic Structures. US Patent US3197927A, filed December 19, 1961, and issued August 3, 1965.

Pottmann, Helmut, Michael Eigensatz, Amir Vaxman, and Johannes Wallner. 2007. *Architectural Geometry*. Exton, PA: Bentley Institute Press.

Resch, Ronald Dale. 1976. Self-supporting Structural Unit Having a Three-dimensional Surface. US Patent US4059932A, filed June 21, 1976, and issued November 29, 1977.

Tenu, Vlad. 2009. "Minimal Complexity." In *Fabricate 2011*, edited by R. Glynn and B. Shiel, 90–93. London: UCL Press.

IMAGE CREDITS

6   The unique nature of the installation encourages visitors to occupy and engage with its subtly morphing geometry (Spaw, 2016, © SHO Architecture).

Gregory Thomas Spaw is an Assistant Professor at the American University of Sharjah in the United Arab Emirates. He has previously held the Ann Kalla Assistant Professorship at Carnegie Mellon University and taught undergraduate and graduate studios, seminars and electives at the University of Tennessee. Concurrent with his academic engagement, Spaw is a principal of SHO, a design collaborative that straddles the territories of teaching, research and practice. His previous professional experience includes work with the award-winning offices of Bohlin Cywinski Jackson, Preston Scott Cohen Inc., and Asymptote. His scholarly pursuits incorporate digital visualization, harnessing parametric workflows, intelligent material fabrication, and responsive environment design.

Lee-Su Huang received his Bachelor of Architecture from Feng-Chia University in Taiwan and his Master in Architecture degree from Harvard University's Graduate School of Design. He has practiced in Taiwan with various firms and in the United States with Preston Scott Cohen Inc. in Cambridge, and with LA.S.S.A Architects in Seoul, Korea. As co-founder and principal of SHO, his research and practice centers on digital design+fabrication

methodology, parametric design optimization strategies, as well as kinetic/interactive architectural prototypes. Lee-Su is currently Lecturer at the University of Florida's School of Architecture, teaching graduate and undergraduate level design studios as well as foundation and advanced digital media/parametric modeling courses.

Jakob Marsico is an interaction designer and media artist. He runs Ultra Low Res Studio, an arts-engineering firm that works with developers and architects to integrate dynamic, experiential installations with the built environment. Jakob currently holds an adjunct instructor position at Carnegie Mellon and is a member of the CoDe Lab in CMU's School of Architecture. He has a BA in Religious Studies from George Washington University and a Masters of Tangible Interaction Design from Carnegie Mellon University.

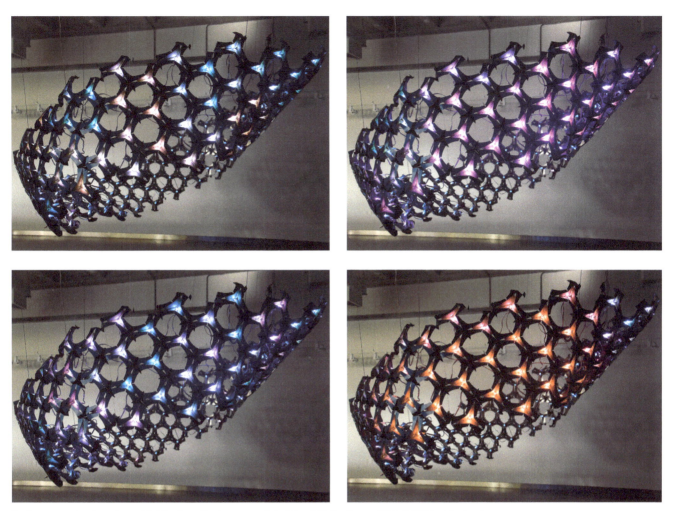

7   Sequence showing animated lighting transitioning across Holo | Morph Redux (Spaw, 2016, © SHO Architecture).

8   Strands of individually-addressable RGB LEDs were mapped, fitted, and animated through the use of a control computer and a Rasberry Pi that translated network packets into low-level SPI protocol (Spaw, 2016, © SHO Architecture).

SYNTETHIC REDUNDANCY
An Adaptive Hi-res Timber Frame

Giovanni Checchia de Ambrosio
Università di Bologna / Co.de.it

Alessio Erioli
Università di Bologna / Co.de.it

1   Synthetic Redundancy: Final proposal.

The ability to manipulate large amounts of data and to embed material proprieties in a simulation process enables the achievement of a novel and richer architectural expression. High-detailed formations, both as structural and aesthetic performative systems, are unveiling the hidden role of materiality in the design process. The embedded feedback between design intent and fabrication technology works as catalyzer for the materialization of the system: conditions like material constraints, connections between pieces, acting forces, boundaries, and voids are directly coded into the system, thus allowing the search for a balanced condition among its space of possibilities.

Synthetic Redundancy is a speculative master's thesis work that probes the architectural and spatial potential of a mereologic system made of lamellar wood components capable of self-organization out of low-level local interaction rules. The aim is to create a highly redundant tectonic system that can be deployed in a 3D space based on environmental conditions and constructive constraints, exhibiting rich articulation and seeking differentiation by means of its organization rather than through the variety of its parts. This logic enables the future implementation of automated processes, from production to construction, whose speed and economy is still unparalleled at the architectural scale.

The environmental information set is used to drive a bespoke variation of a reaction–diffusion system imbued with anisotropic diffusion. Data from structural analysis is used to inform the environmental conditions for the development of the system, fostering

PRODUCTION NOTES

Architect: G.Checchia/A.Erioli
Client: Master's Thesis Project
Date: 2017

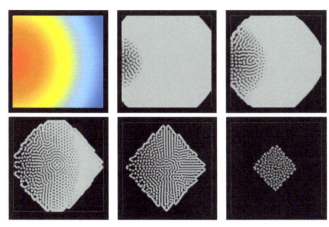

2   RDA: Variation in diffusion based on feed map.

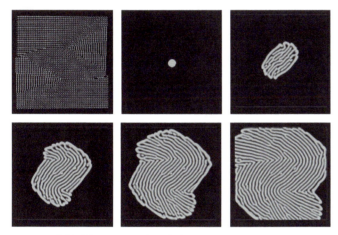

3   Vector field—driven anisotropic variations.

4   Discretization: From load conditions to orientation according to principal stress directions.

remarkable adaptability and directionality features.

The system's tectonics—intended as the realm in which relations amid formal organization and internal logics (structure, function, material system) are established—deploy through the arrangement of a predefined number of construction elements and their topological relations. An initial set of building blocks is first oriented according to principal stress direction, and then, through an iterative feedback loop, each block is able to move, stretch, or orient itself along a fixed set of directions (0°, 45°, 90°).

This second phase, coded like a multi-agent system, has primary importance in the formal and hierarchical organization of the system. Each element can decide whether to connect to a neighbor and follow its trajectory or continue along its own direction, avoiding self-intersection or incoherent shapes. Distributed and selective behavioral triggers like these provoke the emergence of highly differentiated hierarchical configurations, maximizing links and element redundancy from a single element variation.

The multi-agent system behavior overcomes the rigidity of combinatorial logic, strengthening the stability and consistency of the system. The system's tectonic potential is tested first in the generation of archetypical elements, such as beams and columns, and then on more complex assemblies. In this upscaling of the process, a particle-spring system, running in real time along the growth process, has been introduced to qualitatively define the structural stress level for each voxel in the growing structure. This level of information, along with the 3D scalar and vector fields, sets the development conditions for the assembly in a continuous feedback process. The emergence of directional growth patterns, along with richness in detail (connections, sub-structures, hierarchies), enhances the system's differentiation level, adding further depth to its perceptual qualities.

The system remaps the initial reaction–diffusion voxel data, and in a series of spatial/tectonic conditions, further specializes from structural volumetric features towards more superficial/planar cladding, allowing for interfacing

5   Column aggregation, showing the components' articulated deployment without self-intersections.

          Synthetic Redundancy Checchia, Erioli

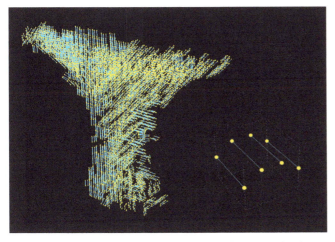

6   The components' orientation phase based on principal stress direction.

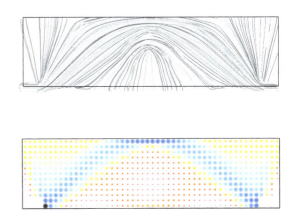

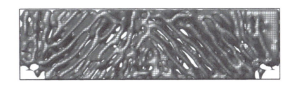

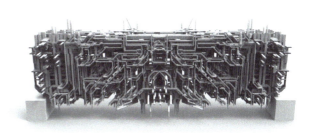

7   Left to right: elements assembly hierarchy, showing angular stiffening.

8   Beam-like test: RDA works as 3D data map driving the system's growth.

with standard building components (interior walls, stairs, doors, windows).

This last level of sophistication adds an important adaptive capacity to a system in which details are means to both embed procedural information and generate richer spatial experiences, fusing structure, space, and ornament in volumetric patterns that emerge as it is deployed. The procedural information itself is the result of fabrication constraints embedded into the growth algorithm, resulting in an intricate reciprocity between design and making.

9   Environmental-driven growth, and the following steps (RD map, orientation and growth).

ACKNOWLEDGMENTS

I would first like to thank my thesis advisor, (here co-author of this work) Prof. Alessio Erioli of the Building Engineering and Architecture School, Università di Bologna. He consistently allowed this paper to be my own work, but steered me in the right direction with his brilliant analysis and suggestions.

REFERENCES

Carpo, Mario. 2011. *The Alphabet and the Algorithm*. Cambridge, MA: MIT Press.

———. 2014. "Breaking the Curve: Big Data and Digital Design." *Artforum* 52 (6): 168–73.

Cheung, Kenneth C., and Neil Gershenfeld. 2016. "Reversibly Assembled Cellular Composite Material." *Science* 341 (6151): 1219–21.

Erioli Alessio. 2010. "Beyond Simulation." *DISEGNARECON* 3 (5): 63–82.

Reiser, Jesse, and Nanako Unemoto. 2006. *Atlas of Novel Tectonics*. New York: Princeton Architectural Press.

Retsin, Gilles. 2016. "Discrete Assembly and Digital Materials in Architecture." In *Complexity & Simplicity: Proceedings of the 34th eCAADe Conference* vol. 1, edited by Aulikki Herneoja, Toni Österlund, and Piia Markkanen. Oulu, Finland: eCAADe, 143–51.

IMAGE CREDITS

All other drawings and images by the authors.

10 Intricacy of detailed hierarchical structures.

11 Detail of floor system and integration with modular elements.

Giovanni Checchia de Ambrosio is an engineer currently working as 3D artist in an Italian architectural practice. His interests are focused on computational design and CG art, and he is constantly struggling to "chase the beauty" in things.

Alessio Erioli is an engineer and Senior Researcher at Università di Bologna, MArch in Biodigital Architecture, PhD in Architectural Engineering. His interests interweave teaching and design ecologies in computational design, focusing on relations among matter, information, agency, space, aesthetics explored through multi-agent based simulations coupled with form-finding strategies, and robotic construction. He is also skilled in computational design, programming, and modeling on several platforms.

Air Hugs: A Responsive Environment

Rachel Dickey
University of North Carolina
Charlotte

Noushin Radnia
University of North Carolina
Charlotte

Alireza Karduni
University of North Carolina
Charlotte

1   Mylar lung inflating in response to the color red.

The Air Hugs installation is a responsive environment that perceives, tracks, and is activated by the color red, moving with passersby and causing the actuated material to produce a calculated gentle breathing, contractions of rustling sounds, and fields of reflection and light. When the large-scale inflatable lungs fill with air, they encase and enclose the space around the body, offering a deliberate, delicate, and gracious hug.

Rekindling the architects' experimental side, the Air Hugs installation treats the gallery as a petri dish for combining space and computation to cultivate contemporary forms of experience. It explores the spatial effects of the large-scale pneumatically actuated lungs controlled with real-time computing and image-recognition techniques. The sensing environment is run with a RaspberryPi, a small single-board computer, connected to a webcam and relay channels, which control the inflation and deflation of the lungs with fans. Red hats are distributed to guests of the installation, which allows for color detection with the webcam mounted 30 feet above the ground for full field of view. Once the system detects red, the lungs closest to the color fill with air and then deflate as passersby leave their proximity. This proximity is based on a three by three grid that aligns with the grid of the lungs and corresponds to the division of images through the image processing code (Figure 5).

Searching through the ideals of the projects from the 1960s, the Air Hugs installation redeploys the inflatable as an imaginative tool for exploring the implications and consequences

2 Installation with responsive inflatable lungs suspended from the ceiling.

3 Two installation guests walking through with red hats.

4 Dancer activating the installation for the first time for the public.

of emerging trends and technologies. It carefully outfits its membranes with a strong, light, plastic, vacuum-metalized film invented by NASA to insulate everything from the Hubble Space Telescope to blankets, rockets, and rovers. This high-tech membrane, which encases the air, brings surface qualities of light, reflection, and sound, and is controlled by computational sensing and actuation.

Reasonable yet absurd, the title draws from the use of air as a primary material and the hug as the convergence of two systems of difference in an affectionate embrace. To conceive of an architecture of air requires a fundamental shift in the structural and atmospheric frames of the discipline from fixed to flexible, hard to soft, static to dynamic, dense to empty. The hug, however, offers an immediate awareness of one's body in relation to other bodies, and of the space—or lack thereof—between them, thus recalibrating human scale and enhancing social interactions. Combined air and hugs offer an otherness, which excites our present temporal existence and moves beyond the rigidity that most often structures our built environments.

This exhibition lines the gallery unapologetically with softness, much like the lining of architecture with the hanging of curtains, placement of carpets, and wrapping of foams around furniture in order to modify a local environment. It does not simply stand in the empty space, but instead fills it with potential, reaching and gesturing outward yearning for reciprocation. The Air Hugs installation asks, how can we find humanity in certain forms (perhaps even forms beginning before language and culture) and reintroduce those forms as means of integrating responsivity and feedback in architecture? How might design and technology provide us with newfound intimacies with ourselves, each other, and the world around us?

ACKNOWLEDGMENTS

This research was conducted at University of North Carolina Charlotte and show cased in the Storrs Gallery as part of the Dense Emptiness Symposium.

Special thanks to the team of research assistants: William Hutchins, Sara Shamloo, Hunter Sigmon, Swathi Sreedharan, and Lina Taheri

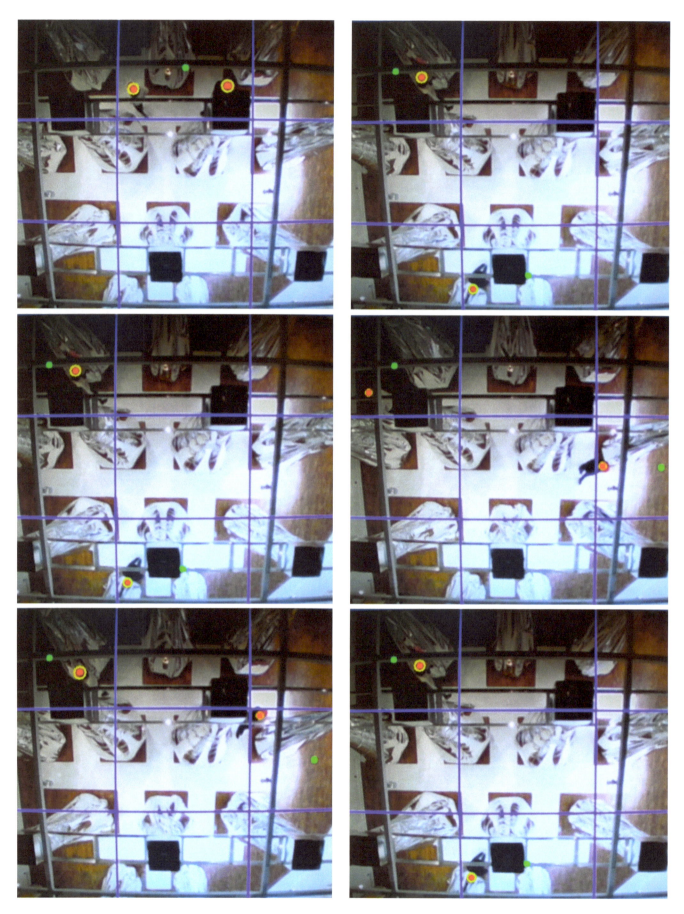

5   Stills from webcam video that tracks red. Green dot shows closest lung.

Air Hugs Dickey, Radnia, Karduni

6   Guest observing her reflection in the mylar. as it inflates around her.

REFERENCES

Lavin, Sylvia. 2011. *Kissing Architecture*. New Jersey: Princeton Press.

Lord, Chip, and Schreier, Curtis. 1973. *Ant Farm's Inflatocookbook*. San Francisco: Self-published.

IMAGE CREDITS

All images by the authors.

Rachel Dickey is an Assistant Professor of Computational Design at the University of North Carolina at Charlotte. She holds a Master of Design Studies from Harvard University Graduate School of Design and a Bachelor of Science in Architecture and Master of Architecture from the Georgia Institute of Technology. Dickey's research explores the intersections between design, technology, and culture.

Noushin Radnia is a teaching fellow at the School of Architecture, University of North Carolina at Charlotte. She holds a dual Masters in architecture and information technology from UNCC. She has pursued her research in the Digital Arts Lab at UNCC in the domain of human and technology relationships with a focus on communication, exploring both digital and analog realms.

Alireza Karduni is a PhD student in the College of Computing and Informatics at the University of North Carolina at Charlotte (UNCC). His research involves creating novel methods and technologies for understanding and impacting the public space. Karduni has a dual MS in architecture and information technology from UNCC and an MS in urban planning and policy from the University of Illinois at Chicago.

7   Image of deflated lungs.

Air Hugs Dickey, Radnia, Karduni

8   Image of fully inflated lungs..

RECALIBRATION   ON   IMPRECISION   AND   INFIDELITY

OPALE: AN EMOTIVE SOFT ROBOTIC GARMENT

Behnaz Farahi
University of Southern
California (USC)

1   This is Opale: An emotive soft robotic garment moves based on emotions of people around. (Nicolas Cambier & Kyle Smithers, 2017).

We tend to respond to people around us through our unconscious facial expressions and bodily movements. When surrounded by smiling people, we often smile back. And when threatened, we often take on a defensive stance. Animals do the same. Dogs, cats, and mice bristle their fur as a defensive mechanism or as a form of intimidation. So why can't we develop clothing that can do the same? For example, how might clothing sense aggression and go into defensive mode accordingly?

Opale is a custom-made fashion item, integrating soft robotics and facial tracking technology, which responds to the expressions of onlookers' faces. Inspired by animal fur, the outfit is composed of a forest of fiber optics embedded in silicon whose fur bristles when under threat, or which purr when stroked. It is equipped with a camera that can detect a range of facial expressions: happiness, sadness, surprise, anger, and neutral. It also incorporates an interactive pneumatic system that can respond accordingly. For example, Opale can respond to "anger" by agitated movements, or to "surprise" by bristling, in order to influence social interaction.

The material development of the Opale project with its forest of fiber optics was based on a study of human "body architecture." Data captured from an analysis of surface curvature of the human body and the underlying contours of the muscles informed the location, density and height of each fiber. The intention was to exaggerate the movement of underlying muscles by having denser and longer fibers following the contours of the muscles.

2   Details of fiber optics in silicone landscape, Opale.

3   Small camera embedded inside the silicone dress.

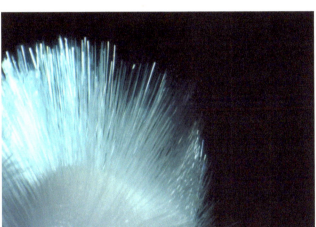
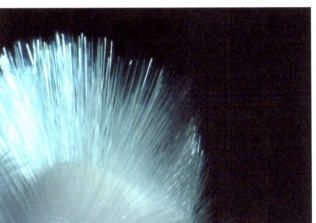

4   Close up of a shoulder pad inflating based on the data from the camera.

5   How might clothing sense aggression, and go into defensive mode?

Opale consists of 52,000 fibers embedded in a silicone base.

The fabrication process for this project consisted of manually inserting fiber optics into the laser cut mounting surface (1/4″ clear acrylic sheet). After placing all the fibers into the surface, the fibers were carefully moved to a bath of silicone (Eco-flex 30). After 48 hours, once the silicone was fully cured, the mounting surface was removed gently from the fiber landscape.

The inflatable behaviors were controlled using a custom designed electrical board attached to an Adafruit Feather microcontroller (M0 with ATSAMD21G18 ARM Cortex M0 processor) capable of controlling an array of six low powered 3-port medical solenoids (LHLA Series). This facilitated the computational control of air pressure and rapid inflation through the Arduino programming environment. As a result, each of the six pneumatic soft composites pockets were capable of providing dynamically controlled texture patterns that could vary in speed and frequency of change. For this, a miniature sized CO_2 capsule (16

gram, LeLand) and a regulator (15 psi output, Beswick) and lithium polymer battery (3.7 V, 2000 mAh) were used.

This project is an attempt to explore the technical possibilities of computer vision and dynamic actuation in order to address psycho-social questions of emotion. It is part of an ongoing research initiative into the relationship between emotional expressions and social interactions. It builds upon the capacity of computer vision to recognize different facial expressions that has already been explored by others, but crucially integrates this system into interactive clothing. Opale is a highly innovative initiative which could open up new opportunities for the worlds of design, fashion and technology. Not only does the smart garment promise to become part of the apparatus of human intelligence but it can also benefit many people with autism who have difficulties recognizing facial expressions. People with autism might be paying attention to what you are saying but be unable to tell if you are happy, sad, or angry. As a result their responses might not match the desired expectation, leading to isolation and rejection by others. Such a system

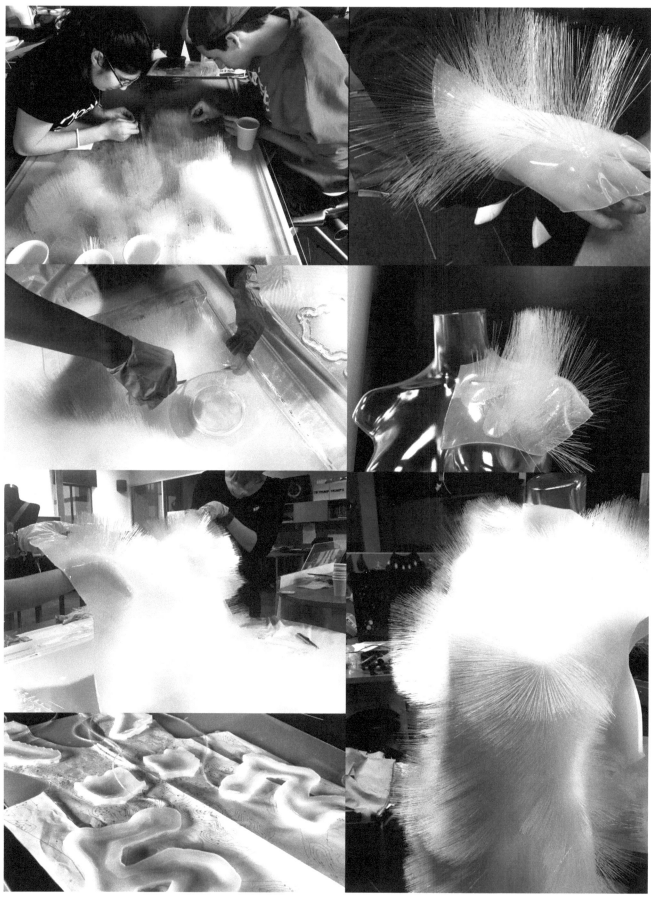

6   Fabrication of the soft robotic dress with landscape of fiber optics.

OPALE Farahi

7   16 g CO_2 capsule and pressure regulator (15 psi output).

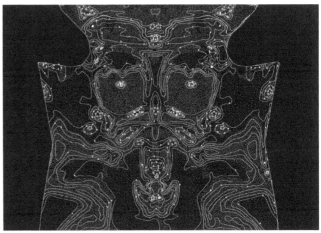

8   Data from surface curvature analysis of the human body informs the location, density and the height of fibers, simulated using Grasshopper.

9   A pneumatic control circuit consisting of six 3-port solenoids valves with coax cable connections.

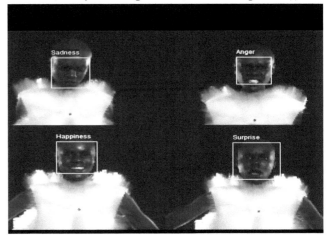

10   Facial tracking camera embedded into the silicone dress, and can detect onlookers facial expressions. (Happiness, Sadness, Surprise and Anger). Behnaz Farahi, 2017.

can help them blend more easily with others and over time learn appropriate responses.

ACKNOWLEDGMENTS

This research is part of a broader ongoing collaboration with Paolo Salvagione and Julian Ceipek. I would like to thank them for their helpful advice and contributions to the production of these works. I would also like to acknowledge the USC Bridge Art + Science Alliance Research Grant program that funded "Opale."

IMAGE CREDITS

Figures 1–5: © Nicolas Cambier and Kyle Smithers, 2017

Figures 6–9: © Behnaz Farahi, 2017

Behnaz Farahi is a designer exploring the potential of inter-active environments and their relationship to the human body working in the intersection of architecture, fashion, and interaction design. She is also an Annenberg Fellow and PhD candidate in Interdisciplinary Media Arts and Practice at USC School of Cinematic Arts. She has an Undergraduate and two Masters degrees in Architecture.

Buoyant Ecologies Float Lab

Adam Marcus
California College of the Arts

Margaret Ikeda
California College of the Arts

Evan Jones
California College of the Arts

Taylor Metcalf
California College of the Arts

John Oliver, Ph.D
Benthic Lab, Moss Landing
Marine Laboratories

Kamille Hammerstrom
Benthic Lab, Moss Landing
Marine Laboratories

Daniel Gossard
Phycology Lab, Moss Landing
Marine Laboratories

1   Buoyant Ecologies Float Lab.

The Buoyant Ecologies Float Lab is a prototype for a new kind of resilient coastal infrastructure. It merges expertise from design, advanced composites manufacturing, and marine ecology to imagine a floating architecture of the future that can exist productively with its surrounding environment. The project, which will be deployed in San Francisco Bay in fall 2018, builds upon three years of applied research, prototyping, and monitoring conducted by a collaborative team of architects, ecologists, and fiber-reinforced polymer (FRP) manufacturers. The large-scale prototype consists of a floating breakwater structure that incorporates a digitally fabricated, ecologically optimized FRP composite substrate with variable topographies that perform both above and below the water.

The research challenges conventional notions of "biofouling"—the unwanted accumulation of marine life on the underside of floating structures—and instead proposes controlled upside-down habitats as an ecological resource. The underwater landscape channels plankton and other nutrients into valleys that provide protected habitats for marine invertebrates of various sizes, helping to promote ecological diversity and support biological growth that in large quantities can help attenuate wave action. In this regard, the project explores how innovations at the micro scale of material performance can initiate vectors of change that will have impacts at the macro scale of coastal resilience.

The project utilizes advanced design computation workflows to integrate ecological criteria into digital, parametric models than can be used to iterate and simulate how

PRODUCTION NOTES

Designer: CCA Architectural
             Ecologies Lab
Fabricator: Kreysler & Associates
Status: Built
Location: San Francisco Bay
Date: 2017

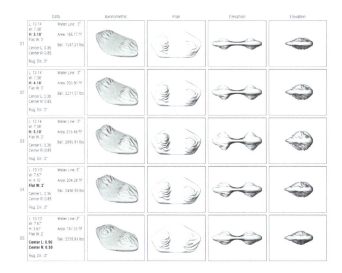

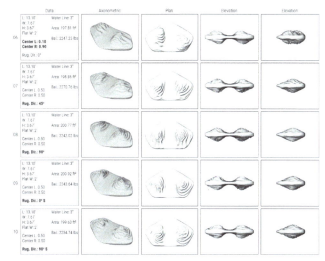

2   Matrix of formal and geometric studies.

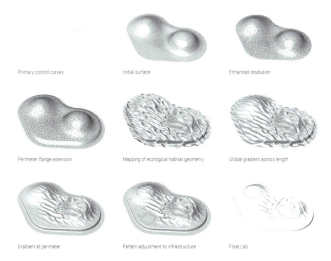

3   Sequence of evolutionary diagrams explaining the Float Lab's formal and geometric logics.

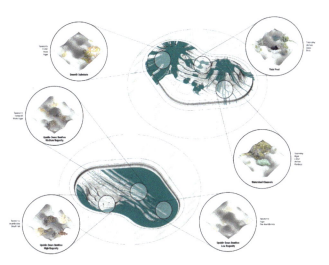

4   Ecological performance, above and below the water, with flow simulations documenting the flow of water across the surface on both the top and bottom sides of the prototype.

the substrate will perform as a diverse marine habitat. Since 2015, nearly two dozen full-scale FRP prototypes have been produced for testing and monitoring different surface geometry, slopes, and dimensional parameters for the "hillocks" and "valleys" along the substrate. Marine ecologist team members have installed duplicates of the prototypes in locations in Monterey Bay and San Francisco Bay to compare how the substrates perform in different environments. Monitoring and documentation of these proof-of-concept prototypes help to establish precise parameters such as shape, dimension, slope, and spacing that can be input directly into a digital model that translates these constraints into optimized topographic landscapes. The use of robotic and CNC machinery to fabricate molds for the FRP substrate allows for a high degree of customization and surface variation.

Embedded within the Float Lab's design and fabrication process is a modular logic that anticipates future deployment at a greater scale. The pentagonal plan geometry allows for a variety of configurations that can accommodate networked archipelagos of wave-attenuating floating breakwaters that help limit coastal erosion. When scaled up, the aggregations also allow for a buoyant urbanism of floating communal habitats. The reliance on reusable molds to mass-produce the FRP composite components provides an economy of scale and material.

Although informed by empirical research, the project also embraces more visionary aspirations, imagining a floating architecture of the future predicated on mutually beneficial coexistence between humans and nonhumans. The floating breakwater concept can apply to different climates and contexts, but it can also scale up to suggest inhabitable,

RECALIBRATION ON IMPRECISION AND INFIDELITY

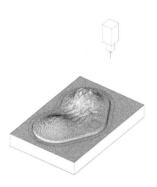 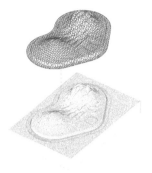  

1. POSITIVE FORM
A robotically controlled router carves the positive form of the Float Lab hull from a block of EPS foam. Integrated file-to-factory workflows ensure precise translation of optimized geometry.

2. FABRICATE REUSABLE MOLD
Fiber-reinforced polymer (FRP) is applied over the positive to create a negative, reusable fiberglass mold to be used for fabrication of the hull.

3. NEGATIVE MOLD
The FRP negative is mounted to a support frame. Foam knockouts are added as needed for hull penetrations, such as the hatch and solar vent.

4. FABRICATE FLOAT LAB HULL
FRP is applied in the negative mold to produce the hull's two identical parts, which are then adhered together with resin. This process can be repeated to produced additional Float Lab modules.

5   Diagram of Float Lab fabrication process, explaining the reusable mold used to fabricate both parts of the hull.

Clustered Aggregation   Hexagonal Aggregation I   Hexagonal Aggregation II

6   Tiling diagrams demonstate the prototypes modular logic and capacity for forming networks or chains of floating breakwaters.

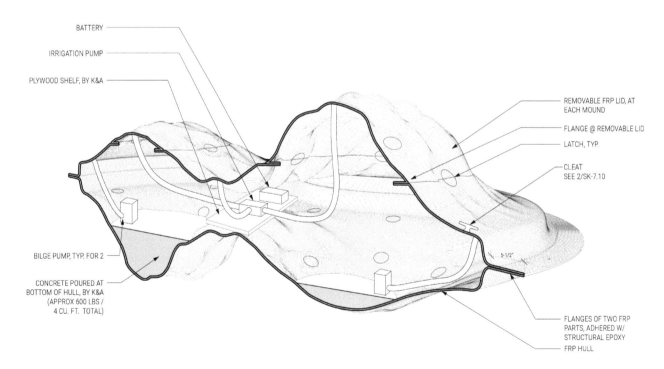

BATTERY

IRRIGATION PUMP

PLYWOOD SHELF, BY K&A

REMOVABLE FRP LID, AT EACH MOUND

FLANGE @ REMOVABLE LID

LATCH, TYP.

CLEAT
SEE 2/SK-7.10

BILGE PUMP, TYP. FOR 2

CONCRETE POURED AT BOTTOM OF HULL, BY K&A (APPROX 600 LBS / 4 CU. FT. TOTAL)

5-1/2"

FLANGES OF TWO FRP PARTS, ADHERED W/ STRUCTURAL EPOXY

FRP HULL

7   Section through Float Lab, showing interior cavity and equipment.

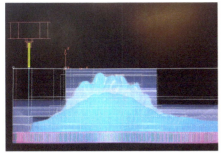

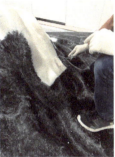

8   Float Lab fabrication process.

9   View of Float Lab from above.

10 Detail view of Float Lab hull.

multifunctional floating structures that provide habitats for humans and animals. The ambition is to leverage design computation and digital fabrication workflows to instigate new models for a whole-system concept of human habitation and ecological resilience in anticipation of the impacts of climate change and sea-level rise.

ACKNOWLEDGMENTS

Project Leaders: Adam Marcus, Margaret Ikeda, Evan Jones

Design Assistants: Taylor Metcalf, Georine Pierre, Jared Clifton

Marine Ecology: Benthic Lab, Moss Landing Marine Laboratories – John Oliver, Kamille Hammerstrom, Daniel Gossard

Fabrication: Kreysler & Associates

Naval Architecture & Engineering: Tri-Coastal Marine

Funders: Miranda Leonard, Kreysler & Associates, Ashland Reactive Polymers, Autodesk Workshop at Pier 9, Port of Oakland

Thanks: Jonathan Massey, Stephen Beal, Tammy Rae Carland, Karen Weber, Dustin Smith, Niko Oliver.

IMAGE CREDITS

All drawings and images by the authors.

Adam Marcus is an Associate Professor of Architecture at California College of the Arts in San Francisco, where he teaches design studios in design computation and digital fabrication and co-directs CCA's Architectural Ecologies Lab. He has previously taught at Columbia University, the University of Minnesota, and the Architectural Association's Visiting School

11 View of Float Lab.

Los Angeles. He directs Variable Projects, an award-winning design and research studio in Oakland, California. Adam is a graduate of Brown University and Columbia University's Graduate School of Architecture, Planning and Preservation, and he currently serves on the ACADIA Board of Directors.

Margaret Ikeda is an Adjunct Professor at California College of the Arts, where she co-directs CCA's Architectural Ecologies Lab. Margaret is a founding partner at ASSEMBLY, a practice whose focus, since 1994, is exploring connections, both in innovative details, materials and assemblies, and in the integration of multiple building specialists into the design process. Her work is notable for forging alliances with community stakeholders that builds a collaborative network for the realization of projects.

Evan Jones is an Adjunct Professor at California College of the Arts, where he co-directs CCA's Architectural Ecologies Lab. Evan founded ASSEMBLY, a Berkeley-based architecture office, with Margaret Ikeda in 1994. ASSEMBLY's projects span in scale from furniture to multistory mixed-use housing. As implied by the name, the firm focuses on connections between physical materials and the collaborative process of design. Its projects have included the design and fabrication of installations and furnishings as well as large-scale commercial work.

Taylor Metcalf is a graduate of Ball State University and California College of the Arts, where he earned his Master of Architecture degree and worked as a research assistant for the CCA Architectural Ecologies Lab. His final project at CCA earned the Masters Thesis jury prize, and he was a co-recipient of the 2017 AIA COTE Top Ten Award for research and design related to floating ecologies. He currently practices at Studio Gang in Chicago.

John Oliver, Ph.D explores disturbances and other processes that influence the organization of benthic invertebrate communities, particularly in soft bottom ecosystems where human activities are major disturbances. He directs the Benthic Lab at Moss Landing Marine Laboratories, which recently discovered one of the most diverse soft bottom communities in the world at the shelf edge in Monterey, and dramatic degradation of inner shelf communities from regional warming in the last 25 years. John also works in freshwater benthic ecosystems, and coordinates a dozen habitat restoration projects in local sand dunes and wetlands in the Moss Landing area.

Kamille Hammerstrom completed an undergraduate degree in Marine Biology at Texas A & M University at Galveston and a master's degree in Marine Science at the University of South Carolina, following an early and intense childhood fascination with blue crabs. Kamille is interested in disturbance and recovery processes in marine environments, from how seagrasses respond to boat hull and propeller damage to how infaunal communities change in response to erosion and tidal restriction. She has participated in research projects in the seagrass-coral banks, eelgrass, tidal, kelp, infaunal communities, hydrothermal vents, and sponge communities.

Daniel Gossard is currently a graduate student at Moss Landing Marine Laboratories. His graduate studies have given him the opportunity to study algal population dynamics within bull kelp forests. Dan will be actively SCUBA diving in multiple bull kelp forests in order to characterize the small scale spatial and temporal distribution of an obligate epiphyte. He is currently in the midst of culturing bull kelp and its epiphyte in order to conduct in situ settlement experiments using the two species.

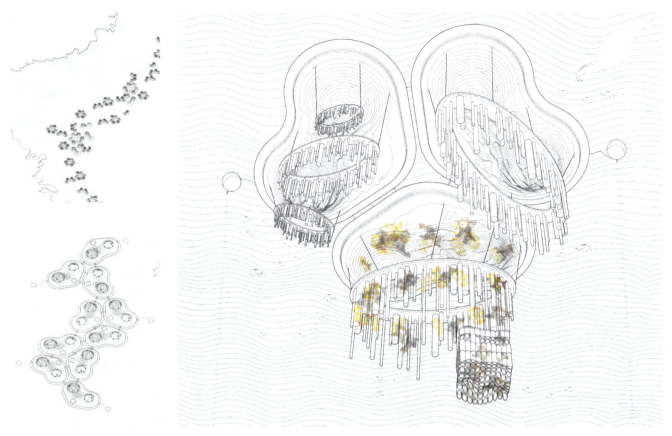

12 These drawings project forward into the future and imagine a larger-scale deployment of floating breakwaters as a means to reduce coastal erosion and the impacts of sea level rise on shorelines. The necklace of buoyant wave-attenuating structures offers an adaptable and reconfigurable alternative to the more conventional fixed and permanent typologies of seawalls and barriers that many cities currently look to as models for coastal resilience.

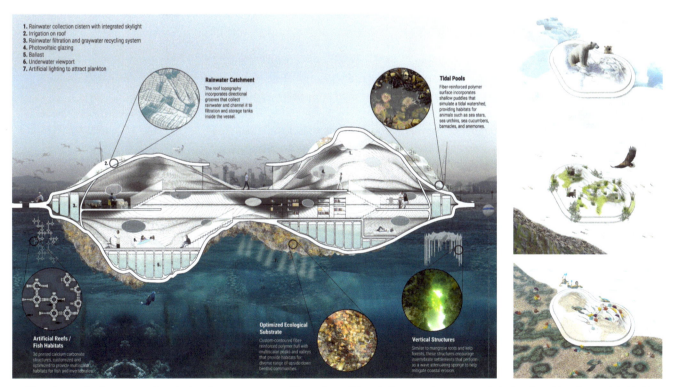

13 These images begin to suggest how the breakwater concept could transfer to different climates and contexts, and also how it could scale up to inhabitable, multifunctional floating structures that provide habitats for humans and animals. The ambition is to instigate new models for a whole-system concept of human habitation as well as ecological resilience in anticipation of the impacts of climate change and sea-level rise.

Image Matters:
Digital to Analog Translations

McLain Clutter
University of Michigan

Cyrus Peñarroyo
University of Michigan

1   Digital patterns translated to. physical wet-plate collodian wall panel prototypes.

Images are everywhere in contemporary culture: illuminated through pixel, embossed in neuron, stored in silicon, and still ever-present in a range of photographic formats.[1] Once theorized primarily as representations of past events or projections of future visions, the amount of physical and digital space they occupy in our world demands that they now be understood as objects in their own right. Indeed, images constitute an increasing proportion of the stuff of everyday reality (Linder 2012). And yet the matter of images remains under-explored. If images are a ubiquitous part of our material world, what is the status of the materiality of images? How might we materialize digital images? What might emerge from translations between the digital and analog milieus? This research explores these questions, following a broad spectrum of theorists from the arts, humanities, and sciences who have recently turned critical attention to the vast proliferation of images within digital culture (Rancière 2007; Flusser 2011 [1985]; Damasio 2010).

Architecture is a uniquely appropriate medium through which to pursue this research. From Kevin Lynch's identification of imageability as the quality that allows one to form a cognitive map of a place (1960), to Venturi and Scott Brown's interest in the imagistic qualities of the American strip (1972), to contemporary work featuring image-embedded facades by Herzog and de Meuron, the role of image is a recurrent topic in architectural discourse. This history is increasingly relevant today. Our every engagement with the built environment is prefigured by expectations colored by images and our contemporary media ecology has tutored audiences in modes of image recognition that are still only dimly

PRODUCTION NOTES

Architect: EXTENTS

Status: Installed exhibition

Date: 2018

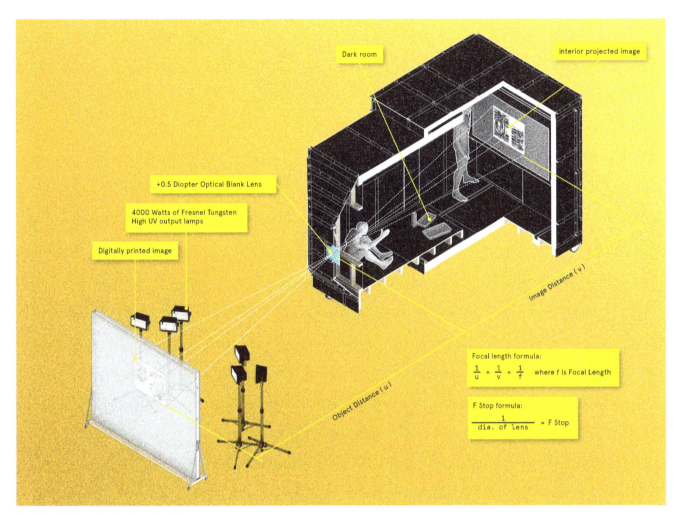

Labels in figure:
- Dark room
- interior projected image
- +0.5 Diopter Optical Blank Lens
- 4000 Watts of Fresnel Tungsten High UV output lamps
- Digitally printed image
- Image Distance (v)
- Object Distance (u)

Focal length formula:
$$\frac{1}{u} + \frac{1}{v} = \frac{1}{f} \quad \text{where f is Focal Length}$$

F Stop formula:
$$\frac{1}{\text{dia. of lens}} = \text{F Stop}$$

2   Optical diagram for image-capturing process.

understood. Such context could revise prior paradigms of architectural legibility and representation, attracting new and heterogeneous audiences. Meanwhile, images have consumed architecture culture and design methodology. While architects produce drawings as the primary instruments of service, we increasingly work in software with raster-logics. We rely on images to perpetuate disciplinary conversations and to communicate to clients and consultants (May 2017). The tempo of architectural production has been tuned to the trending Instagram feed. Now more than ever, we live in a house of images. The pixel is the new brick.

Image Matters explores the matter of architecture in contemporary image culture. The project recovers archaic and materially rich tintype wet-plate collodion photographic processes to produce prototypes for an image-embedded architectural wall panel system. Tintypes use metallic substrates to host layers of chemical and physical reactions, eventually producing a direct-positive photographic image. The resulting prints have unique

visual qualities—they are unmistakably photographic and yet sufficiently distinct from the types of images most commonly circulated today to interrupt habitual consumption. They also have unique physical properties, with texture, depth, and thickness endowing heightened material presence that vastly exceeds that of the typical snapshot or the digital pic. Tintypes are image-objects that evince familiar photographic effects, while obstinately refusing to cede their object-quality to the realm of mere appearances.

Our prints were produced within an occupiable sliding-box camera that is itself a study of the material consequences of image-making. Clad in neoprene, particular attention was paid to the paneling details, which elevate the light and thermal requirements for our imaging process to the level of architectural expression. Aluminum reproductions of these details serve as the substrates for the final products of this phase of our project. These substrates have been photo-sensitized, producing three-dimensional tintypes displaying photographic impressions of digitally

      RECALIBRATION ON IMPRECISION AND INFIDELITY

3   Wet-plate collodion wall panel prototype.

4   Wet-plate collodion wall panel prototype.

5   Wet-plate collodion wall panel detail.

6   Wet-plate collodion wall panel prototype.

7   Wet-plate collodion wall panel prototype.

Image Matters Clutter, Peñarroyo

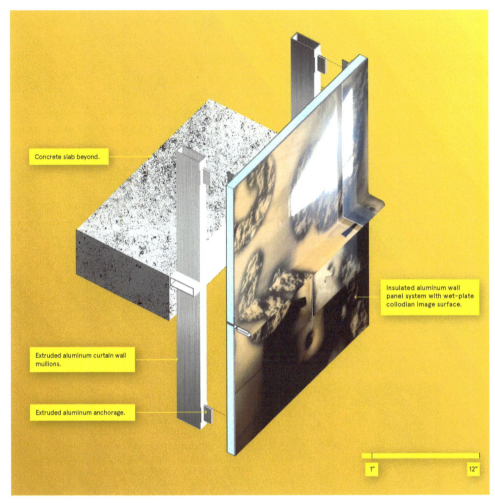

Concrete slab beyond.

Insulated aluminum wall panel system with wet-plate collodian image surface.

Extruded aluminum curtain wall mullions.

Extruded aluminum anchorage.

1" 12"

8 Panel wall system detail.

9 Panel detail.

manipulated material textures. Novel relationships emerge between the digital patterns imaged and the material consequences of the tintype process. The results confuse the flat and the thick, the digital and archaic, precision and imprecision, all in order to disrupt or slow-down image circulation to secure moments of rare attention.

ACKNOWLEDGMENTS
Thanks Michael Amidon and Te-Shiou Chen for design and fabrication assistance.

This project was funded through the 2017 Research Through Making Program at the Taubman College of Architecture and Urban Planning and the University of Michigan Office of Research Artistic Production grants program.

NOTES
1. Here, we allude to recent thought on the nature of images, and their motions through medium and mind, most prominently developed by Hans Belting (2011).

2. We draw on the artist Artie Vierkant's use of the term "image-object" (2010).

REFERENCES
Belting, Hans. 2011. *An Anthropology of Images: Picture, Medium, Body*. Princeton, NJ: Princeton University Press.

Damasio, Antonio. 2010. *Self Comes to Mind: Constructing the Conscious Brain*. New York: Vintage Books.

Flusser, Vilem. 2011 [1985]. *Into the Universe of Technical Images*, translated by N. Roth. Minneapolis: University of Minnesota Press.

Linder, Mark. 2012. "Images and Other Stuff." *Journal of Architectural Education* 66 (1): 3–8.

Lynch, Kevin. 1960. *The Image of the City*. Cambridge, MA: MIT Press.

May, John. 2017. "Everything is Already an Image." *Log* 40: 9–26.

Rancière, Jacques. 2007. *The Future of the Image*, translated by G. Elliot. London: Verso.

Metal plates are coated with a substance called collodion, which is liquid nitrocellulose mixed with two halogen salts, cadmium bromide and ammonium bromide. Gently rocking helps with even distribution. The plates are then placed in a silver nitrate bath where a chemical reaction turns the halogen salts into two photosensitive silver salts, silver bromide and silver iodide. >>>

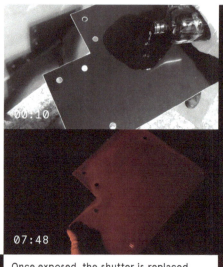

The plate becomes photosensitized after 5 minutes in the silver nitrate bath. It is removed from the bath and positioned on a shelf attached to a pull-down screen. The shutter is opened and the plate is exposed for 6 minutes to the digitally-manipulated pattern outside of the Conditions Room, illuminated by 4000 Watts of artificial lighting. >>>

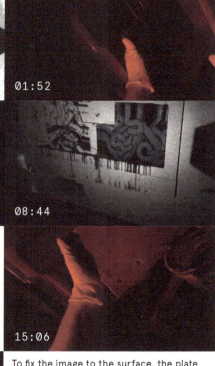

Once exposed, the shutter is replaced and a developer mixture is poured onto the plate for exactly 10 seconds to render the image visible. The wetplate developer contains ferrous sulfate, acetic acid, potassium nitrate, white sugar, and alcohol. To dilute this mixture, 1000mL of developer is combined with 500mL of distilled water. >>>

Overdevelopment can lead to blue streaks in the image and underdevelopment produces dark or foggy results. To halt the development process, the plate is washed for 1 minute using 2 gallons of distilled water. Following the edge of the plate, the water is poured evenly across surface to avoid unwanted marks or black spots. >>>

To fix the image to the surface, the plate is placed in an ammonium thiosulfate rapid fixer bath. To dilute the mixture, 1 part rapid fixer is combined with 3 parts water. After 5 minutes in the fixer, the image appears. The plate is removed, excess liquid is drained off, and the plate is placed on a tray to be taken out of the Conditions Room. >>>

The plate is washed under cold water for 5 minutes and set out to dry. The plate is sprayed with 1 coat of lacquer to help seal the image to the surface. The plate is then bent to replicate the neoprene details on the exterior of the Conditions Room. The bent plates are sprayed with several coats of lacquer to give it a glossy finish. >>>

10 Video stills from the wet-plate collodion development process.

11 Our occupiable sliding box camera.

Venturi, Robert, Denise Scott-Brown, and Steven Izenour. 1972. *Learning From Las Vegas*. Cambridge, MA: MIT Press.

Vierkant, Artie. 2010. "The Image Object Post-Internet." http://jstchillin.org/artie/pdf/The_Image_Object_Post-Internet_us.pdf.

McLain Clutter is an architect, author, and Associate Professor at the University of Michigan Taubman College of Architecture and Urban Planning. Clutter's work focuses on the role of architecture within the multidisciplinary milieu of contemporary urbanism, and the interrelations between architecture and media culture. His writing has been broadly published, and his design and research has been awarded support from the Graham Foundation for Advanced Studies in the Fine Arts, an Architect Magazine R+D Award, an ACSA Faculty Design Award, and other honors. Clutter's book, *Imaginary Apparatus: New York City and its Mediated Representation* was published by Park Books in 2015.

Cyrus Peñarroyo is a designer and educator whose work explores architecture's entanglement with contemporary image culture. He is an Assistant Professor at the University of Michigan Taubman College of Architecture + Urban Planning where he was the William Muschenheim Fellow in 2015–2016. Previously, he taught at Princeton University and Columbia University GSAPP and has worked for LTL Architects, OMA, and Bureau Spectacular. He was Project Lead on Manual of Section, published by Princeton Architectural Press and Cities Without Ground: A Hong Kong Guidebook, published by ORO. Cyrus received his M.Arch from Princeton University and his B.S. in Architecture Summa Cum Laude from the University of Illinois at Chicago.

Rigorously Anexact: Building Bending-Active Bamboo Shells

Kristof Crolla
The Chinese University of
Hong Kong

1   ZCB Bamboo Pavilion, night time event (Michael Law, 2015).

Introduction

The ZCB Bamboo Pavilion, the largest bending-active bamboo shell structure to date, was tied together in Kowloon Bay, Hong Kong, by hand using large raw bamboo poles—the fastest growing, most sustainable construction material naturally available in most of the rapidly developing parts of the world. Without typical architectural drawings, using nothing but steel wire and a century-old knotting technique, a handful of local craftsmen erected the graceful, forty-yard-spanning event space, elegantly placed in a park in the heart of one of Hong Kong's many busy districts. Its hyper lightweight canopy structure, the result of extensive iterative prototyping, modelling, and simulation, weighed only seventy percent more than the weight of the volume of air it covered.

Design

The design maximizes the use of bamboo's unusually high flexibility and strength and is tailored to a local historic craft's typical intuitive additive construction method. The shell structure consists of a bending-active triangulated diagrid, built up from three layers of bamboo that fold onto themselves into three large hollow columns. The design was developed over an iterative series of bamboo prototypes at various scales and digital design models that incorporated physical force simulations. These simulation engines abstracted the forces at play in the analogue studies. Corresponding vector forces were applied on a discretized curve network represented by a spring-particle system. Each curved member in this interconnected network aimed at maintaining its original length and attempted to

PRODUCTION NOTES

Architect: Kristof Crolla / The
            Chinese University of
            Hong Kong
Client: Zero Carbon Building
            of the Construction
            Industry Council
Status: Dismantled
Site Area: 4,575 sq. ft.
Location: Kowloon Bay, Hong Kong
Date: 2015

2   ZCB Bamboo Pavilion by day (Michael Law, 2015).

straighten itself out by pushing back against its anchor points. Macro-level behavior could be perceived similar to what was found in the physical models: the virtual setup would find its force equilibrium in comparable emergent geometries.

Construction

The construction required the development of a stream-lined, semi-automated, low-tech workflow that centred on a computation-driven yet manual labelling method. Bamboo axis lines were digitally unrolled into long straight lines onto which intersection points with other members were mapped out. Simplified drawings and printed sticker labels were used to mark these points onto interconnected canes. These were then lifted on top of a temporary bamboo scaffolding, where they were manually bent and tied into place. Substantial tolerances and material deviations were balanced out into the overall structure that gradually found its own equilibrium shape while being erected. Bending forces in individual curves steadily balanced one another out as the final shape emerged.

The pavilion was covered with a triangulated, tailor-made tension membrane for which the fabrication required detailed onsite measurement of the as-built structure. Three-dimensional scanning was practically impossible given the complexity of the structure and the intricate scaffolding underneath. Instead, a manual method was developed based on the observation that all workers carried smartphones. A shared cloud-based spreadsheet was set up in which triangle edge lengths were fed after manual measurement. From these numbers, the cutting pattern was digitally regenerated. Next, the fabric was cut and welded into one giant sleeve that was draped and fixed onto the bamboo structure.

Conclusion

The ZCB Bamboo Pavilion proves that even within the most primitive construction contexts, design process engineering and computational optimization can yield substantial architectural benefits. Rather than incorpo-rating computer-controlled manufacturing technology that is foreign to craft-based workflows, instituting only

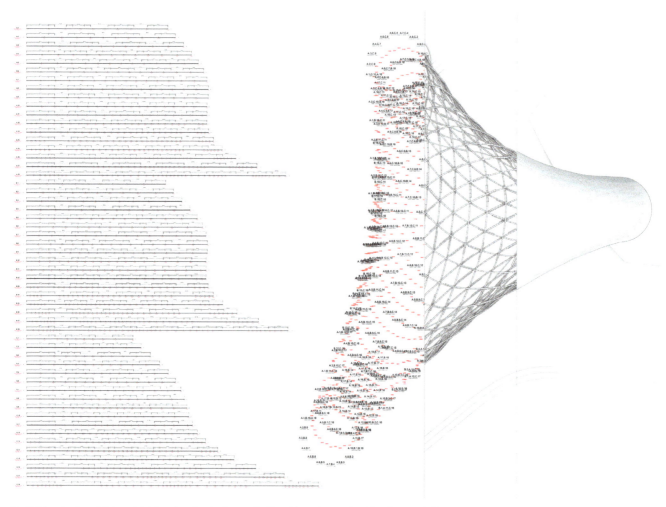

3 Highly selective digital model data extraction for the production of bespoke construction documentation.

slight strategic changes can dramatically expand design delivery opportunities. For this, the role and responsibilities of design architects must be expanded such that they can operate beyond their commonly perceived tasks and be involved in project delivery. Only through participatory action research from conceptual design to construction can practical building implementation information be identified, challenged, and processed for inclusion in a holistic end-to-end design and construction process. Such modes of interactive collaboration allow the digital era's promise of a new relationship between craft and construction to be achieved.

ACKNOWLEDGMENTS

This research was supported by a grant from the Research Grants Council of the Hong Kong Special Administrative Region China: Project No. CUHK24400114, Project Title: Architectural design and building of lightweight, bending-active, bamboo shell structures for Hong Kong, using live physics engines.

Design research team: Kristof Crolla, Adam Fingrut, Ip Tsz Man Vincent, and Lau Kin Keung Jason (CUHK); Goman Ho; Alfred Fong; Vinc Math; Martin Tam; George Chung.

Client project team: Christopher To (CIC); Yan Ip and Margaret Kam (ZCB).

Construction team: W.M. Construction Ltd. (Main Contractor), Sun Hip Scaffolding Eng. Co., Ltd. (Bamboo Construction), Ladden Engineering Ltd. (Fabric Contractor), CONA Technology Co. Ltd. and Brandston Partnership Inc. (Lighting)

REFERENCES

Buildings Department. 2006. *Guidelines on the Design and Construction of Bamboo Scaffolds*. Hong Kong: Buildings Department.

Crolla, Kristof. 2017. "Building Indeterminacy Modelling: The 'ZCB Bamboo Pavilion' as a Case Study on Nonstandard Construction from Natural Materials." *Visualization in Engineering* 5:15.

Crolla, Kristof. 2018. "Bending Bamboo Rules: Beyond Century-Old Typologies." *Journal of Architectural Education* 72 (1): 135–45.

4   Manual bamboo connection and intersection labelling (Kevin Ng, 2015).

5   Individual member installation onto temporary scaffold (Kevin Ng, 2015).

6   Manual bending of bamboo (Kevin Ng, 2015).

7   Matching corresponding intersection labels (Kevin Ng, 2015).

8   Completed bamboo structure (Kevin Ng, 2015).

RECALIBRATION ON IMPRECISION AND INFIDELITY

9 Hand-measuring of fabric triangle edge lengths (Kevin Ng, 2015).

10 Fabrication data input into cloud-based spreadsheet (Kevin Ng, 2015).

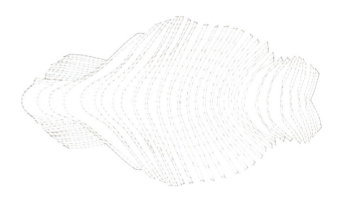

11 Fabric CNC-manufacturing drawing generated from measured edges.

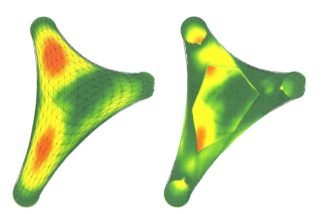

13 Comparative diagram between 3D-scanned as-built structure and digital model: Green = less than 50mm deviation, red = more than 1000mm.

12 Fabric fixing to bamboo structure (Kevin Ng, 2015).

14 ZCB Bamboo Pavilion by day (Michael Law, 2015).

Dunkelberg, Klaus. 1985. *IL31 Bamboo. Bambus als Baustoff. Bauen mit pflanzlichen Stäben*. Stuttgart: Institute for Lightweight Structures, University of Stuttgart.

Hidalgo-López, Oscar. 2003. *Bamboo: The Gift of the Gods*. Bogotá: Oscar Hidalgo-López.

Janssen, Jules J.A. 1995. *Building with Bamboo, A Handbook*. London: Intermediate Technology Publications.

Piker, Daniel. 2013. "Kangaroo: Form Finding with Computational Physics." *Architectural Design* 83 (2): 136–37.

Kristof Crolla is an architect who combines his architectural practice, Laboratory for Explorative Architecture & Design Ltd. (LEAD), with his position as Assistant Professor in Computational Design at the Chinese University of Hong Kong (CUHK) School of Architecture. He is currently based in Hong Kong, where his work has received numerous design, research and teaching awards and accolades, including the RMIT Vice-Chancellor's Prize for Research Impact—Higher Degree by Research. He is best known for the projects "Golden Moon" and "ZCB Bamboo Pavilion," for which he received the World Architecture Festival Small Project of the Year 2016 award.

IMAGE CREDITS

gateHOUSE_GARDEN

Michael Hughes
American Univ. of Sharjah

William Sarnecky
American Univ. of Sharjah

1   View from the southwest (I. Ibrahim, June 2017).

The gateHouse_Garden tests digital fidelity at the frontier of building scale, where less precise tolerances imposed by manual assembly, extreme weather, site-based logistics, limited budget, and multiple material interfaces conspire to subvert computational accuracy that can be proven in smaller, more controlled environments and scales (furniture/sculpture). Located in a region where service personnel endure long shifts under challenging circumstances, the project seeks to elevate basic human comforts while simultaneously extracting exuberant delight out of a small-scale design opportunity.

Context
Situated on an unnaturally landscaped campus in an otherwise arid environment notable for extreme high temperatures (+40° C/110° F is common throughout the five months of summer), the project references and transforms regional vernaculars to mitigate solar gain through passive cooling strategies. In this harsh environment campus security guards are expected to remain outside their small, 10 sq. ft. conditioned space for 70% of their 12-hour shift, despite the fact that existing gatehouses provide no exterior solar protection or shade.

Light, Shade + Water
The new gatehouse incorporates an exterior parasol inspired by the local mashrabiya to mitigate solar gain on the interior air-conditioned booth while simultaneously creating a pair of exterior living spaces. Composed of steel bar grate, the exoskeleton shades a

PRODUCTION NOTES

Architect: AUS DB Team
Status: Built
Site Area: 1,000 sq. ft.
Location: Sharjah, UAE
Date: 2018

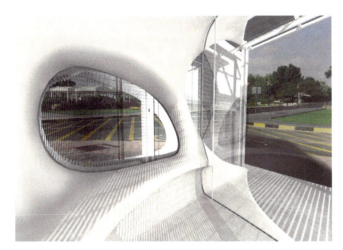

2   Booth interior looking NW to "front porch" and street.

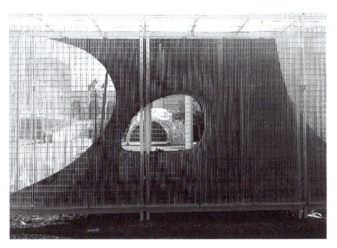

3   South Elevation with wood booth installed (M. Hughes, December 2017).

4   Existing gate house (M. Hughes, September 2016).

cross-ventilated observation porch adjacent to the gate checkpoint on the north side. The fritted glass roof panels contribute shading and are designed to be swapped with solar panels when the local electrical grid can support net metering. A second, larger shaded space on the south provides respite and water for the often under-appreciated members of the campus community, guards and landscape workers, who toil long hours outside in difficult conditions.

Precedent

The inherent visual permeability of the bar-grate mashrabiya balances the dual role of the security guard to see and to be seen while the etymology of the word contributes to the expanded program. Commonly understood as an architectural screen associated with privacy and shadows, the term Mashrabiya derives from the original Arabic word "mashrab," meaning a place to drink water. This project relinks the two manifestations of the word, creating a shaded and screened shared drinking space/garden, or in other words a "Mae Sabeel." This part of the project program evolves from a modified expression of the shade

and ventilation provided by a mashrabiya, combined with this earlier poetic reference to a shared drinking space.

Standards + Deviations

Within the standard, mass-produced bar grate, a series of custom "deviations" address specific pragmatic and programmatic requirements such as signage, seating, and increased visual access for the guard. Conceived through parametric computational studies, these localized modifications leverage efficiencies of material mass production while selectively deploying custom CNC-plasma cut and traditional, analog craftsmanship in the steel assembly.

A similar set of deviations animate the wood booth to accommodate and integrate the desk, drawer, water fountain, and HVAC duct, while a third set of deviations, including a ripple in the flooring, formally link the wood booth and bar-grate exoskeleton.

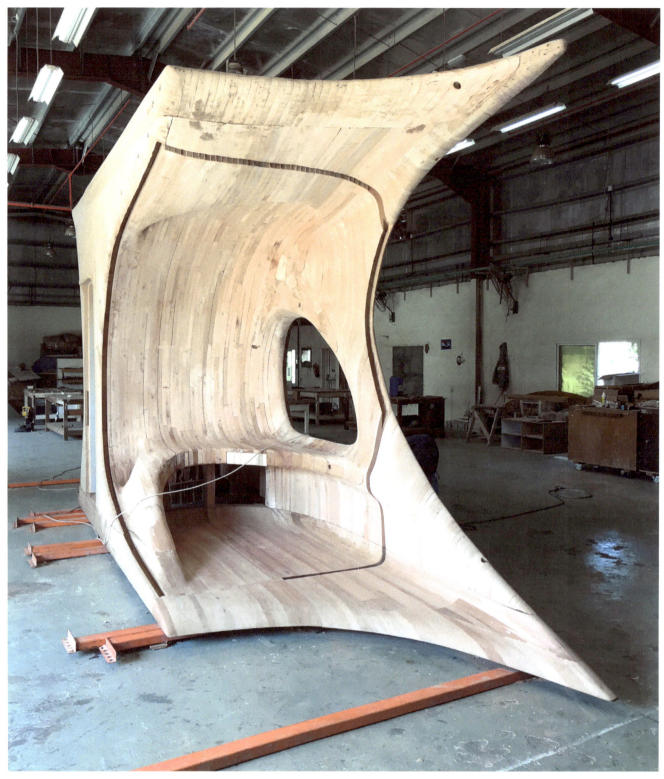

5 Wood booth assembly (M. Hughes, January 2018).

gateHouse_Garden Hughes, Sarnecky

6　Custom bar-grate bench install (M. Hughes, April 2017).

7　Bar-grate bench (M. Hughes, April 2017).

8　Bar-grate "Floor Ripple" during assembly (M. Hughes, April 2017).

9　Completed "Floor Ripple" (M. Hughes, January 2018).

Assembly Process

The monolithic, solid wood structure combines enclosure, insulation, and weather protection in a single system that also accommodates the sculpting of complex curvatures that register simultaneously on the interior and exterior. The milled surfaces result from a normative serial section approach of simple contour cuts combined with localized surface milling where necessary to minimize the amount of surface sanding required after assembly. Finger joints provide connection details and registration between the individual pieces, comprising a single lamination while pin connections provide registration between the laminations. Glued and screwed connections provide mechanical strength and clamping force particularly where extreme curvature prevented traditional clamping techniques.

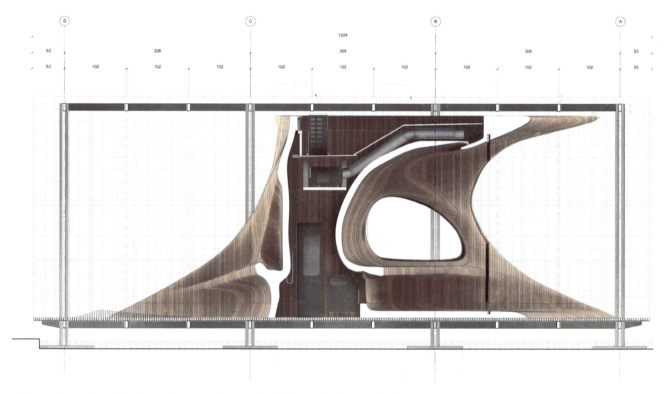

10 Section through mechanical room between north guard booth (right) and south maesabeel (left)

IMAGE CREDITS

Figure 1: © Ibrahim Ibrahim, June 2017

Figure 12: © Basil Al Tahar, June 2017

All other drawings and images by the authors.

Michael Hughes is a Professor in the Department of Architecture at the American University of Sharjah. He is also a licensed architect and principal of Catovic Hughes Design. His research, teaching, and creative activities involve community outreach, tectonics, and material exploration. These interests inform a pedagogical agenda focused on an integrated approach to architectural education that emphasizes hands-on learning, sustainable practices, and civic responsibility.

William Sarnecky is an architect, furniture designer and educator. Currently residing in Tucson, Arizona, Sarnecky spent eleven years teaching as Associate Professor of Architecture at the American University of Sharjah in the UAE. He is currently a Visiting Professor of Practice at AUS one semester per year while maintaining a design practice with areas of research including digital fabrication, furniture design and the "architecture of immediacy." Prior to his academic career, Sarnecky worked in award winning design practices Brooks Scarpa Architecture and Belzberg Architects. He is a licensed architect and holds an M Arch from the University of New Mexico.

11 Mae Sabeel (M . Hughes, January 2018).

12 Sign embedded in custom bar grate (B. Al TAhar, June 2017).

Patio de las Jacarandas

John Brennan
A. Zahner Company

Jo Kamm
A. Zahner Company

1   The Patio de las Jacarandas provides a place to gather in Aguascalientes. (Jaime Navarro © 2015).

Jacaranda Pavilion

This project demonstrates a workflow combining custom automated geometry analysis tools and manual edits to the artwork. The artwork consists of two layers of decorative metal panels, representing the branches and leaves of the Jacaranda tree. The branch layer is suspended by cable connections to the leaf layer above (Figure 4). The project was executed in 522 quarter-inch unique panels, waterjet-cut in Kynar-coated aluminum, covering approximately 17,000 ft² (1,580 m²). Since the project was executed in two phases of approximately similar size, it is possible to compare the process and results of the auto-mation aids. In simple numbers, the effort for the task was cut approximately in half from 800 to 400 hours. This includes the time to develop the analysis and augmentation tools.

In the Phase 1 workflow, each panel was edited separately and completed before starting the next, making it time consuming and tedious, and increasing the risk of manual errors. In the revised Phase 2 workflow, large groups of panels were edited together. This increased overall consistency of the artwork by allowing the geometry edits to be completed by a single operator looking across the whole pattern at the same time. The repetitive basic edits and tedious checks were automated, making the results of these operations consistent (Figure 6).

Initial processing was needed to clean up the artwork files for fabrication. The waterjet stream has a width of 0.040″, which would produce undesirable blowouts of the material

PRODUCTION NOTES

Architect:	José Luis Jiménez García & Arturo Revilla Guerra
Artist:	Jan Hendrix
Client:	Government of the State of Aguascalientes
Status:	Complete
Site Area:	17,000 sq. ft.
Location:	Aguascalientes, Mexico
Date:	2015–2017

2   Site plan showing phases 1 and 2 of construction. (John Brennan © 2016).

3   Phase 1 courtyard view (Jaime Navarro © 2015).

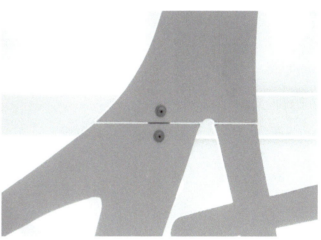

4   Jacaranda tree referenced for the canopy layers (Jaime Navarro © 2015).

5. Splice joint detail between panels (Mariana Guerra © 2015).

if a cut passed into a long corner or a narrow throat. A set of analysis tools was devised to deconstruct the linework geometry and identify areas that met these conditions. A sampling algorithm evaluated the artwork inside the boundary for unsupported tributary areas below a multi-variate threshold of length, width, number, and distance of nearby connections. A sampling "hatch" test evaluated drop areas for throat clearance of the nozzle stream. At the same time, it was necessary to maintain aesthetic consistency with the artwork so that alterations were not disruptive to the design intent. Due to the subjective aspects of the alterations, it was not feasible to fully auto-mate the editing process.

Once the geometry was cleaned and ready for fabrication, the next challenge was in adapting the cleaned artwork to the structural constraints of the panelized system. Through automation we highlight the problems created by dividing panel boundaries. These divides created loose or weak parts, which had to be either eliminated, extended, or widened (Figures 8 and 9).This required manual alterations

to the artwork to connect the problem areas so that they would not be loose or weak. The cable connections required the top and bottom layers to overlap, and that the areas surrounding the connection be strong enough to distribute the weight of the panel (Figures 10 and 11). Additionally, splice plates for the lower panels needed to be placed and aligned with the lower geometry manually,

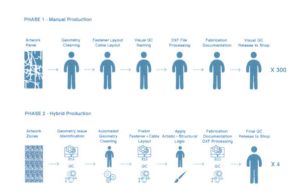

6   Automation and agile user collaboration workflow
(John Brennan © 2017)

RECALIBRATION ON IMPRECISION AND INFIDELITY

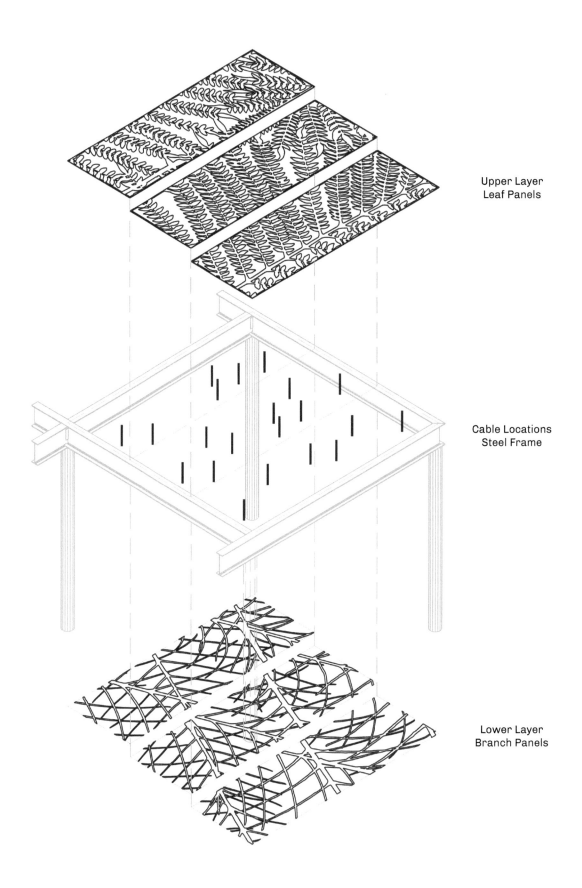

Upper Layer
Leaf Panels

Cable Locations
Steel Frame

Lower Layer
Branch Panels

7   Axon-panelized system layering (John Brennan © 2017).

Patio de las Jacarandas Brennan, Kamm

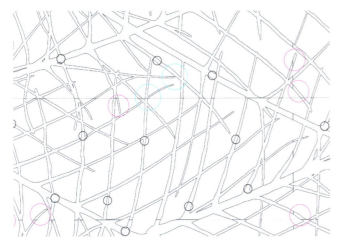

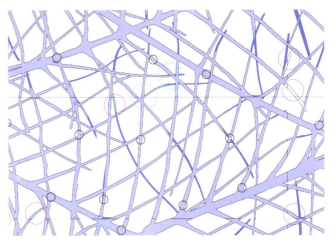

8   Lower Panels - Analysis tool identifying (pink) Loose Parts, (cyan) Weak Joints, (black) Cable Locations (Jo Kamm © 2018)

9   Lower Panels - The User manually extended, shifted, and thickened geometry; to support the cable locations, loose parts and weak areas and to work as a whole (Jo Kamm © 2018)

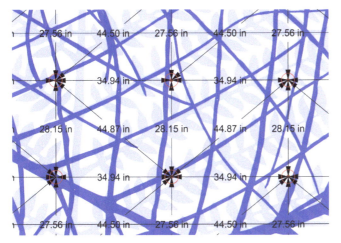

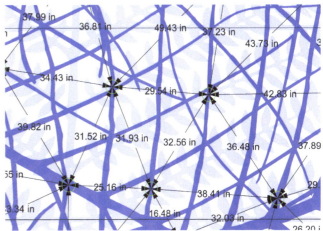

10 Lower & upper panels overlap with ideal cable spacing laid out. Dimensions across panels give live feedback to follow structural constraints (Jo Kamm © 2018)

11 Final placement of fasteners, splice plates, and cable locations. All are overlapped to test structural constraints followed prior to fabrication. (Jo Kamm © 2018)

12 Panels assembled in Zahner Shop for full-size mock-up.
(A.Zahner Co © 2015).

13 Panel Installation of Phase 1. (Mariana Guerra © 2015).

while evenly spaced fasteners for the upper panels needed to be placed with automation. The authors developed a hybrid combination of automated conditional recognition scripts and manual edit processes. This precipitated a set

of tools to augment the manual tasks: visual feedback for maintaining structural constraints, identifying areas in need of editing due to fabrication constraints, generating shop drawings and cut files, and maintaining quality control

RECALIBRATION ON IMPRECISION AND INFIDELITY

14 Night photograph on the street side of Patio de Las Jacarandas (Oscar Hernandéz © 2017).

throughout the process.The promise and progression of computational design in architecture is often towards increasing automation and abstraction, replacing both simple and complex, analytical tasks. However, there is still a significant cost to setting up complex automation, which suggests an intermediate position where computation and manual tasks by an operator can work together in an agile workflow. In suggesting a continued role for the human operator, this design methodology disrupts the assumption that computation is necessarily progressing toward total automation. This hybrid approach is particularly appropriate for medium-sized projects—the ones that are big enough to make automation desirable, but not so big as to allow for the development time to create a completely automated solution. This project is an example of this hybrid approach, using computational tools along with human direction to achieve a complex goal in a timely manner.

ACKNOWLEDGMENTS

We want to thank the architects José Luis Jiménez García and Arturo Revilla Guerra for their vision in creating this public space in the city. To Jan Hendrix for your fresh and innovative art. To the photographers Jaime Navarro and Oscar Hernandéz for their beautiful photos. And to Mariana Guerra and Paul Martin for working through the engineering and project management in Kansas City and Aguascalientes.

John Brennan is a production engineer who provides architectural design for fabrication at Zahner. He has a masters in architecture from the University at Buffalo and is involved in public art in Kansas City through his company Hello Architecture.

Jo Kamm provides algorithmic design and process automation for Zahner. As a graduate of Kansas City Art Institute, Kamm maintains a studio art and design practice exploring generative patterns through sculpture and drawing.

15 Day photo of courtyard (Jaime Navarro © 2015).

RECALIBRATION ON IMPRECISION AND INFIDELITY

Confluence Park

Andrew Kudless
Matsys / California College of
the Arts

1   View of the BHP Pavilion at Confluence Park from the south. (Casey Dunn, 2018).

Overview

Located along the Mission Reach section of the San Antonio River, Confluence Park is an educational park focusing on the critical role of water in the regional ecosystems. The park consists of 3.5 acres of native planting, a 2000 square foot multipurpose building, a 6000 square foot central pavilion, and 3 smaller "satellite" pavilions dispersed throughout the park. The central pavilion is composed of 22 concrete "petals" that form a network of vaults that provide shade and direct the flow of rainwater into an underground cistern used for the park's irrigation. The design of the pavilion was inspired by the way many plants in the region direct rainwater to their root system through harnessing the structural efficiency of curved surfaces. Each petal was cast on site using a modified tilt-up construction technique and digitally fabricated fiberglass composite molds and then lifted into place in pairs to form structural arches. The pavilion embodies our deep interest in the integration of form, fabrication, and performance.

Pavilion Geometry

The development of the central pavilion focused on creating an inspirational and aspirational space that helped communicate the client's mission in providing environmental education on the topic of water conservation. Using the biomimetic principle of looking towards nature for inspiration, the pavilion geometry is inspired by some plants' use of doubly curved fronds to cantilever out, collect rainwater and dew, and redirect the water towards its root stem. A modular system of concrete "petals" was developed that collected

PRODUCTION NOTES

Architect: Lake Flato Architects +
            Matsys
Client: San Antonio River
            Foundation
Status: Completed
Area: 6,000 sq. ft.
Location: San Antonio, TX
Date: 2014 - 2018

2   Night photo of pavilion interior. Each petal is a half-arch. The pavilion is composed of 22 petals that make up 11 structurally independent arches. (Casey Dunn, 2018).

3   The pavilion at dusk with the custom pentagonal concrete pavers in the foreground. (Casey Dunn, 2018).

4   Water is funneled off of the pavilion roof and down the petals to their bases where the water is collected in an underground cistern. (Casey Dunn, 2018).

rainwater and funneled it to the petals' columnar bases and then on to a central underground cistern.

In developing these petals, one of the central concerns was to make sure that they were modular yet seemingly non-repetitive. The design uses the Cairo tile, an irregular pentagon, as the underlying base grid in order to resolve the tension between cost-effective modularity and the desire for spatial richness. The pentagon is subdivided into 5 triangles in a way that results in only three unique modules: two asymmetrical triangles that are mirrors of each other and one equilateral triangle.

From this irregular triangular base grid, a parametric model was used to create the three-dimensional solids of each petal. Structurally, each petal is half of an arch which starts out as a 16″ thick column and tapers to a 4″ deep curved roof. The double-curvature of the surface geometry helps with the structural rigidity of the petal. Each petal is connected to its paired half-arch by two structural pin joints. The petals' capacity to shed water in the proper

direction was tested through water-flow analysis using particle simulations.

Pavilion Construction

The three petals' formwork was fabricated off of 5-axis CNC milled forms. After milling the foam forms, a 2″ thick composite structure composed of inner and outer layers of fiberglass composite with a central core of balsa wood was applied. The formwork was then shipped to the site and positioned in a way that it could be cast as a modified tilt-up wall construction. This avoided the need for a fully enclosed form, which decreased the cost and allowed the top and bottom surfaces to have radically different finishes: the bottom is cast against the smooth fiberglass while the top is broom-finished, with the broom strokes aligning with the direction of the water flow.

Paver Geometry

The Cairo tile geometry was reused at a much smaller scale for the thousands of concrete pavers used throughout the park. Four different inlay patterns were developed for the

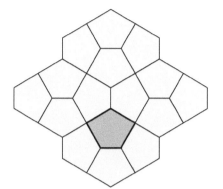

1. Base pentagonal grid

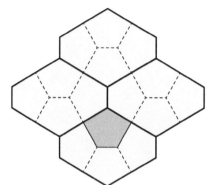

2. Four pentagons form hexagonal grid

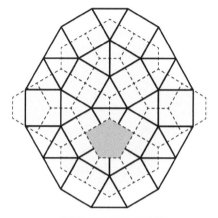

3. Dual of the pentagonal grid is formed with a combination of equilateral triangles and squares

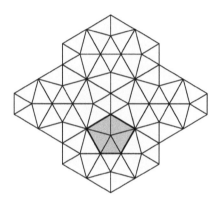

4. Each pentagon is subdiveded into smaller triangles

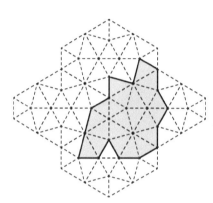

5. An irregular selection of triangles is made to create the outside roofline

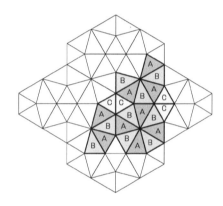

6. This new triangular grid is composed of only three types of triangles

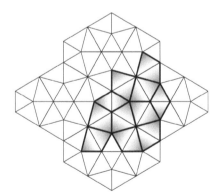

7. Triangles are paired into arches made of either an A-B or C-C combination

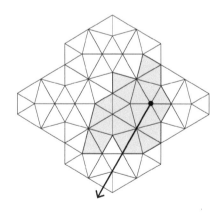

8. The grid is orientated to create a large space directed towards the confluence of the river and creek

5   Plan diagram of pavilion geometry (© Matsys).

6   The patterns for the formwork were digitally fabricated from foam using both 7-axis robotic mills and 5-axis gentry mills. (Cade Bradshaw and Stuart Allan, 2017).

7   Works at the fiberglass composite fabricator making the formwork used for the concrete petals. The formwork is shown here upside down. The forms are composed of inner and outer layers of fiberglass with an inner-core of balsa wood.(Cade Bradshaw and Stuart Allan, 2017).

8   The fiberglass composite forms were delivered to the site and positioned for a modifed version of tilt-up concrete construction. PVC pipes were inserted into the mold to create a field of 1″-2″ diameter holes in the concrete. Each of these mini-skylights is capped with a small acrylic disk.

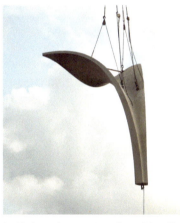

9   Each petal was cast on-site and then lifted into place and attached to its paired half-arch. (Cade Bradshaw and Stuart Allan, 2017).

pavers, such that a larger network of branching curves is created. This network is aperiodic and references the bifurcations and deltas of the local watershed.

ACKNOWLEDGMENTS
Confluence Park was a highly collaborative project. The design of the park was led by Matsys, Lake|Flato Architects, and Rialto Studio. The structural engineers were Architectural Engineering Collaborative and the mechanical engineers were CNG. Kreysler & Associates fabricated the composite formwork and SpawGlass were the general contractors. The client was the San Antonio River Foundation with Stuart Allen as the client's project manager.

Andrew Kudless is a designer based in San Francisco, where he is an Associate Professor at the California College of the Arts. In 2004, he founded Matsys, a design studio exploring the emergent relationships between architecture, engineering, biology, and computation. He holds a Master of Arts in Emergent Technologies and Design from the Architectural Association and a Master of Architecture from Tulane University. The work of Matsys has been exhibited internationally and is in the permanent collections of the San Francisco Museum of Modern Art, the Centre Pompidou in Paris, and the FRAC Centre in Orleans, France.

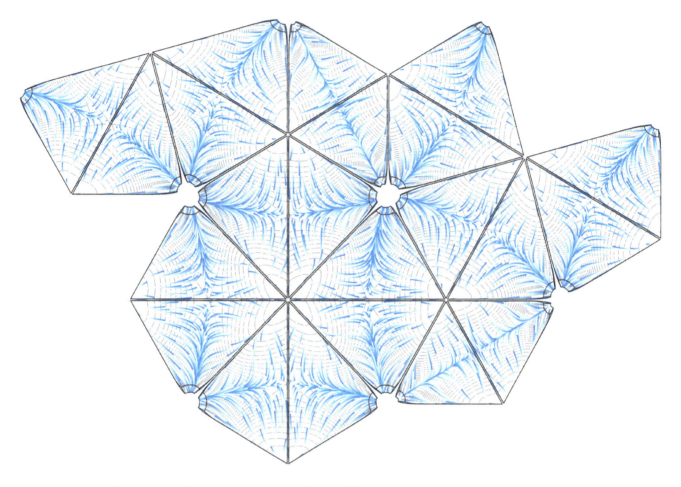

10 Roofplan of the pavilion with overlay of rainwater flow simulation. (Matsys, 2015).

11 BHP Pavilion at Confluence Park looking south towards the San Antonio River. (Casey Dunn, 2018).

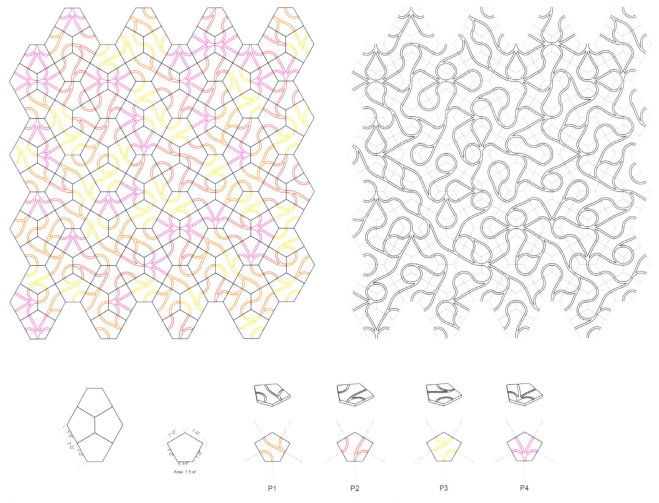

P1   P2   P3   P4

12 Geometric definition of custom pentagonal concrete pavers for Confluence Park. (Matsys, 2016).

13 Mitchell Street entrance to Confluence Park showing custom pentagonal pavers. BHP Pavilion is in the background. (Casey Dunn, 2018).

FABRICARTE: Vaulting, Craft, and Construction

M. Wesam Al Asali
University of Cambridge

Dr. Michael H. Ramage
University of Cambridge

1   FabricArte (2018).

Craft in the building industry is usually considered to be limited to decorative arts and regarded as labor intensive. Using the Mediterranean technique of thin-tile vaulting, artisans can convert tiles into utilitarian and expressive structural elements (Huerta 2003). Handmaking's place alongside modern construction is central to this experiment, in which the design explores the interface between craft, computation, and construction in thin-tile vaulting.

FabricArte is a three-vault pavilion built for the Ceramic Expo Valencia 2018. Expo regulations require short on-site construction. The project explores prefabrication by building the vaults off site, then slicing it into pieces and transferring it to the site for reassembly. The cut geometry was inspired by Gothic vaulting, commonly seen in the historic buildings of Valencia, where modular units mirror, repeat, and array to compose the main structure (Catalán 2009). As a result, the vault manufacturing was optimized for a rapid in-situ construction, but it also avoided using heavy machinery, and the process remained handmade.

Design

The architecture of the pavilion shows two systems of structures, in tension and compression, integrated into three modules. The transition from full-height to flat vault tests spatial and structural properties of geometry and demonstrates different possible uses of unreinforced ceramics for both expressive standalone structures and vaulted slab systems

PRODUCTION NOTES

Client: ASCER (Tiles of Spain)
Status: Built
Site Area: 350 sq. ft.
Location: Valencia, CEVISAMA
Date: 2018

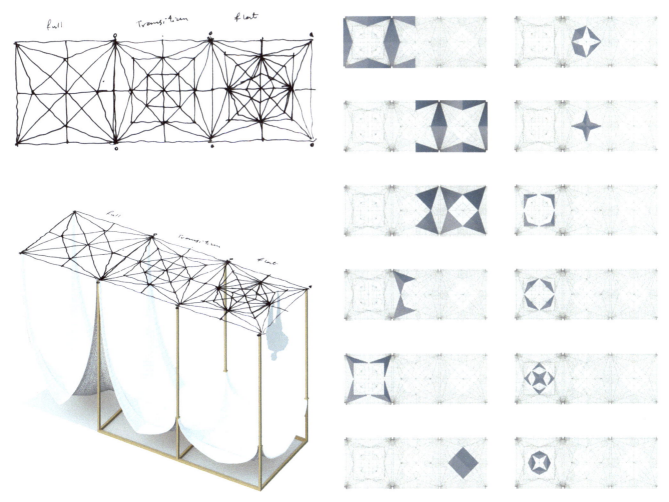

2   Concept sketch: three modules of vaults (2017).

3   Construction optimization study (2017).

that could be used in housing. While the added soffit layer of tiles hid the gothic patterns of cuts, the flooring of the pavilion reflects the lines as a diagram of the process of manufacturing.

Construction: Tile vaulting

The technique (Bóvedas tabicadas) is rooted in Valencia. The oldest document mentioning this craft is a 1382 letter from King Peter IV of Aragon, describing builders in Valencia using a rapid and efficient vaulting technique (Huerta 2001; Ochsendorf 2010).

Tile vaulting uses fast-setting mortar and the planar positioning of the tiles to make a first layer before adding more layers of tiles and cement, hence it needs no shuttering or extensive formwork (Ramage 2007).

The vaults were three layers thick, but only one layer was built off site and sliced, making the transportable pieces lighter. We used molds that marked the outline of a quarter of each vault; the molds were used for the off-site making,

transport, and reassembly. Thanks to the cutting pattern inspired by Gothic vaulting, heavy parts of the vault were below whereas lighter pieces were above, making reassembly easier for the builders.

Tile vaulting has been revived and transferred to new contexts as an affordable method of construction to build thin-tile shell structures made from local materials, usually from earth found on site and shaped into unfired earthen tiles (Ramage, Ochsendorf, and Rich 2010).

In Valencia, the tradition of tile vault and stair making continues thanks to masonry masters who keep it alive (Al Asali 2016). The team worked closely with one of those master builders, Salvador Gomis Aviño. During the collaboration with the builders, the project showed the benefits of iteration between design and craft, where each discipline influenced and improved the other.

The structural analysis of the vault was made using graphic statics with help from particle-spring system, but an analog

4   FabricArte: bottom-up view (2018).

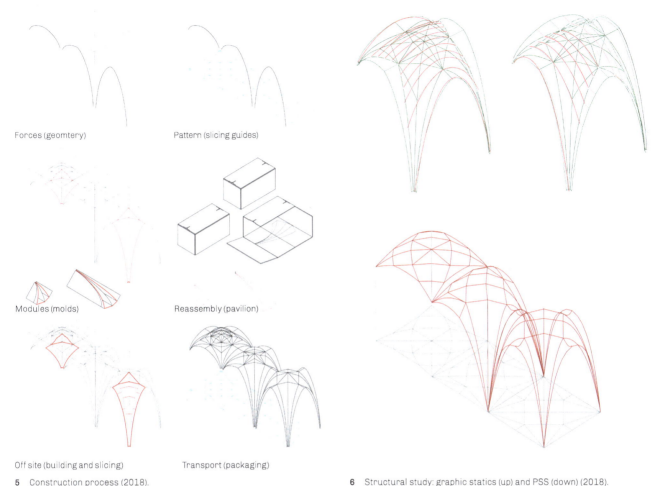

Forces (geomtery)

Pattern (slicing guides)

Modules (molds)

Reassembly (pavilion)

Off site (building and slicing)

Transport (packaging)

5   Construction process (2018).

6   Structural study: graphic statics (up) and PSS (down) (2018).

hanging chain model was made for better communication with the builders. The calculations of the cuts were digitally studied based on the height and weight of each piece, but in situ conditions altered the cuts for quicker construction without compromising the overall design. For the construction of the mold and the discussion about tile coursing, virtual reality models and pictures were exchanged when physical attendance was not possible.

Conclusion

Vaults in prefabrication in modern construction are not a new subject (Muñoz and Fernández 2014), but this experiment proposes a modus operandi that is driven by craft without compromising design decisions.

Manufacturing of building components is usually imagined as accompanied by heavy machinery, cranes, and advanced tools. FabricArte challenges this image by constraining all manufacturing phases to the scale of the hand and pushing the construction industry towards a more inclusive approach to craft, where complex geometries can still be achieved without the extensive use of computation.

ACKNOWLEDGMENTS

The authors would like to thank Salvador Gomis Aviño and his team for collaboration on this project and building the vaults, Oliver Hudson for the structural calculations of the metal structure, and Jordi Font de Mora (Grupoom) for building them. The authors are grateful to Ana Martínez Balaguer (ASCER), Javier Mira Peidro, Laura Vilalta Ibane, and Jorge Corrales García from ITC (Instituto de Tecnología Cerámica) for supplying the needed materials for the construction, and Salvador Tomás Márquez for helping in the construction. M. Wesam Al Asali is receiving Cambridge Trust-Saïd Foundation funding for his PhD. The project was administrated by Light Earth Designs.

7 Vault building and cutting in workshop (2018).

8 Vaults cut for piece transport (2018).

9 Vault piece reassembly on site (2018).

10 Internal and external cladding of vaults (2018)..

REFERENCES

Al Asali, M. Wesam. 2016. "Tools and Technology in Traditional Architecture: A Study of Thin Tile Vaulting." Master of Philosophy thesis, University of Cambridge.

Catalán, Arturo Zaragozá. 2009. "A propósito de las bóvedas de crucería y otras bóvedas medievales." *Anales de Historia del Arte* 19 (Extra): 99–126.

Huerta, Santiago. 2003. "The Mechanics of Timbrel Vaults: A Historical Outline." In *Essays on the History of Mechanics*, edited by Antonio Becchi, Massimo Corradi, Federico Foce, and Orietta Pedemonte, 89–134. Birkhäuser Basel.

Muñoz, Julián García, and María de los Ángeles Beltrán Fernández. 2014. "La prefabricación de bóvedas de ladrillo. Una utopía latino-americana." *Rita_revista indexada de textos académicos* 2: 92–99.

Ochsendorf, John. 2010. *Guastavino Vaulting: The Art of Structural Tile*. New York: Princeton Architectural Press.

Ramage, Michael H. 2007. "Guastavino's Vault Construction Revisited." *Construction History* 22: 47–60.

Ramage, Michael H., John Ochsendorf, and Peter Rich. 2010. "Sustainable Shells: New African Vaults Built with Soil-Cement Tiles." In *Proceedings of the International Association for Shell and Spatial Structures Symposium*, edited by Alberto Domingo and Carlos Lazaro, 1512–20. Valencia: IASS.

IMAGE CREDITS

All drawings and images by the authors.

11 FabricArte: exterior (2018).

12 FabricArte: interior (2018).

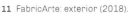

M. Wesam Al Asali is an architect and PhD candidate at the Centre for Natural Material Innovation at the University of Cambridge. His research focuses on design, manufacturing, and craft training and transfer in thin-tile vaulting. Wesam studies craft and technology in building practice of thin-tile vaulting and its potential in postwar reconstruction. He graduated in 2007 from Damascus University and pursued an MPhil in architecture and urban studies at the University of Cambridge in 2016. He has experience in practice in Syria, Denmark, Spain, and the UK. In 2010, He co-founded IWLab in Damascus to be a place for studies in architecture, culture, and urban heritage.

Dr. Michael H. Ramage leads the Centre for Natural Material Innovation at Cambridge University, and is an architectural engineer and Reader in the Department of Architecture, a fellow of Sidney Sussex College, and a founding partner of Light Earth Designs. He studied architecture at MIT, and worked for Conzett Bronzini Gartmann in Switzerland prior to teaching at Cambridge. His current research is focused on developing low-energy structural materials and systems in masonry, better housing in the developing world, and improved engineered timber and bamboo through natural material innovation. He receives research funding from the Leverhulme Trust, the Engineering and Physical Sciences Research Council, the Royal Society, the British Academy, and industry.

RECALIBRATION ON IMPRECISION AND INFIDELITY

RECALIBRATING
Material + Production systems

CCFF: Catenary Concrete Funicular Formwork

Jonathan Rule
University of Michigan /
MPR arquitectos

Ana Morcillo Pallares
University of Michigan /
MPR arquitectos

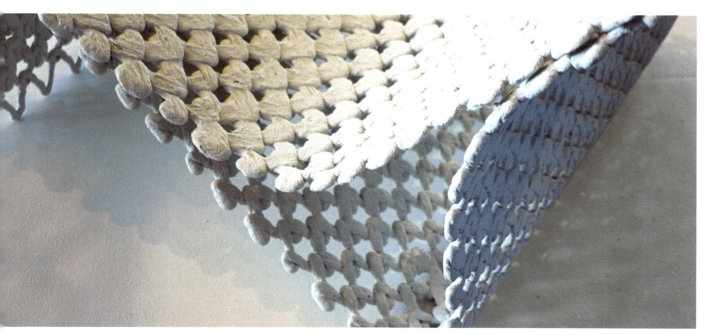

1   Catenary concrete chair prototype.

Today architectural workflows for the development of complex geometries and their translation to physical objects mainly rely on computational processes. The generation of form has become intrinsically tied to computer simulation in response to datasets and external information. Prior to the advent of these technologies, forms were generated and understood through analogue methodologies that depended on the behavior of the material in response to a set of physical conditions. The ambition of the research is to investigate high-/low-tech possibilities for generating form and space at the interstices of the digital and the handmade. The study leverages the use of physical catenary and funicular modeling in conjunction with the precision of robotic concrete extrusion for the development of pattern-based thin concrete screens.

PRODUCTION NOTES

Architect: MPR arquitectos
Year: 2018
Site: Ann Arbor, MI
Location: LRA Gallery
Material: Concrete

Nervi:Recalibration of Material Practice

"It may be noted that although reinforced concrete has been used for over a hundred years and with increasing interest during the last decades, few of its properties and potentials have been fully exploited so far. Apart from the unconquerable inertia of our own minds, which do not seem to be able to adopt freely any new ideas, the main cause of this delay is a trivial technicality: the need to prepare wooden forms" (Pasqualino 2015).

With these words, Pier Luigi Nervi questions material practices with respect to the use of concrete. It is a statement of provocation for disrupting standard practice in favor of alternative methods for working with this material. Like Nervi, other architects and

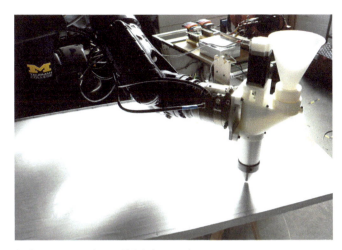

2   Concrete extruder and fabric formwork.

3   Detail of concrete extrusion on canvas.

4   Detail of final catenary screen.

engineers during this time were also attempting to push the boundaries of concrete by reconceiving this a priori heavy and brutal material as something light, delicate, and thin. Within this vein of thought, and in an attempt to explore new possibilities for material practice, the research on CCFF attempts to break away from our preconceived notions of how to work with concrete.

Methodology

The research began with the intention of revisiting the "hanging cloth reversed" method developed by the Swiss engineer Heinz Isler. This method takes advantage of the plasticity of the material in its initial state for physical form finding. However, instead of creating a continuous shell, the intention was to create a permeable shell using a continuous pattern. To begin, glass fibre reinforced concrete mixes were manually deposited onto a canvas formwork through pastry bags. This process allowed for an understanding of the material's consistency, but was limited by our ability to accurately deposit repeatable patterns. This difficulty led to the exploration of tools and techniques for

3D printing that resulted in the development of a concrete extruder for a six-axis robotic arm. Through the integration of robotic motion control, the extrusion process became more precise, allowing for intricate interlayering and repetition of patterns across a flat canvas formwork. Once the entire concrete pattern was deposited, the canvas and concrete together are lifted from the print bed and suspended, allowing the concrete to cure in a catenary form. The type and density of patterning, along with the GFRC mix and the physical catenary form-finding process, influenced the tensile and compressive integrity of the screen shell.

Conclusion

While fabric-formed concrete has been around for some time, the manipulation of material through computational processes allows for innovation in the production of complex patterns and geometries using low-/high-tech fabrication processes. The result of the research becomes a recalibration of Isler's process and a demonstration of the delicacy that concrete can achieve through material

5　View of sample catenary patterns suspended in gallery.

　　　　　　　　　CCFF Rule, Morcillo Pallares

6   Pastry bag extrusion test.

7   Initial catenary test.

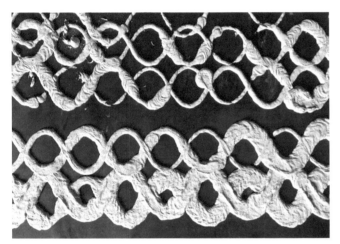

8   Robotically extruded concrete tests.

9   Robotically extruded pattern test.

computation and physical form finding for the production of catenary screens. The combination of fabric formwork and concrete extruding is not a replacement for conventional ways of casting, but questions the methods traditionally associated with it. At the same time the research intends to offer new approaches to form making, permeability, and weightlessness that can be achieved through 3D-printing concrete.

ACKNOWLEDGMENTS

CCFF: Catenary Concrete Funicular Formwork was made possible by a grant from the Taubman College of Architecture and Urban Planning at the University of Michigan.

The robotic control uses Super Mater Tools developed by Wes Mcgee as a graphic user interface for Rhinoceros (www.rhino3d. com), a program developed by Robert McNeil.

The research would also like to acknowledge the participation and collaboration by the following students of Taubman College of Architecture and Urban Planning at the University of Michigan:

Olaia Chivite Amigo, Niloufar Emami, Vanessa Flebbe, and Panquat Kyesmu

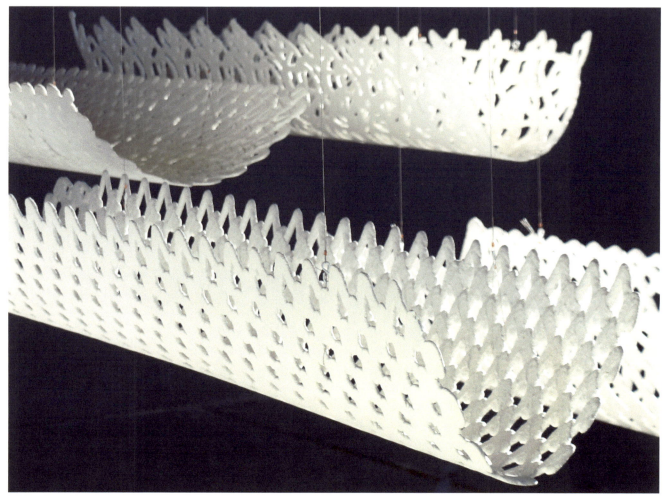

10 Suspended concrete catenary screen samples.

REFERENCES

Solomita, Pasqualino. 2015. *Pier Luigi Nervi Vaulted Architecture : Towards New Structures*. Bologna: Bononia University Press.

Chilton, John, 2000. *Heinz Isler*. London: Thomas Telford.

Orr, John, Mark Evernden, Antony Darby, and Timothy Ibell., eds. 2012. *Proceedings of the Second International Conference on Flexible Formwork*. Bath, UK: University of Bath.

Rael, Ronald, and Virginia San Fratello. 2018. *Printing Architecture: Innovative Recipes for 3D Printing*. New York: Princeton Architectural Press.

West, Mark, 2017. *The Fabric Formwork Book: Methods for Building New Architectural and Structural Forms in Concrete*. London: Routledge.

IMAGE CREDITS

All drawings and images: © Moricllo Pallares and Rule, 2018

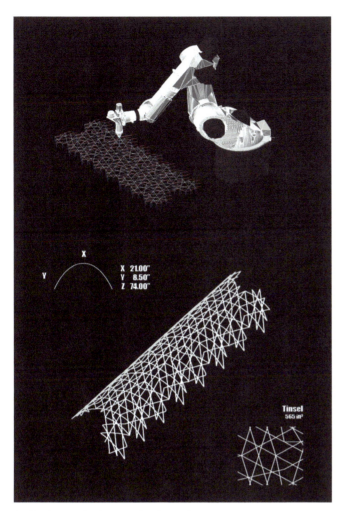

11 Continous toolpath pattern development

12 Suspended catenary screen.

Jonathan Rule is an Assistant Professor of practice at the University of Michigan, Taubman College of Architecture and Urban Planning. He has been practicing architecture in Spain since 2008 and is a co-founder of the studio Morcillo Pallares + Rule Arquitectos. Jonathan received a Bachelor of Science in Architecture from the State University of New York at Buffalo, a Master in Architecture from the Harvard Graduate School of Design, and a Professional Homologation from the Escuela Tecnica Superior de Arquitectura de Madrid.

Ana Morcillo Pallares is an Assistant Professor at the University of Michigan, Taubman College of Architecture and Urban Planning, where she was the 2014-2015 Walter B. Sanders Fellow. Ana holds a PhD from the Escuela Tecnica Superior de Arquitectura de Madrid and a professional degree in architecture from the Escuela Tecnica Superior de Arquitectura de Valencia. She is a licensed architect in Spain where she has been a principal at Morcillo Pallares + Rule arquitectos since 2004.

Wearable Biosensor

Simulating Biotic Growth Patterns and Sensing Environmental Toxins

Nancy Diniz
Rensselaer Polytechnic Institute
Augmented Architectures

Christine Marizzi
Cold Spring Harbor Laboratory,
DNA Learning Center

Frank Melendez
City College of New York, CUNY
Augmented Architectures

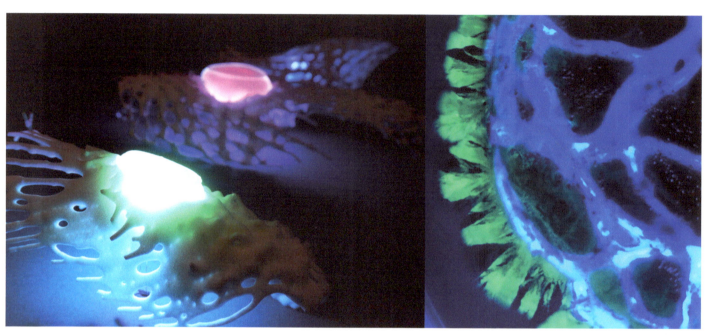

1   Wearable device prototypes exhibited (left) and detail of the bioflurescent bacteria (right), (2018, © Augmented Architectures).

Overview

This architectural research project, titled *Wearable Biosensor*, explores the integration of bacterial biosensors within wearable body architectures as a means of detecting environmental toxins. It is hypothesized that the collected environmental data can be visually expressed through an augmented reality interface. The project builds upon ongoing research that is predicated on interdisciplinary collaborations within the fields of architecture and biology.

Various growth experiments that explore the patterns, forms, and morphologies of living organisms were established as a design methodology framework. *E.coli* bacteria and *Physarum polycephalum*, also known as slime mold, were grown under specific conditions within various parameters, allowing for a set of criteria in which to assess their unruly natural growth and behavior. This behavior was further investigated using computational simulations to generate the design of the architectural devices. The devices house *E.coli* bacteria, which have very specific nutrient needs, a rapid reproduction rate, and a very short life cycle, making them an ideal source of pollution assessment as part of a wearable biosensor. Using DNA cloning technology, genes expressing fluorescent proteins are used as reporters under the control of an inducible promoter, resulting in a bioflorescent effect. Using augmented reality, environmental toxins can be visualized as quantitative data through a mobile phone app interface. Through the use of these architectural devices, users can better understand the specified pollutants that are present in their surrounding environment.

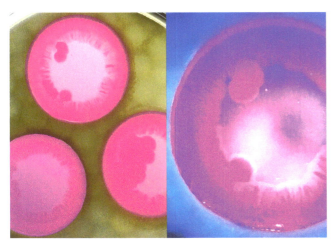

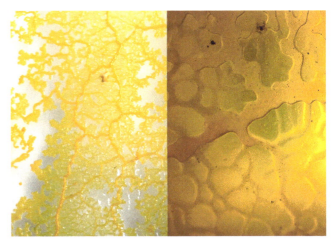

2 *E.coli* bacteria genetically modified to produce magenta bioflorescence.

4 *P. polycephalum* growth pattern details.

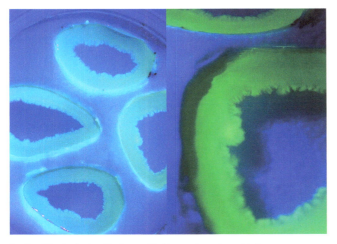

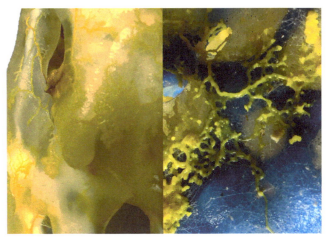

3 *E.coli* bacteria genetically modified to produce green bioflorescence.

5 *P. polycephalum* growth pattern on 3D printed scaffolds.

Biotic Growth Experiments

Bacterial biosensors help to easily detect the presence or absence of environmental toxins (like sulfur dioxide, sulfur, and metal ions). Cells like microalgae or *E.coli* bacteria can act as so-called bioreceptors due to their high sensitivity to the surrounding environment and rapid response to external stimulants. Bacterial biosensors are created by DNA cloning technology followed by bacterial transformation. DNA cloning allows the production of a specific protein by expressing specific genes at high levels in *E.coli*. For example, genes coding for fluorescent proteins like the green fluorescent protein (GFP) can be used as a reporter gene under the control of an inducible promoter. To express genes that produce reporter proteins, a full-length double-stranded cDNA is isolated. Next, the double-stranded cDNA is inserted into an expression vector, which is adapted to function in *E. coli*. To express the protein in *E. coli*, the cDNA must be transcribed from an *E.coli* promoter. A promoter is a region of DNA that initiates (or signals) the expression of the reporter gene. The promoter T7, derived from a bacteriophage, is typically used. In our project, we imagine that binding of the environmental toxin (small molecules like sulfur dioxide, sulfur, and metal ions) to the promoter region is acting as the signal to produce GFP. As an effect the bacteria produce GFP and emit a green light visible under UV light (Figures 2 and 3).

Physarum polycephalum, also known as slime mold, is a unicellular, multinucleate organism that relies on reactive navigation to explore its environment. When the slime mold senses attractants, such as food, the oscillation frequency in the area closest to the food increases, causing cytoplasm (this is the jellylike material that makes up much of a cell inside the cell membrane) to flow toward the attractant (Figure 4). A group of Japanese researchers has shown that *P. polycephalum* can find the shortest route connecting two food sources when placed in a maze with two oatmeal flakes (Nakagaki, Yamata, and Tóth 2000). In a 2010 paper, *P. polycephalum* created a network similar to the existing Tokyo train system when oatmeal flakes were dispersed to represent towns on a map of the Tokyo metropolitan area (Tero et al. 2010). In this project we explored the aesthetic

RECALIBRATION ON IMPRECISION AND INFIDELITY

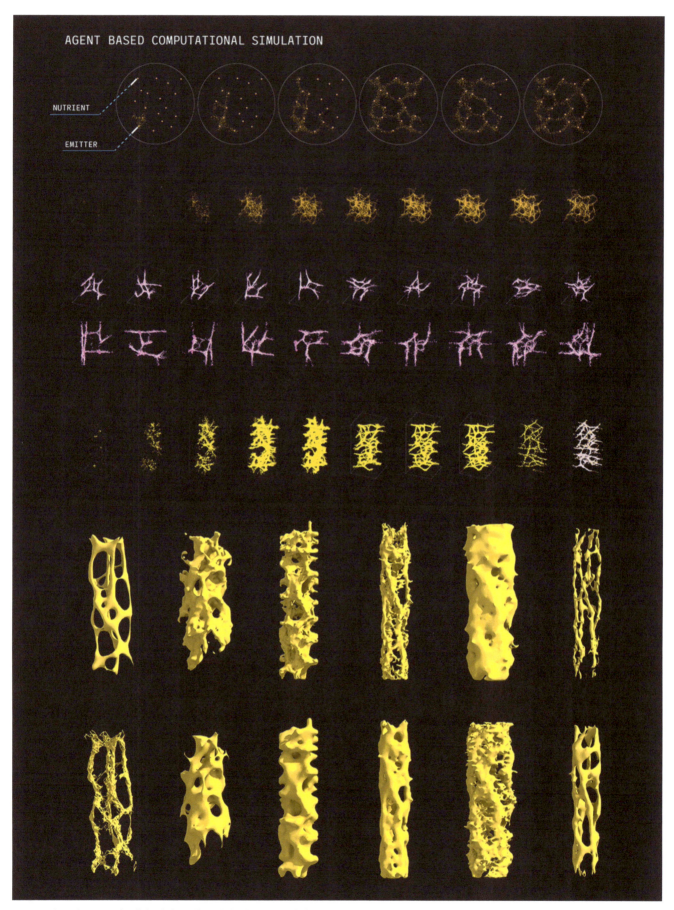

AGENT BASED COMPUTATIONAL SIMULATION

NUTRIENT

EMITTER

6 Agent-based computational simulation stills and digital model renderings based on the *P. polycephalum* growth experiments.

Wearable Biosensor Diniz, Marizzi, Melendez

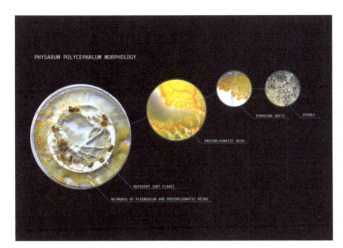

7   *P. polycephalum* morphology.

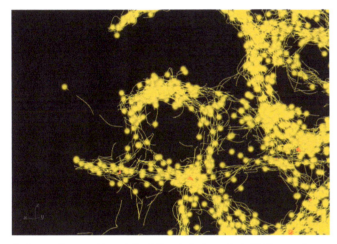

8   Image of an agent-based simulation study generated with Physarealm.

9   Renderings of the wearable devices and their locations on the body.

and navigational ability of the slime mold growth behavior in different configurations of 2D- and 3D-printed scaffolds coated in agar, and strategically placing oat flakes as nutrients to understand patterns of growth (Figure 5). These experiments were important to understand how efficient networks could be formed in our design. The *P. polycephalum* plasmodia were maintained in the semi dark boxes at 22°C on large 1% agar plates embedded with 10% (wt/vol) rolled sterilized oat flakes. Original cultures were obtained from Carolina Biological Supplies, and laboratory stocks were subcultured onto new agar-oat plates every 3 or 4 days (Figure 7).

Agent-Based Simulations

This project looks to biological formations to provide insight into the rules that define complex systems. The complexity of patterns generated in nature have a tendency to self-organize and arrange themselves systematically. This complexity is created out of clear principles (Leach 2004). Building upon knowledge from the growth experiments, a number of computational models were generated

to simulate the behavior of the slime mold growth patterns and self-organizing qualities based on a clear set of rules (Figure 6). These simulations are based on the stigmergic mutli-agent algorithm (Jones 2015), which yields emergent and self-organizing behavior through agents and actions. (Ma and Yidong 2017). Organizations of stigmergy can be found in the collective behavior of bacteria, slime mold, and insects, such as ants and termites. The project utilizes an open source visual programming tool called Physarealm, which was developed for simulating *P. Polycephalum* within Rhino's visual programming editor, Grasshopper. (Ma and Yidong 2017) (Figure 8).

Design Application

The agent-based simulations served as a bio-inspired process to generate the forms and structures of devices that can be worn on the body, and serve as architectures that provide a liminal space between the body and the environment. The optimization of geometry provided by the simulations yields a structural scaffold that incorporates material efficiencies through porous surfaces that can

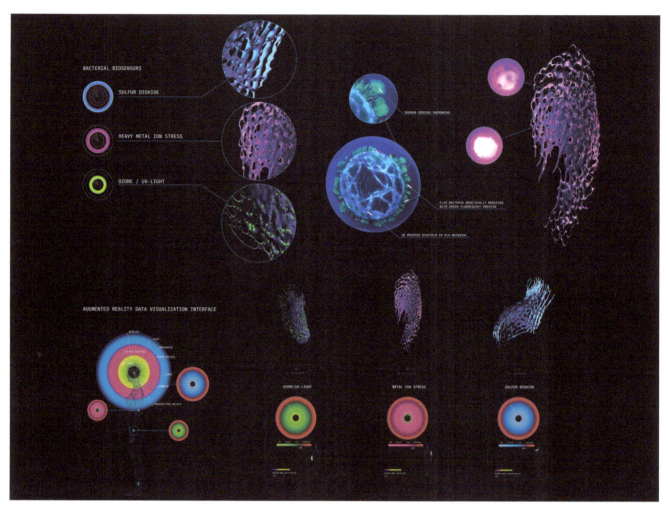

10 Diagrams of the bacterial biosensors and the proposed augmented reality data visualization interface used to display levels of environmental toxins.

contain the biosensors: biofluorescent bacteria (Figure 11). The 3D-printed devices are designed to fit on various parts of the human body (Figure 12) by strategically locating the emitter and attractor points of the agent-based simulations in relation to the muscular and circulatory systems of the body. The bespoke devices are intended to serve as wearable body architectures that augment the body by providing the user with data pertaining to environmental toxins through the use of a hypothesized augmented reality, data visualization interface (Figure 10). As environmental toxins within the atmosphere increase, the *E.coli* bacteria glows to indicate the levels of sulfur dioxide, UV light levels, and heavy metals. This serves as a responsive, architectural interface that provides information about invisible, ephemeral phenomena, and enhances the sensing capabilities of the user.

REFERENCES

Jones, Jeff. 2015. *From Pattern Formation to Material Computation: Multi-agent Modelling of Physarum Polycephalum*. Cham: Springer.

Leach, Neil. 2004. "Swarm Tectonics" In *Digital Tectonics*, edited by N. Leach, D. Turnbull and C. Williams, 70–77. New York: Princeton Architectural Press.

Ma, Yidong and Wieguo Xu. 2017. "Physarealm: A Bio-inpired Stigmergic Algorithm Tool for Form-Finding." In *Protocols, Flows, and Glitches: Proceedings of the 22nd Annual Conference of the Association for Computer-Aided Architectural Design Research in Asia*, edited by P. Janssen, P. Loh, A. Raonic, and M.A. Schnabel, 499–509. Suzhou, China: CAADRIA.

Nakagaki, Toshiyuki, Hiroyasu Yamada, and Ágota Tóth. 2000. "Intelligence: Maze-solving by an Amoeboid Organism." *Nature* 407 (6803): 470.

Tero, Atsushi, Seiji Takagi, Tetsu Saigusa, Kentaro Ito, Dan P. Bebber, Mark D. Fricker, Kenji Yumiki, Ryo Kobayashi, and Toshiyuki Nakagaki. 2010. "Rules for Biologically Inspired Adaptive Network Design." *Science* 327 (5964): 439–42.

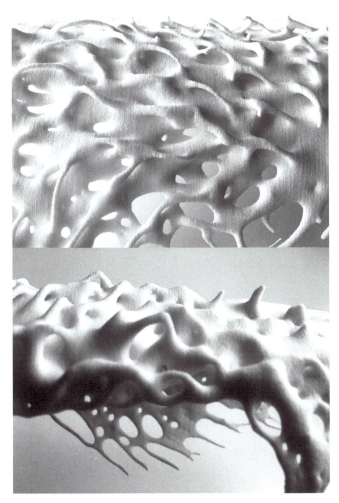

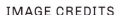
11 Detail photographs of the 3D-printed wearable devices.

12 Photograph of the wearable devices (2018, © Augmented Architectures).

IMAGE CREDITS

Figure 1-11: 2018, © Augmented Architectures

Figure 12: model: Renata Venturelli, 2018 © Augmented Architectures

Nancy Diniz is a registered architect and founder of Augmented Architectures, NY. Nancy has been awarded several fellowships, namely NYSCA/Storefront, MacDowell Colony, EYEBEAM, Seoul Art Space Geumcheon and FCT. She holds a BArch from Lusiada University and a Masters and Ph.D. from the Bartlett Graduate School, UCL. She is an affiliated researcher at ISTAR Digital Living Spaces Lab, ISCTE, Lisbon, Portugal, and at WSNL Wireless Sensor Network Lab, XJTLU, Suzhou, China. Nancy is currently an Assistant Professor at Rensselaer Polytechnic Institute, NY and has previously held permanent academic positions in the US, China, the UK, Italy, and Portugal.

Christine Marizzi graduated from the University of Vienna with a Ph.D. degree in microbiology and genetics for investigating

unique stem-cell mutant of the plant model *Arabidopsis thaliana*. Her current position is Urban Barcode Program Manager at Cold Spring Harbor Laboratory's DNA Learning Center in New York. With 12+ years in urban and international education, she dedicates her time, energy, and intellect to help students realize their greatest potential in STEM fields and provides traditionally under-represented minorities with multiple entry points to academic and professional careers in STEM disciplines.

Frank Melendez is an architectural designer, educator, and partner of Augmented Architectures, NY. He has co-organized and co-curated symposia and exhibitions including *DATA & MATTER*, Venice, Italy, 2018 and *Material Interactions*, New York, NY, 2017. His awards include a MacDowell Colony Fellowship, 2017 and the George N. Pauly Jr. Fellowship, Carnegie Mellon University, 2013. Frank is an Assistant Professor at The City College of New York, CUNY. He holds a BArch from the University of Arizona and an MArch from Yale University. His professional practice experience includes working at Frank O. Gehry & Associates and Urban A&O.

RECALIBRATION ON IMPRECISION AND INFIDELITY

Bioactive Knits

Fiber-based Bio-receptive Architectural Composite Materials for
Augmented Knitted Tectonics with Graded Material Distribution

Bastian Beyer
Royal College of Art London/
ArcInTex ETN

Daniel Suárez
Berlin University of the Arts,
ArcInTex ETN

1   Detail bioreactor and textile structure.

The project explores the distinct textile tectonics and structural potential of bio-solidified
composites through traditional knitting techniques with non-uniform materials. A hand-
crafted soft textile column is gradually transformed into a rigid structure by an active
textile microbiome of *Sporosarcina pasteurii*, inducing a calcite matrix on fiber level.
The fabrication system hereby can be understood as an architectural mediator staging an
explorative multi-actor fabrication process, allowing the interdependent inputs from the
digital, the microbiological, as well as the human body to merge into one co-creating entity.

Knitted fabrics are extremely adaptive textile structures which can be produced with wide-
ranging properties (Eadie and Ghosh 2011) depending on various parameters, such as the
fabric geometry, yarn material, and machine or hand dexterity, thus defining the behavior
and performance of the resulting structure. These versatile systems have attracted
interest as a material for architectural applications mainly as structural reinforcement
for composites or as elastic membranes (De Araujo, Fangueiro, and Hu 2011; Duhovic and
Bhattacharyya 2011; Pamuk 2016).

In contrast to industrial knitting machinery, which is generally bound to a limited material
palette as well as a specific technology which struggles to process very coarse or non-uniform yarns, craft techniques are very suitable, due to the manual interaction, for the
exploration of these materials.

PRODUCTION NOTES

Architect: Bastian Beyer,
            Daniel Suárez
Date: 2018

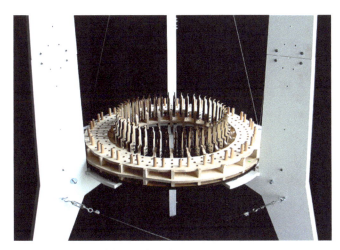

2   Base structure with hand-knitting loom setup.

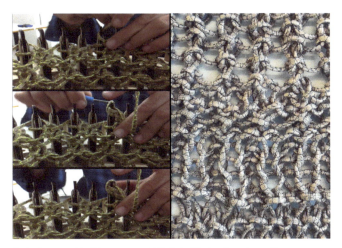

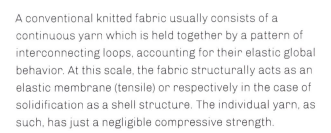

3   Left, manual knitting process / Right, knitting pattern transitions.

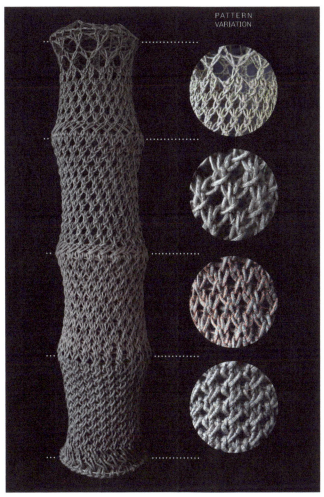

4   Pattern distribution within the structure.

A conventional knitted fabric usually consists of a continuous yarn which is held together by a pattern of interconnecting loops, accounting for their elastic global behavior. At this scale, the fabric structurally acts as an elastic membrane (tensile) or respectively in the case of solidification as a shell structure. The individual yarn, as such, has just a negligible compressive strength.

However, this relationship changes with an increase in yarn diameter and augmentation of the knitting pattern in relation to the whole textile structure. Once the individual yarn sections are able to sufficiently bear compressive loads, the structural system can be understood as a (textile) space frame.

Further exploring this concept, a 160 cm tall textile column was conceptualized, applying 4 distinct knitting patterns according to the expected compressive loads throughout the structure.

A graded continuous yarn was developed which consisted

of a jute fiber core and a permeable polyester sleeve. The thread, with an overall length of 450 m, gradually decreased in diameter from approximately 9 mm to 5 mm in order to increase the material deposition at the base whilst reducing material in the top section of the structure. A customized circular hand-loom, which can be mounted to the modular base structure of the installation, facilitated the knitting process.

The finished structure was mounted inside the bioreactor, similarly compatible with the base structure of the installation, which provided a controlled and enclosed environment for the bacterial calcification to occur. A biologically induced mineralization process is understood as a bio-geo-chemical reaction of a living microorganism with its immediate environment. It can be found in soils across the world as well as in microbial mats both at sea and on land, solidifying granular materials through microscopic calcite links (Dupraz et al. 2009; Esnault Filet et al. 2012). In the context of this project, this process was applied to a medium-scale textile structure for the first time.

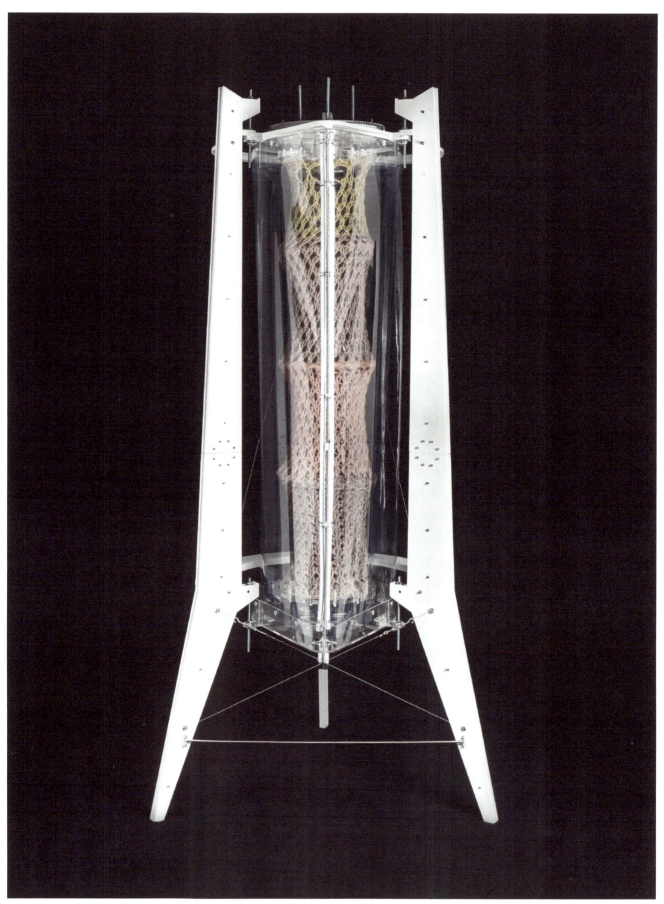

5   Bioreactor setup and textile structure before treatment.

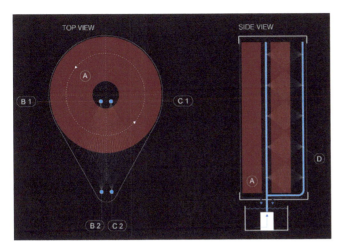

6 Irrigation System: (A) sample area, (B) 1/2-Bacteria irrigation system, (C) 1/2-Calcium chloride/Urea irrigation system, (D) Sprinkler.

7 Irrigation process, sprinkler detail (Figure 6, element D).

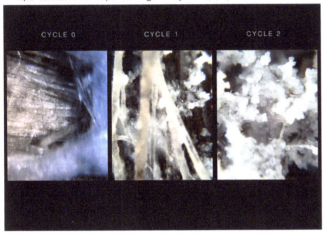

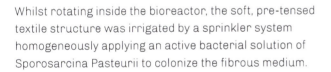

8 Calcification after 1/2 cycles, 100x magnification.

9 Detail calcified knitted loop (after treatment).

Whilst rotating inside the bioreactor, the soft, pre-tensed textile structure was irrigated by a sprinkler system homogeneously applying an active bacterial solution of Sporosarcina Pasteurii to colonize the fibrous medium.

Subsequently, the second irrigation system applied a Calcium chloride/Urea solution to trigger the bacterial calcite precipitation (Biocalcis process, Esnault Filet et al. 2016). This alternating treatment was repeated 8 times over a period of three days, gradually establishing a load-bearing calcite matrix within the fibrous system.

The generated active textile microbiome hereby adds another layer to the material hierarchy consisting of the time-based inter-relation between a living microorganism, its "host" material and its environment which could potentially be utilized for future bio-receptive and sustainable materials for architectural design.

ACKNOWLEDGMENTS

The authors would like to thank:

Annette Esnault Filet (Soletanche Bachy) and the Biocalcis Team who contributed to the Project extensively with their knowledge and experience in the field of bio-calcification and providing the bacteria for the tests.

Brice Desvages (Soletanche Bachy) who was a great support supervising the biochemical processes on site.

The textile research center EURECAT in Canet de Mar, Spain for the competent consulting in regards to textile technology as well as facilitating the fabrication process.

Albert Palen for the photography of the final installation.

This project has received funding from the European Union's Horizon 2020 research and innovation programme under the Marie Sklodowska-Curie grant agreement No. 642328.

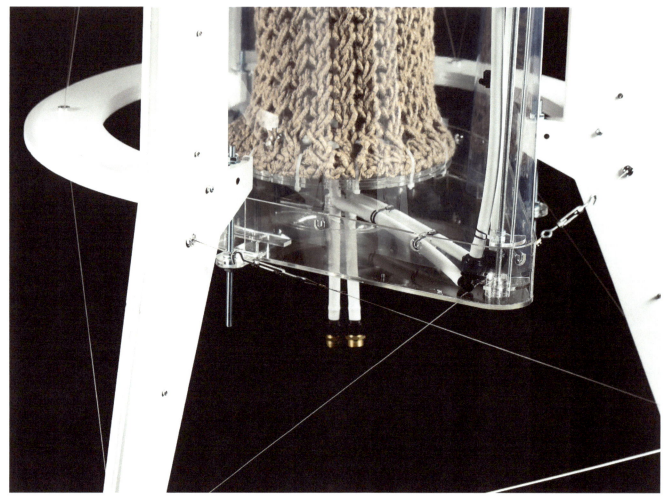

10 Installation detail, bioreactor, textile structure, irrigation system.

REFERENCES

De Araujo, Mario, Raul Fangueiro, and Hong Hu. 2011. "Weft-Knitted Structures for Industrial Applications." In *Advances in Knitting Technology*, edited by K. F. Au, 136–70. Cambridge, UK: Woodhead. doi:10.1533/9780857090621.2.136.

Duhovic, Miro, and Debes Bhattacharyya. 2011. "Knitted Fabric Composites." In *Advances in Knitting Technology*, 193–212. doi:10.1533/9780857090621.2.193.

Dupraz, Christophe, R. Pamela Reid, Olivier Braissant, Alan W. Decho, R. Sean Norman, and Pieter T. Visscher. 2009. "Processes of Carbonate Precipitation in Modern Microbial Mats." *Earth-Science Reviews* 96 (3): 141–62. doi:10.1016/j.earscirev.2008.10.005.

Eadie, Leslie, and Tushar K. Ghosh. 2011. "Biomimicry in Textiles: Past, Present and Potential. An Overview." *Journal of the Royal Society: Interface* 8 (59): 761–75. doi:10.1098/rsif.2010.0487.

Esnault Filet, Annette, Ira Gutjahr, Jean-François Mosser, Leslie Sapin, and Khalil Ibrahim. 2016. "A Novel Grouting Process for the Reinforcement of Low Permeability Soils with the Use of Biocementation by Biocalcis ®." In *Proceedings of the 19th Southeast Asian Geotechnical Conference and 2nd Association of Geotechnical Societies in Southeast Asia Conference*. Kuala Lumpur, Malaysia: AGSSEA.

Esnault Filet, Annette, Jean-Pierre Gadret, Memphis Loygue, and Serge Borel. 2012. "Biocalcis and its Applications for the Consolidation of Sands." In *Proceedings of the Fourth International Conference on Grouting and Deep Mixing*, edited by L. F. Johnsen, D. A. Bruce, and M. J. Byle, 1767–80. New Orleans, LA: Grouting and Deep Mixing. doi:doi:10.1061/9780784412350.0152.

Pamuk, Gulsah. 2016. "Development of Tubular Knitted Fabric-Reinforced Composite Pipes." *Journal of Industrial Textiles* 45 (5): 944–56. doi:10.1177/1528083714545393

IMAGE CREDITS

Figures 1, 5, 10: © B. Beyer, photography by Albert Palen
All other drawings and images by the authors © B. Beyer, D. Suàrez.

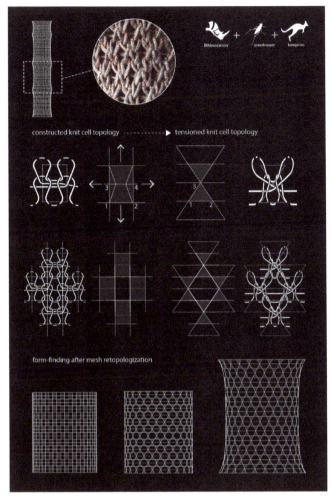

11 Column section study of retopologized mesh according to knitting pattern and mesh relaxation.

12 Bio-calcified, self-supporting composite structure after treatment.

Bastian Beyer is an architect and researcher at the Royal College of Art London and part of the Marie Curie ArcInTex Network (EU/H2020) which promotes interdisciplinary research within the fields of Architecture, Textiles and Interaction Design. His research investigates new approaches towards materiality and assembly systems with the focus on bio-derived matrices for textile-based composites. In this context, he explores how tailored active microbiomes within textile structures can influence and alter their behavior through biological activity.

Daniel Suarez is an architect and Marie Curie Fellow / Ph.D. Candidate at Berlin University of Arts as part of ArcInTexETN. His research explores augmentation processes focused on translating textile operations from the physical to the digital domain by means of human-machine interactions. The aim is to manipulate such textile digital tectonics in correspondence with possibilities of design offered by CAD/CAM processes. This textile tectonics develops innovative knitting paradigms for non-conventional textile materials and unexplored fabrication processes, hence allocating new domains for future spatial and architectural applications. Before joining ArcInTexETN Daniel worked as a practitioner for more than 12 years.

RECALIBRATION   ON   IMPRECISION   AND   INFIDELITY

Robotic Needle Felting

Tsz Yan Ng
Wes McGee
Asa Peller
University of Michigan,
Taubman College of
Architecture and Urban
Planning

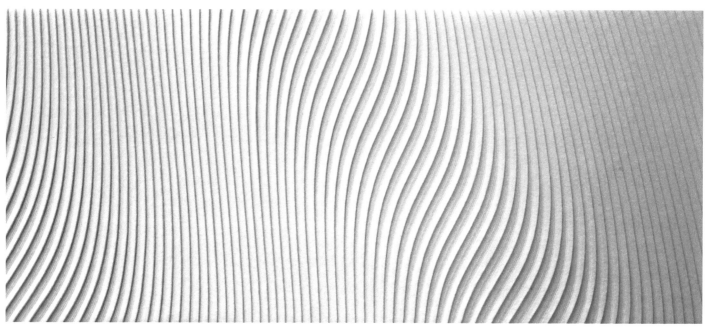

1   Shiplap texture with 1 1/2" wide, 1/8" thick F10 natural felt.

Robotic Needle Felting explores the development of an additive manufacturing technique for nonwoven textiles. Nonwoven textiles, such as felt, can be natural materials (wool), synthetic polymers (polyester), or blends of the two. These textiles have numerous performative aspects for architectural applications, including excellent acoustic absorption, thermal insulation, and tactile characteristics. Nonwoven textiles can be manipulated by a process called needle felting, whereby barbed needles punch through layers of material, entangling the fibers and creating a mechanical bond. This process binds the material together seamlessly without the addition of sewn thread or chemical adhesives, making this technique a more environmentally friendly process.

Needle felting can range in scale from handcraft techniques with a single needle to large-scale industrial web processing. Integration into a robotic process not only enables precision and speed in manufacturing but also extends needle felting as a three-dimensional process, especially for surfaces with complex geometries, allowing for local differentiation of stiffness and other properties across a homogeneous solid. Through a customized digital workflow, formal and material properties can be varied at a local level within a component. By developing a fully integrated design-to-production methodology for influencing these properties, this research opens a wide range of potentials for nonwoven textiles in architectural applications. The project involves three areas of development: the tooling for robotic felting, the digital workflow that enables the formal and material properties to be specified computationally and embedded into the machine code, and

PRODUCTION NOTES

Designers: Tsz Yan Ng, Wes McGee,
          and Asa Peller
Site: Ann Arbor, MI
Location: Annex Gallery
Year: 2018

2   View of exhibition (from left to right), samples of composite felting tests, 2 x 4 ft acoustic panels, video footage of various robotic felting processes, and foreground, bench with felted surface.

prototypes of architectural elements such as acoustic panels and furniture demonstrating different techniques and processes.

Additive manufacturing (AM), commonly known as 3D printing, has revolutionized the design to production workflow in a wide range of disciplines. While AM processes have been developed for a wide range of materials, from ceramics to plastics to metals, there have been very few investigations into their application with textiles. While notable examples exist, such as weaving and 3D knitting, these processes impose limitations on the resulting part thickness and fiber density. Given the unique capacity of felt to be seamlessly "added" into a cohesive solid, it presents a unique opportunity to investigate the potentials of an AM approach to layer nonwoven textiles into a composite material.

The prototypes explored three techniques resulting in different material and formal qualities: quilting, shiplap, and shingle. For these techniques, layers of material were felted together onto a foam substrate. An automatic feed, cut, and restart system facilitated both shiplap and shingle techniques, producing unique patterns and varying overlap between individual felt tapes. In working with nonwoven textiles, the behavior of the fibers in the needle punching process presents a multitude of factors that need to be considered and ultimately incorporated into the process control to achieve sufficient bonding between layers. In some prototypes, a nonwoven thermoplastic textile was used together with other natural felt materials to both create varied ribbed textures and to enhance overall stiffness by heat setting after felting. Overall, the ability to digitally simulate the specific choreography of the multiple functions occurring in the tool as well as to incorporate the geometric limitations imposed by the motion of the robot was critical to the successful realization of the prototypes. Potential applications of these various techniques include acoustic panels and furniture components, and ongoing research is planned to explore the acoustic performance of various textures as well as the structural performance of felted composite systems.

3   Acoustic panels with quilted texture.

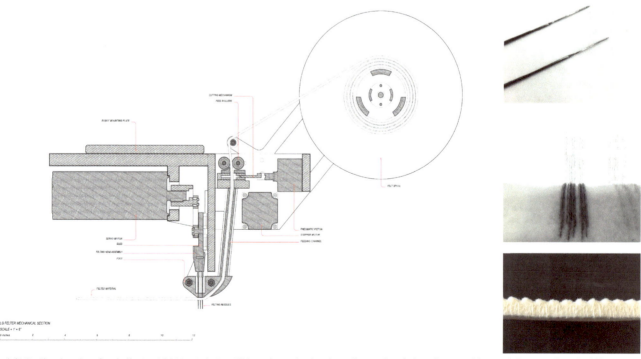

4   (left) Section drawing of end effector, (right top to bottom) Triangular and twisted needles, surface below after punching, and close-up of meshed fibers.

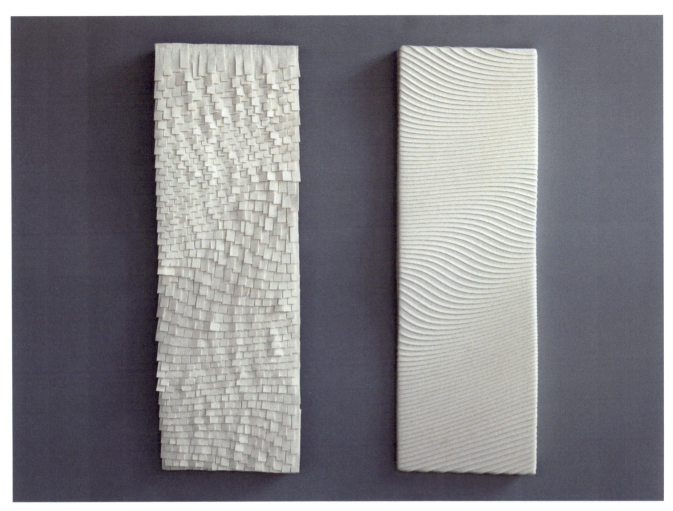

5   2 x 6 ft acoustic panels with shingle and shiplap textures.

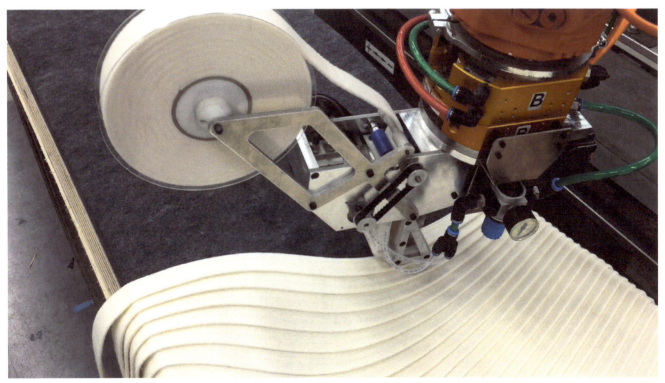

6   Shiplap technique with F10 natural wool being felted onto substrate for acoustic panels.

7 Baked panel with 30 degrees shiplap front and -30 back.

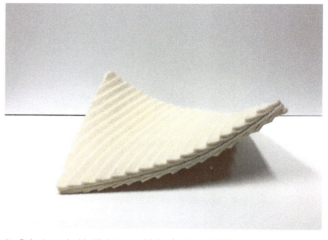

8 Baked panel with 45 degrees shiplap front and -45 back.

9 Baked panel with single-sided curved shiplapped paths.

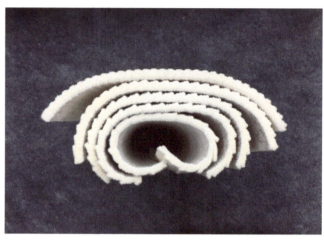

10 Series of felted panels showing curvatures controlled by varying overlap.

11 Strips of felt being laid for shingle process.

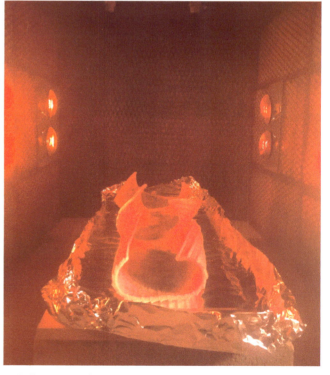

12 Baking process of composite panels with nonwoven thermoplastic textile.

Robotic Needle Felting Ng, McGee, Peller

13 Wavy shiplap texture with "lift" created by tightness of the curved paths.

14 Approximately 2 ft diameter pouf with grey 1/16″ thick F55 felt strips.

ACKNOWLEDGMENTS

Robotic Needle Felting was made possible through the generous support from the Taubman College of Architecture + Urban Planning, University of Michigan. Additional support was received through the University of Michigan Office of Research.

Design Team: Tsz Yan Ng, Wes McGee, and Asa Peller

Research Assistant: Rachel Henry. Production Assistants: Jared Monce, Drew Bradford, and Carlos Pompeo

Portions of this text were previously published in McGee, Wes, Tsz Yan Ng, and Asa Peller. 2018. "Hard+Soft: Robotic Felting for Nonwoven Textiles." In *Robotic Fabrication in Architecture, Art and Design*, edited by J. Willman, P. Block, M. Hutter, K. Byrne, and T. Schork. Cham, Switzerland: Springer.

Tsz Yan Ng is an Assistant Professor in Architecture at Taubman College, University of Michigan. She was the Walter B. Sanders Fellow at the University of Michigan (2007-08) and the Reyner Banham Fellow at the University of Buffalo (2001-02). Ng's practice includes architectural designs and installations in visual art. Common to both practices are projects that deal with questions of labor in its various manifestations, with special focus on techniques in clothing manufacturing and concrete forming.

Wes McGee is an Assistant Professor and the Director of the FABLab at the University of Michigan Taubman College of Architecture and Urban Planning. His work revolves around the interrogation of the means and methods of material production in the digital era, through research focused on developing new connections between design, engineering, materials, and manufacturing processes as they relate to the built environment.

Asa Peller is a Lecturer in Architecture and the Manager of the FABLab at the University of Michigan Taubman College of Architecture and Urban Planning. He is an artist, designer, and craftsperson, with a focus on integrating manufacturing processes with robotic techniques of production.

WAFT

Shelby Elizabeth Doyle
Iowa State University

Erin Linsey Hunt
Iowa State University

Kelly Devitt
Iowa State University

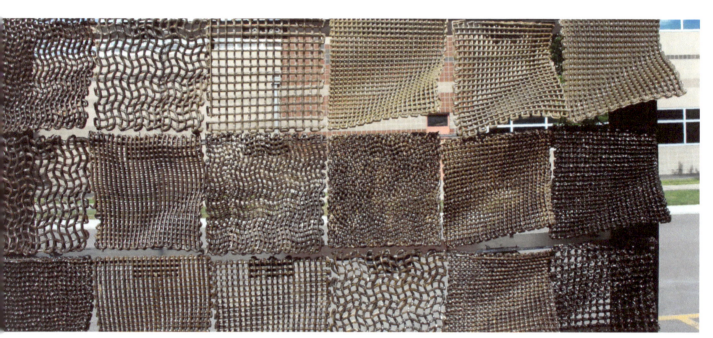

1   WAFT final mock up assembled.

Introduction

WAFT is an interdisciplinary collaboration between researchers in architecture, computation, and ceramics. The project integrates traditional slump molding techniques and handmade glazes with computationally designed and 3D-printed ceramic tiles and CNC milled molds. WAFT is the result of an ongoing partnership at the Iowa State University (ISU) Computation + Construction Lab (CCL) between the departments of Architecture and Arts & Visual Culture at ISU's College of Design. The project relies upon digitally assisted fabrication: the combination of manual and digital fabrication practices. WAFT leverages both ceramic knowledge and digital fabrication capabilities to create designs that neither discipline could produce in isolation.

Background

Clay's plasticity makes it an ideal material for exploring the complex geometries made possible by digital tools: from facades by Building Bytes (2018) to the Cabin of Curiosities by Emerging Objects (Goldberg 2018). In parallel, the scholarship of architectural ceramics continues to develop and includes events such as the 2015 Data Clay Symposium and books such as *Printing Architecture: Innovative Recipes for 3D Printing* (Rael and San Fratello 2018).

This research began with a close examination of the innovative techniques and evocative aesthetics presented in "Clay Non-Wovens: Robotic Fabrication and Digital Ceramics,"

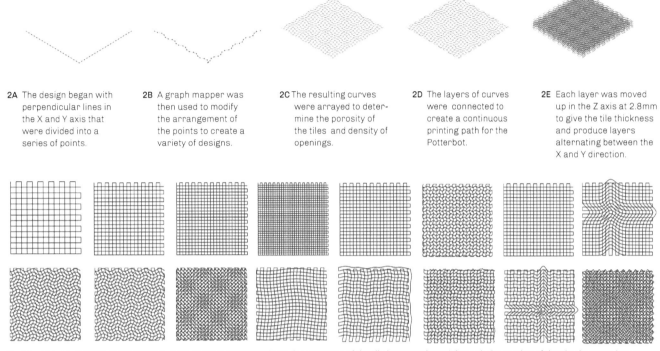

2A The design began with perpendicular lines in the X and Y axis that were divided into a series of points.

2B A graph mapper was then used to modify the arrangement of the points to create a variety of designs.

2C The resulting curves were arrayed to determine the porosity of the tiles and density of openings.

2D The layers of curves were connected to create a continuous printing path for the Potterbot.

2E Each layer was moved up in the Z axis at 2.8mm to give the tile thickness and produce layers alternating between the X and Y direction.

2   Layers were printed in pairs of 2, 4, or 6 creating a weave where the structure of the tile is strengthened through the overlap of the clay between layers.

specifically, the notion of clay as a "structural fiber rather than a tool for solid construction" (Rosenwasser, Mantell, and Sabin 2017). WAFT then deviates from "Clay Non-Wovens" by exploring the possibilities of three-axis ceramic printing combined with slump molding, a less cost prohibitive method than robotic fabrication. The goal was to build upon lessons learned to create a low-cost method for interdisciplinary experiments in architectural ceramics. This process included the integration of ceramic knowledge, such as clay bodies, custom glazes, and slump casting, with parametric design, such as controlling the porosity, depth, and surface curvature of each tile. The design and production of a full-scale mock-up concluded this phase of research.

Process

The tile design process required the customization of several digital tools which were integrated into a single digital workflow using Grasshopper for McNeel Rhinoceros. The tiles were designed using graph mappers to customize the gradient and density of patterning for each tile. Layers were printed in pairs of 2, 4, or 6, creating a weave where the structure of the tile is strengthened through the overlap of the clay between layers. Tile size remained consistent at X-6″ (252 mm) by Y-6″ (252 mm) and layer height for the clay remained constant at Z-0.11″ (2.8 mm); each tile took approximately ten minutes to print. G-code for the Potterbot was produced directly from Grasshopper using the Xylinus plug-in. Tiles were printed using a variety of custom polygonal and star-shaped 3D-printed ABS nozzles on the 3D Potterbot 7 (3DP7) by Deltabot which has an envelope of X-17″ (432 mm), Y-14″ (356 mm), and Z-19″ (483 mm). A mid-range stoneware was used throughout the process. The clay arrives as a premixed dry body and is then mixed with water and pug milled to printing consistency. Printing begins with running a "prime" g-code which runs until the clay begins extruding. Once "priming" is complete, the specific tile g-code is selected, and the Potterbot homes automatically to X and Y in relation to the start code. Z-zero is manually established by the user. The extrude speed and move speed are written in the code but the user can override these as necessary through the print process

3 Hardware was attached to the fired tiles using apoxie clay. From the non-glazed (interior) a variety of light conditions and views are created.

4 Combining the material knowledge of slump molding with the computational intelligence of 3D printing produced a gradient of results.

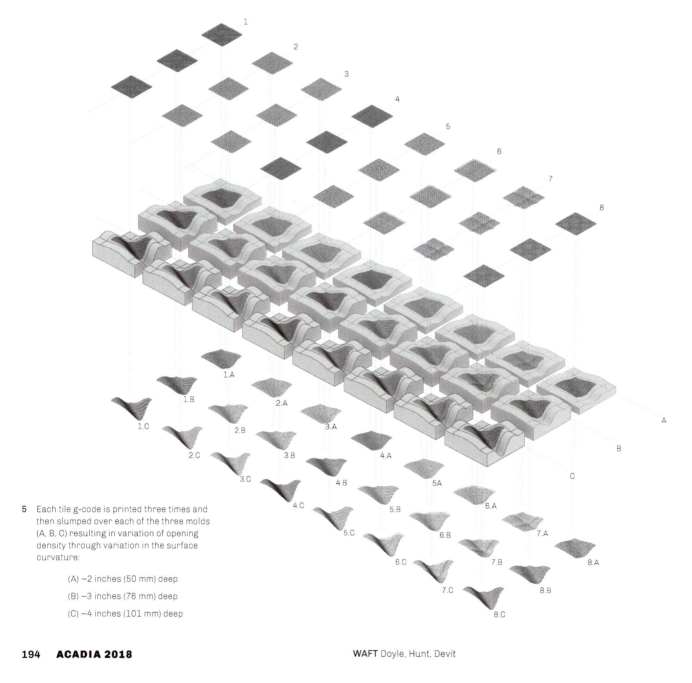

5 Each tile g-code is printed three times and then slumped over each of the three molds (A, B, C) resulting in variation of opening density through variation in the surface curvature:

(A) ~2 inches (50 mm) deep

(B) ~3 inches (76 mm) deep

(C) ~4 inches (101 mm) deep

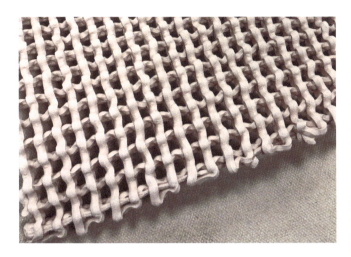

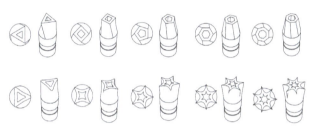

6 Custom 3D printed polygonal and star-shaped ABS nozzles for the Potterbot were designed to produce additional depth and patterning in each tile.

7 Color variation was produced by altering the quantity of glaze additives to produce a gradient of colors across the final thirty-six tiles.

to accommodate variations in clay consistency. A layer of plastic wrap was placed on a dampened acrylic bed and smoothed with a potter's rib (Sheffield very soft red rib 0) before each tile printed, allowing the tile to be picked up on the sheet of plastic wrap and then draped over one of three reusable CNC'd rigid insulation slump molds (A) ~2 inches (50 mm) deep, (B) ~3 inches (76 mm) deep, or (C) ~4 inches (101 mm) deep. Slump molds are concave forms over which clay slabs are draped to create reproducible forms such as plates or bowls. When producing slabs by hand, textured slabs or rollers are used to imprint upon the clay prior to slumping. In this case, the texturing is produced through the ceramic 3D printing process and the introduction of custom 3D-printed nozzle geometry, then the clay is slumped by hand. The tile is left on the slump mold until it is dry enough to be self-supporting. Then the tile is flipped and the plastic removed allowing the mold-side of the tile to dry at the same time as the upward facing-side which prevents cracking due to uneven drying rates. Then the tiles are bisque fired in an electric kiln to 1900 degrees Fahrenheit, cooled, waxed on the interior facing side, and glazed on the exterior facing side with a handmade transparent based glaze made with Mason Stain 6600 (Black CoCrFeNi) and

Rutile (TiO2) colorants. Color variation was produced by altering the quantity of glaze additives to produce a gradient of colors across the final thirty-six tiles. After the tiles were dry enough to touch, they were placed back into the kiln and fired to cone 6 (2232 degrees Fahrenheit). To complete this research phase, a full-scale façade mock-up was constructed from thirty-six tiles which were assembled in a grid from lightest (top) to darkest (bottom) and from smallest curvature (2″) to greatest curvature (4″) Each tile was attached to an L-bracket with apoxie clay and then attached to the plasma-CNC-cut steel frame using machine screws, washers, and nuts to create an adjustable attachment for each tile in the assembly. The material costs for the mock-up were quite low totaling approximately one-hundred dollars (twenty dollars for each of the following: clay, firing, eleven-gauge steel, concrete, hardware and adhesives).

Conclusions and Next Steps
This research integrates traditional slumping techniques with a parametric approach to digital fabrication resulting in a low-cost digitally assisted method of manufacturing through the merging of hands-on experience with

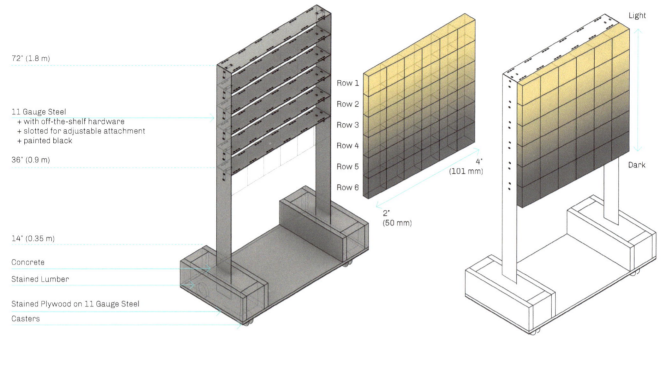

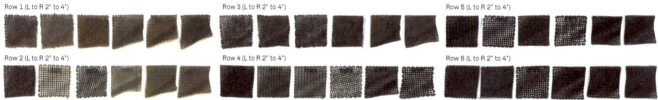

8 A full-scale substructure was constructed using plasma-CNC-cut steel and off-the-shelf hardware to allow for testing tile assemblies and the develople-ment of attachment details. The tiles were hung from lightest to darkest glazing and from smallest curvature to greatest curvature.

computational methods. Or in the terms of this conference "mediating between an 'ideal' precision/accuracy obtainable through digital methodologies, and the imprecision and infidelity of the physical/material world around us, simultaneously acknowledging the interrelated importance of both analog and digital processes, and privileging neither one over the other." As this collaboration continues, the next design steps will be the development of custom surface treatments and the design of parametrically controlled glazing patterning to explore the evaporative cooling potential of clay (Lilley 2012).

REFERENCES

Building Bytes. 2018. http://www.buildingbytes.info/

Goldberg, Mackenzie. 2018. "3D printed Oakland cabin proves the architectural (and aesthetic) possibilities of additive manufacturing." *Archinect*, March 14, 2018. https://archinect.com/news/article/150054399/3d-printed-oakland-cabin-proves-the-architectural-and-aesthetic-possibilities-of-additive-manufacturing

Lilley, Brian, Roland Hudson, Kevin Plucknett, Rory Macdonald, Nancy Yen-Wen Cheng, Stig Anton Nielsen, Olympia Nouska, Monika Grinbergs, Stephen Andematten, Kyle Baumgardner et al. "Ceramic Perspiration: Multi-Scalar Development of Ceramic Material." In *Synthetic Digital Ecologies: Proceedings of the 32nd Annual Conference of the Association for Computer Aided Design in Architecture*, edited by Jason Kelly Johnson, Mark Cabrinha, and Kyle Steinfeld, 97-108. San Francisco: ACADIA.

Rael, Ronald, and Virginia San Fratello. 2018. *Printing Architecture: Innovative Recipes for 3D Printing*. New York: Princeton Architectural Press.

Rosenwasser, David, Sonya Mantell, and Jenny Sabin. 2017. "Clay Non-Wovens: Robotic Fabrication and Digital Ceramics." In *Disciplines & Disruption: Proceedings of the 37th Annual Conference of the Association for Computer Aided Design in Architecture*, edited by Takehiko Nagakura, Skylar Tibbits, Mariana Ibanez, and Caitlin Mueller, 502–11. Cambridge, MA: ACADIA.

IMAGE CREDITS

All photos, drawings, and images by the authors.

9   WAFT completed assembly.

ACKNOWLEDGMENTS

This work was made possible by the Computation + Construction Lab (CCL) an initiative of the Department of Architecture at Iowa State University. Additional support was provided by: the ISU Office of the Vice Provost for Research, the ISU Department of Architecture, ISU Department of Arts & Visual Culture, and the Daniel J. Huberty Faculty Fellowship.

Shelby Elizabeth Doyle, AIA is an assistant professor of Architecture and Daniel J. Huberty Faculty Fellow at the Iowa State University College of Design. Doyle was hired under the ISU President's High Impact Hires Initiative to combine digital fabrication and design/build at ISU. This led to the development of the ISU Computation & Construction Lab (ccl.design.iastate.edu). She holds a Master of Architecture degree from the Harvard Graduate School of Design and a Bachelor of Science in Architecture from the University of Virginia.

Erin Hunt is the ISU Computation & Construction Lab Associate where she oversees operations and conducts research. Her research interests include construction applications for additive manufacturing technologies, specifically 3D printing. Erin plans to pursue an advanced degree in digital fabrication and computational design. She was an Undergraduate Research Assistant with the ISU CCL and she holds a Bachelor of Architecture degree from Iowa State University.

Kelly Devitt is a Ceramic Research Assistant for both the ISU Computation & Construction Lab and the ISU Integrated Visual Arts Department. Her research explores Cone 6 and High Fire glazes, the use of different clay bodies and consistency in ceramic 3D printing, and her personal work explores large sculptural forms. She holds a Bachelor of Fine Arts degree from Iowa State University and plans to pursue an advanced degree in ceramic arts.

Elemental | Ornamental

Asa Leland Peller
Wes McGee
Taubman College of
Architecture and Urban
Planning

1   Detail of the translucent qualities of porcelain and the relationship between topology and bead geometry.

Elemental | Ornamental is an ongoing research project focused on the development of ceramic-based 3D printing technologies for a range of architectural, design, and manufacturing applications. Inspired by the speculations of Viollet-le-Duc and the use of cast iron in the work of Henri Labrouste, Hector Guimard, and Louis Sullivan, this project began as an investigation into robotically fabricated ceramic molds for casting metal. The work has diverged along a number of interrelated trajectories, including material research, mold production and aluminum casting, computational design and toolpathing techniques, and product design.

As engineered material compounds, clay bodies have a range of physical and chemical properties. Clay is a non-Newtonian fluid, which presents several challenges for 3D printing. Differences in water content and granularity affect the pressures required to extrude it, and this also impacts layer bonding and bead quality. The first end effector, a ball-screw-driven piston extruder, is excellent for continuous printing, but back-pressure produces substantial start and stop delays. A second system combined three types of pump technologies, which made it possible to move clay from a remote unit to the end effector on the robot at high (>1000 psi) pressure. A servo-controlled progressive cavity pump at the point of deposition allows for precise control of the printing process. It is synchronously controlled via a custom PLC interface, which allows the tool to be programmed as an external robot axis. A third, hydraulically driven piston is currently in development.

PRODUCTION NOTES

Designers: Asa Peller, Wes McGee
Status: Current Research
Location: Ann Arbor, MI
Date: 2017-2018

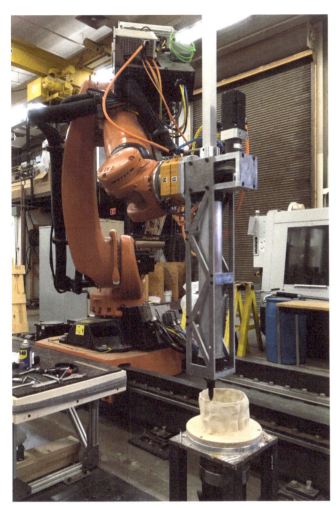

2   Screw-driven piston extruder, printing on an external rotary axis.

3   Robotically printed refractory molds, pre-heated before casting.

4   The molds are boxed in sand to insulate them during the pour.

Investment casting is a technique that has been in existence for almost 8000 years. This process entails the production of a wax model, which is coated with a refractory ceramic material. The wax is melted from the shell, and liquid metal is poured into the resulting cavity. The research builds on this method through the development of robotically printed ceramic molds, simultaneously eliminating the need to produce a positive while also simplifying the production of compound molds for larger or geometrically complex components. A refractory clay body is used for its ability to resist thermal fluctuations, retaining its strength at high temperatures. The prototypes generated are intended to represent potential sections and surface treatments of non-standard structural members.

Additionally, the work explores several computational strategies related to toolpath generation. As opposed to typical layer slicing used in 3D printing, approaches which generated paths in the surface domain were explored. This has the advantage of producing continuous, smooth curves, but typically results in layers of variable thickness. During the path generation phase, this layer thickness is continuously calculated and stored in a custom data object, exposed by the SuperMatterTools plugin for Rhino. This data object is later processed into the robotic code and used to control the extrusion rate synchronously with the robot position.

Finally, the research explored the material qualities of porcelain, as demonstrated by a series of light fixtures and vessels. Porcelain is fine-grained and plastic, making it possible to produce very thin and narrow layers, which offers a fine print resolution. Due to low water content, it is stiff, making it possible to print faster, taller, and with greater cantilevers. Porcelain is also an excellent medium for transmitting light, and the pieces highlight design explorations in textures and forms found in nature. Infidelity, misregistration, and imprecision are inherent qualities of clay, and this project seeks to mask the precision of computation and digital fabrication within a material that is constantly resisting control.

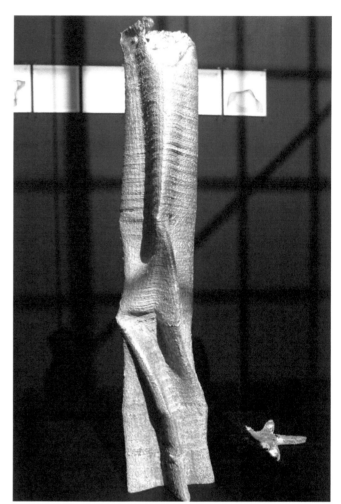

5   Aluminum flake from a failed mold.

6   Scale column study, Cast aluminum.

7   Cross section study. Cast aluminum.

8   Tube section study, Cast aluminum.

9 Porcelain lamp fixture.

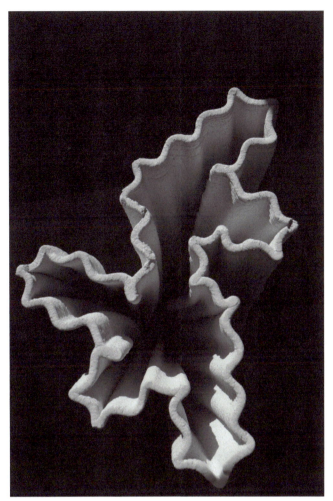

10 Refractory mold for aluminum.

11 Daylit study. Extrusion rates increase over gaps between layers.

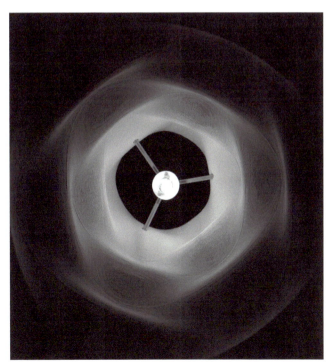

12 Porcelain lamp fixture.

RECALIBRATION ON IMPRECISION AND INFIDELITY

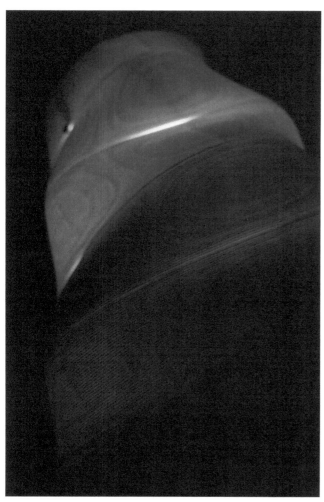

13 Wobbly vase. Radiating surface ridges generated from robot backlash.

14 Detail. Porcelain mold for aluminum. Column study.

15 Deformations due to robot backlash.

16 Lamp interior.

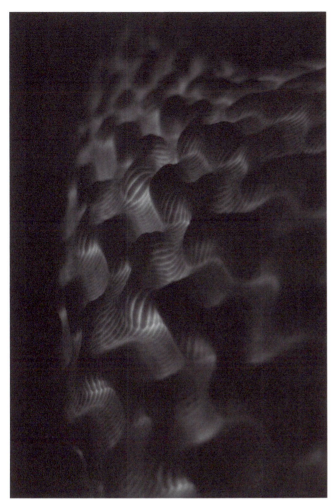

17 Extrusion detail. Bulges due to robot-induced changes in the part.

18 Lamp detail.

ACKNOWLEDGMENTS

Elemental | Ornamental was made possible by the generous support of Taubman College of Architecture and Urban Planning. Special thanks to Matt Bierl, Rahul Attraya, Max Neisweinder, Tyler Van Kirk, Dan Tish, Mick Kennedy, and John Leyland.

IMAGE CREDITS

All drawings and images by the authors.

Asa Leland Peller is a Lecturer in Architecture and the FABLab Manager at the University of Michigan Taubman College of Architecture and Urban Planning. A designer, artist, and craftsman, he melds experiences in traditional and digital methods of making. His work at the university is focused on integrating robotic techniques of production within current manufacturing and fabrication processes.

Wes McGee is an Assistant Professor and the Director of the FABLab at the University of Michigan Taubman College of Architecture and Urban Planning. His work revolves around the interrogation of the means and methods of material production in the digital era, through research focused on developing new connections between design, engineering, materials, and manufacturing processes as they relate to the built environment.

EndlessColumns

Variable 3D-Printed Ceramic Molds for
Cast Architectural Elements

T. Shan Sutherland
Clemson University

William Marshall
Clemson University

Dave Lee
Clemson University

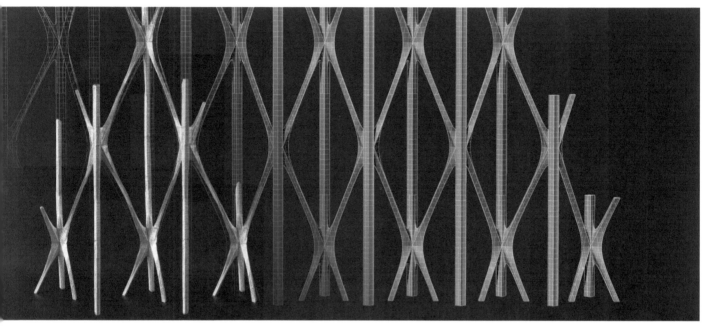

1   Lattice system cast from 3D-printed ceramic molds (Authors 2018).

Abstract

This ongoing project examines the potential to utilize 3D-printed ceramic technologies to
produce variable, positive-less molds for the production of architectural elements in cast
metal. The research addresses the formal limits and fidelity issues of gel extrusion; computationally assesses the variable infidelities involved in the drying, vitrification, and casting
process; and assesses the technical limits of cold-mold, gravity-cast metal. The examples
produced show the potential for this process to realize architecture which simultaneously achieves both structural gracility and ornamental complexity efficiently and with a
constrained capacity for serial variability.

History

Ceramic molds have been used for the past 5700 years for the production of bespoke metal
objects. Though capable of achieving both scale and accuracy, traditional slip-painted, "lost
wax" methods of ceramic shell casting are unsuitable for the mass production of architectural elements because of the time and materials involved in destructed positive mold
production. In comparison, cast metal elements were employed in many exquisite architectural works during the Art Nouveau and Neo-Gothic periods. These larger works used
reusable green sand (sand mixed with bituminous clay and water) as a mold medium, and
a durable, reusable wood positive. The method was adopted from the industrial arts of the
day, and was suitable for serial production of single parts in the ornate yet repetitive style
of the era.

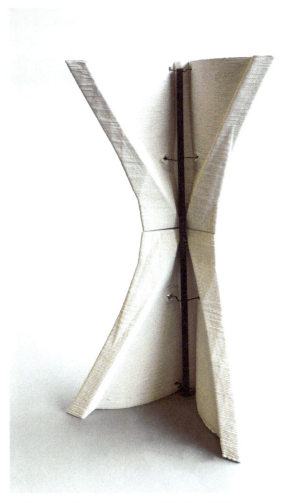

2   Two piece 3D-printed ceramic mold (Authors 2018).

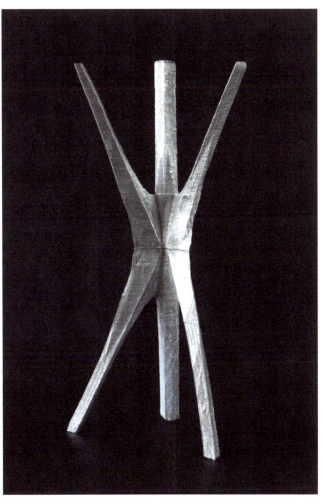

3   Cast aluminum module (Authors 2018).

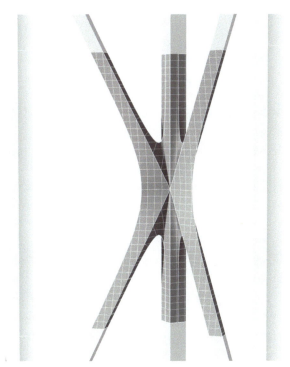

4   Module geometry (Authors 2018).

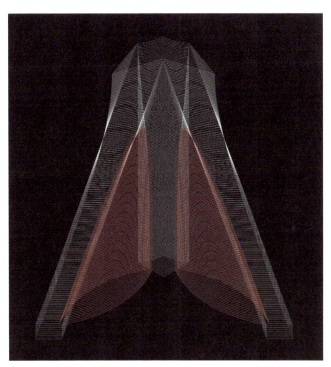

5   3D printer toolpath (white=mold, red=printed support) (Authors 2018).

RECALIBRATION ON IMPRECISION AND INFIDELITY

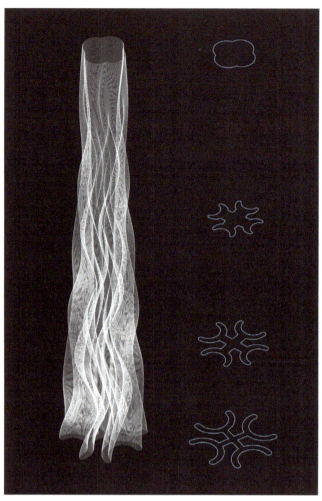

6 Change in moments of inertia at various cross sections of Column (Authors 2018).

7 3D-printed ceramic mold for Column (Authors 2018).

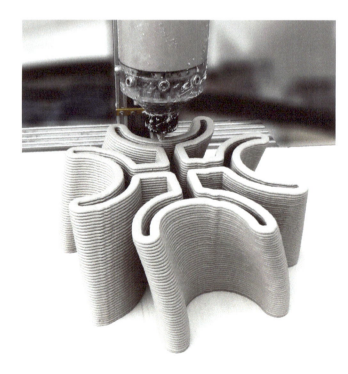

8 Molds are printed from one continuous line of clay using a Potterbot 3D ceramic extruder (Authors 2018).

9 Pouring aluminum into 3D-printed ceramic mold (Authors 2018).

Endless Columns Sutherland, Marshall, Lee

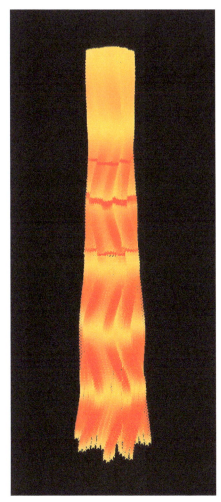

10 Material overhang analysis (Authors 2018).

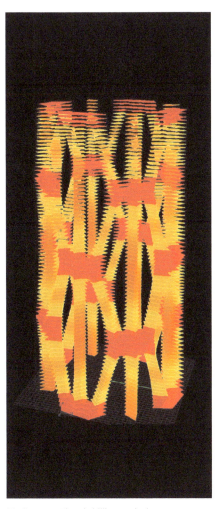

11 Cross sectional chilling analysis (Authors 2018).

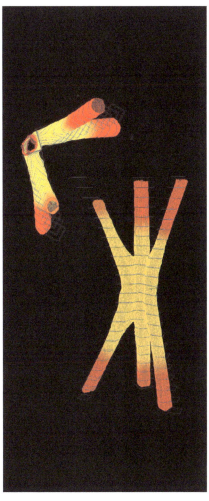

12 Material deflection analysis (Authors 2018).

Materials and Methods

Our technique represents a hybrid of green sand and ceramic shell casting, which circumvents the need for a destructible or reusable positive. The use of a thin-shelled (4–8 mm) printed ceramic void packed into a reusable, thermally resistant green sand mold allows for a serial, efficient casting method with a capacity for the rapid production of unique or variable parts.

The ceramic shells were printed using a Potterbot 3D Ceramic extruder and stoneware. The printer and media combination proved effective when printing simple cylindrical forms with low degrees of overhang and limited traversing. To overcome the process limitations, and to explore non-cylindrical formal typologies, we developed methods for modeling integrated support systems and controlled traverse paths (Figure 5).

Individual part size was relatively small, compelling us to explore the aggregation of several part molds. Although this process allowed for greater variability between each part, serial modular parts were produced to assess the predictability and fidelity of the process for different geometric forms.

Computation

In addition to using a standard Rhino 3DM-to-Cura slicer, We used Grasshopper to assess the printability, castability, and fidelity of the mold and cast. We developed methods to qualitatively analyze the cross-sectional areas of all members showing forms that are likely to chill during casting (Figure 10). Finally, we assessed cross-sectional areas of a final scan of the cast object in relation to the original model to evaluate shrinkage and torsion (Figure 11).

13 Lattice column multi-piece stacked ceramic molds (Authors 2018).

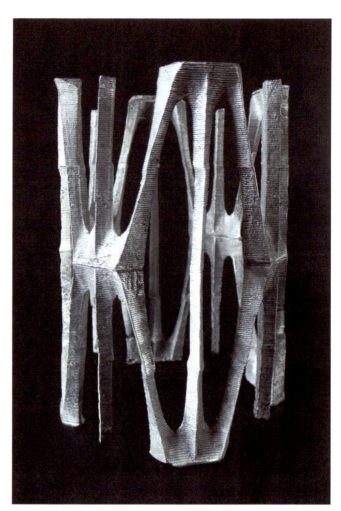

14 Lattice column aluminum cast (Authors 2018).

15 X module system ceramic mold (Authors 2018).

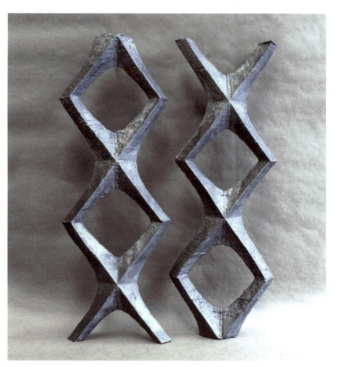

16 X module system iron casts (Authors 2018).

Endless Columns Sutherland, Marshall, Lee

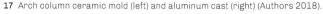

17 Arch column ceramic mold (left) and aluminum cast (right) (Authors 2018).

18 Perforated column ceramic mold (left) and bronze cast (right) (Authors 2018).

19 Iron pour (Authors 2018).

Conclusions

There are many obstacles to overcome before thin-shell 3D printed molds can provide a viable, predictable method for building component production. Significantly, it is necessary to control moisture and temperature at every step in the production process. Even with extensive precaution, rates of shrinkage and predictable patterns of warping must be accounted for in order for parts to be produced in a sufficiently predictable manner for complex aggregations (Figure 1). We feel that the inherent variability of the amorphous material can be overcome with technical rigor, while the predictable changes to the geometry inherent to the process can be overcome with accurate data collection and increasingly sophisticated computational modeling.

ACKNOWLEDGMENTS

The authors would like to acknowledge the Clemson Architecture Department and Architecture Foundation for financial contributions to support research and travel. We would like to acknowledge Valerie Zimmany, Daniel Bare, and Connor Atwood from the Clemson Ceramics department for their assistance with ceramic materials and techniques. Also, we would like to thank the Cody Belvin and Mason Blackwell of the Clemson Digital Design Studio and the Architecture Materials Lab for their essential contributions.

Shan Sutherland is a Lecturer of Architecture and the manager of the Digital Design Studio and the Materials Lab at Clemson University. His research explores the potential combinations of traditional craft techniques and computationally aided design. His research has been published in the proceedings of ACADIA 2016 and FABRICATE 2017.

William Marshall is an undergraduate student in the Clemson School of Architecture. He has been lead fabricator on several published research projects.

Dave Lee is an Associate Professor of Architecture at Clemson University where he leads the Computational Design Group, a transdisciplinary research team dedicated to the exploration of emergent technology, processes, and techniques in architecture. He is the 2018-2019 Clemson Creativity Professorship recipient.

PHOTOPTOSIS

Christoph Klemmt
Orproject/University of
Cincinnati

Rajat Sodhi
Orproject

1   Photoptosis (Kateryna Iakovlieva, © Orproject 2017).

In computational architecture, iterative algorithms such as agent-based simulations or growth simulations can generate interesting, complex geometries. However, while those geometries often present some functional aspects, their use in building designs usually result in various practical requirements that demand the algorithm's output geometry to vary in specific locations. Instead of postprocessing and adjusting the geometry after being generated in order to suit those practical requirements, we propose to incorporate a logic of spatial deformation in the algorithm that is able to increase or decrease the likelihood of geometry being generated in specific areas. The algorithmic calculations in this curved space, similar to the curved space that is used in the general theory of relativity to describe gravity (Weinberg 1972), then become an easily controllable tool for the designer.

The method has been applied to the design of Photoptosis, a sculpture that consists of a triangulated, tree trunk–like stainless steel surface, onto which a set of side-glowing fiber optics cables has been grown algorithmically like the veins of ivy on a tree. The geometries of both the stainless steel surface as well as the fiber optics cables have been developed through computational algorithms that digitally simulate the growth of veins and plants. This venation algorithm, originally developed at the University of Calgary (Runions et al. 2005; Runions, Lane, and Prusinkiewicz 2007; Runions 2008), simulates plants' need to reach the sunlight, or of leaves' veins to supply every cell with nutrients. In doing so, the growth of the branches or the veins slowly expands to cover a large area.

PRODUCTION NOTES

Architect: Orproject
Team: Christoph Klemmt,
            Rajat Sodhi
Production: Structural Engineering:
            Bollinger & Grohmann
            Metalwork:
            Winterberg Metall
Client: Private
Location: Düsseldorf, Germany
Date: 2017

2   Detail Stainless Steel Surface (Kateryna Iakovlieva, © Orproject 2017).

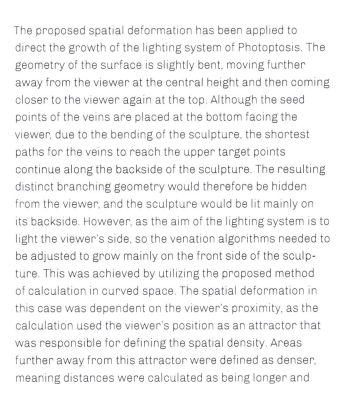

3   Detail Fiber Optic Cables (© Orproject 2017).

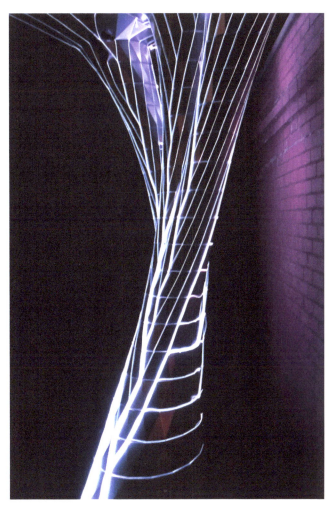

4   Detail Fiber Optic Cables (© Orproject 2017).

The proposed spatial deformation has been applied to direct the growth of the lighting system of Photoptosis. The geometry of the surface is slightly bent, moving further away from the viewer at the central height and then coming closer to the viewer again at the top. Although the seed points of the veins are placed at the bottom facing the viewer, due to the bending of the sculpture, the shortest paths for the veins to reach the upper target points continue along the backside of the sculpture. The resulting distinct branching geometry would therefore be hidden from the viewer, and the sculpture would be lit mainly on its backside. However, as the aim of the lighting system is to light the viewer's side, so the venation algorithms needed to be adjusted to grow mainly on the front side of the sculpture. This was achieved by utilizing the proposed method of calculation in curved space. The spatial deformation in this case was dependent on the viewer's proximity, as the calculation used the viewer's position as an attractor that was responsible for defining the spatial density. Areas further away from this attractor were defined as denser, meaning distances were calculated as being longer and

therefore less likely for the growth. A very simple manipulation of the space was enough to cause the algorithm to grow the main branches of the network on the front side instead of the back.

The structure is made from 100 stainless steel, 3 mm thick panels that have been CNC cut and CNC bent to their respective shapes. The structural engineering managed to utilize only this thin steel surface as the sole structural element without the need for a primary structure. In order for the surface not to deform, additional stainless steel strips were placed in line with the flanges of the panels as stiffeners, and the lower areas required additional bolts along the flanges to connect two rows of steel segments. The lighting is achieved through the use of side-glowing fiber optics cables. The bundle of 200 cables starts at the bottom of the sculpture and then branches out to reach every node on the stainless steel surface.

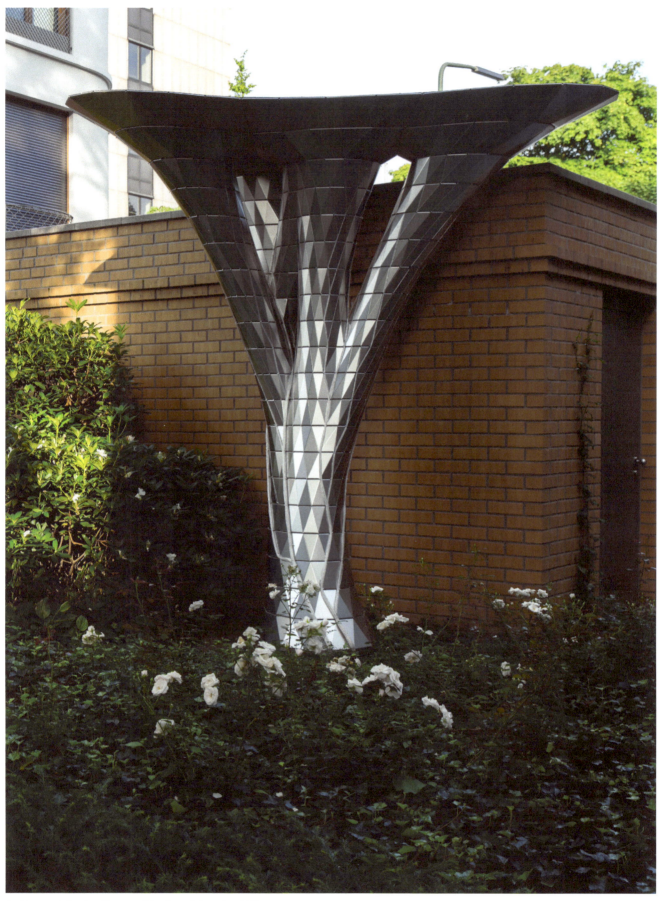

5   Photoptosis Daytime (Kateryna Iakovlieva, © Orproject 2017).

6   Construction Detail (© Orproject 2017).

REFERENCES

Runions, Adam. 2008. "Modeling Biological Patterns Using the Space Colonization Algorithm." M.Sc. thesis, University of Calgary.

Runions, Adam, Martin Fuhrer, Brendan Lane, Pavol Federl, Anne-Gaëlle Rolland-Lagan, and Przemyslaw Prusinkiewicz. 2005. "Modeling and Visualization of Leaf Venation Patterns." *ACM Transactions on Graphics* 24 (3): 702–11.

Runions, Adam, Brendan Lane, and Przemyslaw Prusinkiewicz. 2007. "Modeling Trees with a Space Colonization Algorithm". In *Proceedings of the Third Eurographics Workshop on Natural Phenomena*, 63–70. Prague, Czech Republic: NPH.

Weinberg, Steven. 1972. *Gravitation and Cosmology: Principles and Applications of the General Theory of Relativity.* New York: Wiley.

IMAGE CREDITS

Figures 1, 5, 7, 8: Kateryna Iakovlieva, © Orproject 2017.

All other photographs by the authors.

Christoph Klemmt graduated from the Architectural Association in London in 2004. He has worked amongst others for Zaha Hadid Architects, where his responsibilities were focused on the company's Soho Galaxy, Wangjing Soho, and Leeza Soho projects. He is Assistant Professor at the University of Cincinnati, where he received a grant to set up the Architectural Robotics Lab, and he is co-directing the AA Visiting School at the Angewandte in Vienna. In 2008 Christoph Klemmt co-founded Orproject, an architect's office specialising in advanced geometries with an ecologic agenda. Orproject has exhibited at the Palais De Tokyo in Paris, the China National Museum in Beijing, and the Biennale in Venice.

Rajat Sodhi received his diploma from the AA in London in 2007 and the DRL masters in 2009. He has worked with 1-to-One for Herzog & de Meuron, Foster + Partners, Morphogenesis Architecture Studio, and Le Groupe Arcop. He has lectured and given workshops at the Architectural Association, the University of Westminster, and the Indian Institute of Technology in New Delhi. His interest lies in developing computational geometry and exploring material formations inspired by nature's inherent optimisations.

7   Photoptosis Twilight (Kateryna Iakovlieva, © Orproject 2017).

8   Photoptosis Twilight (Kateryna Iakovlieva, © Orproject 2017).

RECALIBRATION ON IMPRECISION AND INFIDELITY

Delight: Lattice Cloud

Dr. Jason Lim Teck Chye
Singapore University of Technology and Design /
TakahashiLim A + D

1   The lattice cloud in the Singapore Pavilion (Tomohisa Miyauchi, 2018).

A Cloud of Light

The centerpiece of the Singapore Pavilion for the 2018 Venice Biennale is a cloud of light manifested as a crystalline lattice knotted out of acrylic strands. The realized structure exhibits geometric precision with its computed form, yet registers elements of the human touch arising out of a manual fabrication process.

A common material—acrylic—was selected for the structure because of its optical qualities. The project explored ways to transform standard acrylic rods through thermal deformation. Using a heat gun, separate rods could be tied together once they become pliant and fixed in place after they cool off. As the rods remain continuous, their ability to transmit light is preserved. Moreover, the refractive and reflective qualities of the material are accentuated at the bends. The invention of this knotted tectonic was a major step towards realizing the cloud's desired visual effects.

The project also explored crystalline structures, first, for their ability to fill a space efficiently, and second, for their regularity, which was important considering the structure had to be manually fabricated. Two crystal systems—one with a primitive cubic (cP) Bravais lattice and another with a face-centered (cF) cubic Bravais lattice—were further studied. Knots were developed for each system out of three and two strands, respectively, with the latter being simpler and requiring less material. Consequently, a decision was made to base the cloud on a diamond cubic structure following the face-centered (cF) lattice.

PRODUCTION NOTES

Designer: TakahashiLim A + D
            Genome Architects
Client: Design Singapore Council
            Urban Redevelopment
            Authority of Singapore
Status: Completed
Site Area: 2, 700 sq. ft.
Location: Venice, Italy
Date: 2018

2   Initial knotting studies using string.

3   **Study model of** two acrylic rods knotted together.

4   Light entering one end (top of image) of an acrylic rod is emitted at the other end (bottom left of image).

The configuration of the diamond cubic structure was studied within the Rhinoceros-Grasshopper environment. A Python script was written to create bounding boxes to represent the four tetrahedrally coordinated basic components found within a unit cell of the lattice. The structure is sized by adjusting the number of unit cells in three orthogonal directions, which are established as adjustable parameters. A target form for the structure is defined as a boundary representation, and bounding boxes outside the region are culled. Following a placeholder design pattern, a block describing a tetrahedral module with 2 knotted strands is instanced across the collection of remaining boxes, which serve in this case as proxy objects. Various configurations of the structure were generated in this way and evaluated based on fabrication and aesthetic considerations—the time and cost to produce a required number of modules, and how the structure is viewed from various vantage points and is sited within the space .

The finalized lattice design had an extruded triangular form with chamfered edges. With the help of students (as part

of a fabrication workshop) and construction workers, it took four weeks to produce the 1420 tetrahedral modules necessary to assemble the structure. Several issues arose during the manual production process. Rod ends were drilled for a dowel to be inserted, and hairline cracks sometimes formed, leading modules to snap under load. Knots varied in tightness, affecting the modules' shape and assembly tolerances. Some rods were overheated, causing bubbles to form on their surface. Due to infidelity in the production process, at least ten percent of modules had to be rejected on structural, assembly, and aesthetic grounds. The cloud structure was successfully assembled in two weeks and was more structurally rigid than anticipated. An interactive program, together with custom electronics, was also developed to control how light is transmitted through the structure in response to the presence of visitors and to video content projected onto the floor. Further steps to be taken in this project include expanding the range of crystalline structures investigated and developing a simulation of the knotting process as a first step towards a digitally controlled fabrication process.

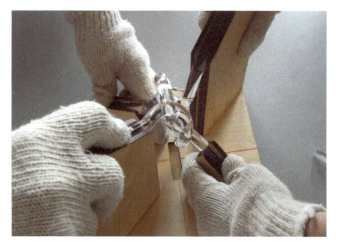

5   Two acrylic rods are pressed into a tetraheral configuration using a wooden jig after they are heated.

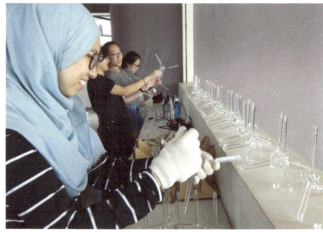

6   Students in a fabrication workshop inspecting completed tetrahedral modules for defects.

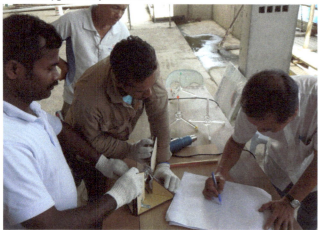

7   Giving fabrication instructions to worker.

8   Assembly of a partial mockup for load testing.

ACKNOWLEDGMENTS

The curatorial team for the Singapore Pavilion comprised Dr. Erwin Viray (Lead), Dr. Jason Lim, Ms. Wu Yen Yen, Dr. Chong Keng Hua and Mr. Tomohisa Miyauchi. We would like to thank DesignSingapore Council and the Urban Redevelopment Authority of Singapore for commissioning the project.

We would also like to thank Tinker Tanker, who was responsible for the interaction design, and all students from the Singapore University of Techology and Design (SUTD), National University of Singapore (NUS) and Singapore Polytechnic (SP) for participating in the fabrication workshops.

REFERENCES

Glazer, Mike. and Miles Kemp. 2016. *Crystallography: A Very Short Introduction.* Oxford: Oxford University Press.

Smith, Cyril Stanley. 1983. *A Search for Structure: Selected Essays on Science, Art and History.* Cambridge, MA: MIT Press.

Woodbury, Robery Robert Aish, and Axel Killian. 2007. "Some Patterns for Parametric Modelling." In *Expanding Bodies: Art, Cities,* *Environment, Proceedings of the 27th Annual Conference of the Association for Computer Aided Design in Architecture*, edited by B. Lilley, and P. Beesley, 222–229. Halifax, NS: ACADIA.

IMAGE CREDITS

Figures 1 and 12: © Tomohisa Miyauchi,2018

Figure 13: © Singapore Pavilion, 2018

All other drawings and images by the author.

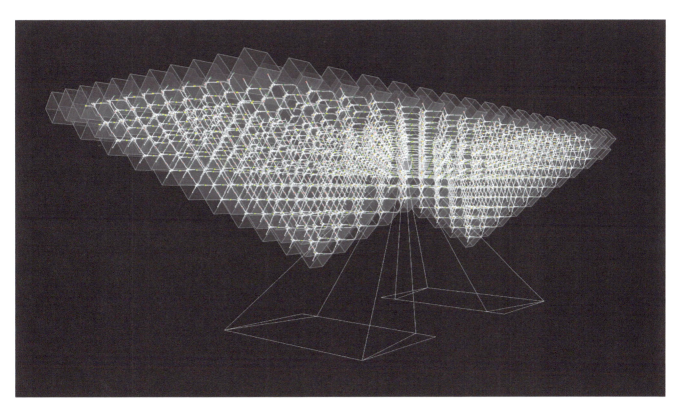

9 Custom python scripts were written to generate and study the geometry of the cloud structure, which is derived from a face-centered cubic Bravais lattice.

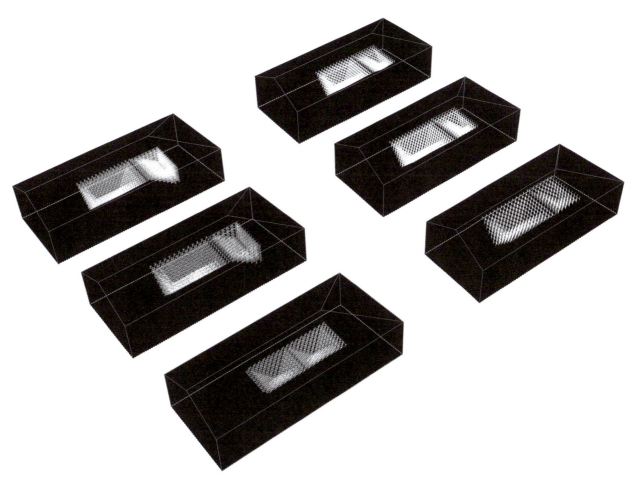

10 Variations of the cloud structure were generated computationally for evaluation.

11 The lattice cloud is aasembled on site with the entire structure suspended from the ceiling rafters.

Jason Lim Teck Chye is co-founder and director of TakahashiLim A
+ D, a Singapore-based design consultancy that leverages cutting-
edge technology to create new spatial experiences, with projects
encompassing art, interiors, and interaction design. He received
his doctorate from ETH Zurich at GramazioKohler Research,
and graduated with Bachelor of Architecture and Master of
Engineering degrees from Cornell University and Stevens Institute
of Technology respectively. Jason is currently an adjunct Assistant
Professor of Architecture and Sustainable Design at the Singapore
University of Technology and Design (SUTD), where he focuses on
design computation.

12 The cloud is programmed with interactive lights that respond to visitors as well as video content projected onto the floor (Tomohisa Miyauchi, 2018).

13 Light is captured at the knots in the cloud as light is transmitted through the lattice (Singapore Pavilion, 2018).

RECALIBRATION ON IMPRECISION AND INFIDELITY

ACCUMULUS

Lavender Tessmer
Massachusetts Institute of
Technology

Jason Butz
Gould Evans

1   ACCUMULUS: completed installation.

ACCUMULUS is hidden within the cantilevered void above the entryway of the
Contemporary Art Museum St. Louis. Composed of over seventeen thousand wire and
plastic parts, its variety of transparent and translucent materials reflect and scatter
sunlight throughout the day, casting textured shadows on the surfaces below. ACCUMULUS
is initially obscured by the walls of the cantilevered volume, but the active light and shadow
it creates are visible from a distance. With its volumetric accumulation of many small
shapes and textures, the installation deliberately contrasts the heavy and planar surfaces
of the museum building.

As a result of the use of linear material (hand-cut wire) and the method by which it is manually joined to sheet material, ACCUMULUS has very large assembly tolerances and a great
amount of overall variation, which contributes to the ease of assembly and takes advantage
of the system's ability to self-correct. Though the modeled geometry is rigid and predeter-
mined to fit within the site volume, the final configuration of elements contains unpredicted
variety, as the material reacts to physical forces as well as the inexact process of making.
Tolerance adds variation and complexity to the rigid geometry of the structural grid without
compromising the spatial effects of the materials.

The installation's visual and structural integrity remain unaffected by large tolerances, as the digital model is not meant to provide the exact appearance of the finished
object, but rather the approximate configuration of all of its parts. Though the project is

PRODUCTION NOTES

Client: Contemporary Art
             Museum St. Louis
Status: Temporary/Completed
Location: St. Louis, MO
Date: 2015

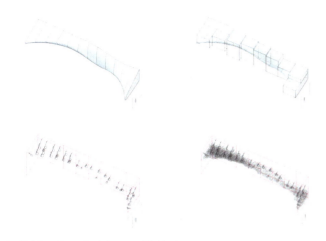

2   Division of massing into assembly blocks.

3   Site location inside cantilevered exterior void.

4   View into cantilevered corner.

parametrically generated and a hybrid of manual and mechanical production methods, finished assembly has rich variation, as the enormous quantity of individual pieces conceals human error and improvisation.

The dimensions of the digital model are iteratively calibrated through measurements of physical prototypes by recording the locations of the interlocking points between the two materials. In the final configuration, the digital model is tuned closely enough to the physical outcome to predict the approximate size of the installation within the bounding box of the site. During installation, the assembly adjusts through its ability to stretch or compress to meet key anchor points, enabling dimensional adjustments to be made during the final installation process.

The initial number of possible geometries in the parametric model is unlimited; however, the selected design forgoes the idea that the source of complexity comes from gradually shifting shapes and chooses instead to limit the number of types to a finite set that is easy to visually

differentiate. While the former method necessitates a vast system of labeling to describe the correct location of each of the parts, the latter requires a simple awareness of the differences between a small set of pieces and a basic set of instructions about how they are sequenced.

The parametric model contains the ability to control how many different variations exist in the project—extending either the size of the workforce or the timeframe of the assembly could create an opportunity to recalibrate the complexity by adding or subtracting from the set of variations.

The role of technology throughout the project's design process is to temper and calibrate the intricacy of the digital model to match the resource of the mechanical and manual workforce, and the installation's production methods and material composition demonstrate the complementary roles of machined and manual labor.

     RECALIBRATION ON IMPRECISION AND INFIDELITY

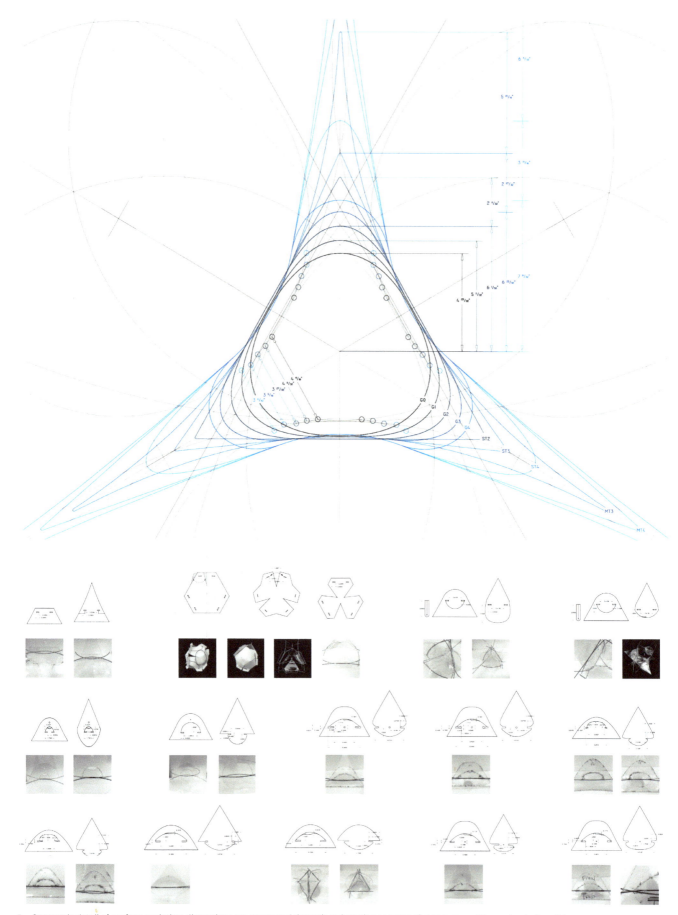

5   Geometric detail of surface variation; dimensions are generated through an iterative process of measurement from physical models.

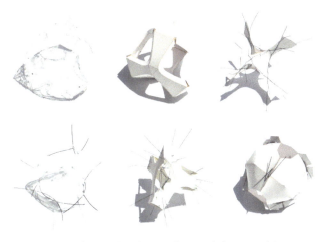

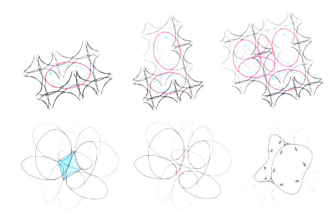

6   Study models of connections between linear and sheet materials.

7   Process of generating surface locations from the grid of circular loops.

8   Snapping surfaces onto wire during assembly.

9   Assembly detail showing interlocking wire loops.

ACKNOWLEDGMENTS

ACCUMULUS is designed and constructed by students in the
Graduate School of Architecture and Urban Design at Washington
University in St. Louis—Chun Liu, Lingfeng Zhang, Joseph
Vizurraga, Jay Bassett, Qian Huang, Boxun Hu, John Patangan, Alex
Melvin, Jeffrey Lee, Yue Zhang—under the direction of Lavender
Tessmer and Jason Butz.

IMAGE CREDITS

Figures 1 and 4: © Stan Strembicki, 2015

All other drawings and images by the authors.

Lavender Tessmer is currently a student in Design and
Computation (SMArchS) at the Massachusetts Institute of
Technology and a research assistant in the Self-Assembly Lab.
Her work explores the disciplinary boundary between art and
architecture, as well as the relevance of craft in digital modes of
design. She received her Master of Architecture from Washington
University in St. Louis in 2011, where she taught as a lecturer from
2012 to 2017. Her most recent work includes Spectroplexus, an
installation at the St. Louis Lambert International Airport, designed
with her spring 2017 graduate architecture studio; and Hedge, a
site-specific installation (with Jason Butz and Nathaniel Elberfeld)
exhibited at the Contemporary Art Museum St. Louis from August
through December 2017.

Jason Butz received a a Bachelor of Arts in Architecture from
Clemson University in 2010, and a Master of Architecture from
Washington University in St. Louis in 2012. During his academic
career, he participated and placed in a number of design
competitions, was awarded the St. Petersburg prize for best
undergraduate work, the AIA Certificate, and was nominated for
the Widmann Award for best graduate work. Upon graduating,
he worked at Cannon Design on a variety of typologies, including
higher education, corporate commercial, and healthcare for
projects all over the world, including Miami, Rio de Janeiro, and
locally in St. Louis. His projects went on to receive several local and
regional AIA awards. While working full time, he also taught in the

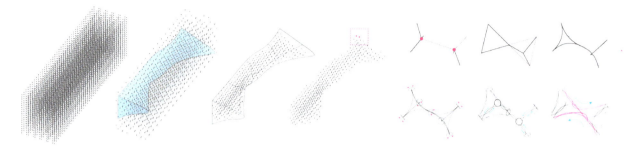

10 Digital process of arriving at the volumetric form from a 3D array of points and the generation of interlocking circular loops

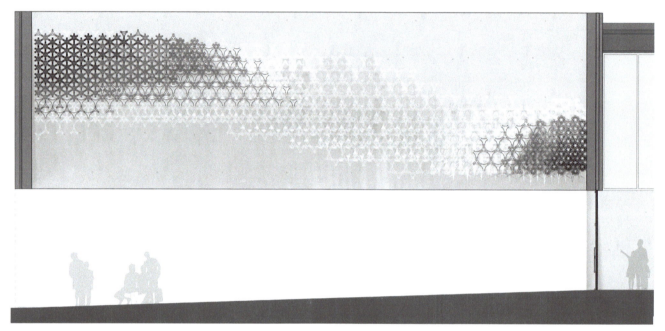

11 Longitudinal section.

Sam Fox School of Design and Visual Arts at Washington University in St. Louis. His classes included seminars on parametric design and three digital fabrication studios co-taught with Lavender Tessmer. In 2017, Jason moved to New Orleans and began working for Gould Evans Architects, exploring new project types, including multi-family residential and adaptive reuse, and developed projects that went on to win local AIA awards. In the Fall of 2018 he will begin teaching a seminar at Tulane University.

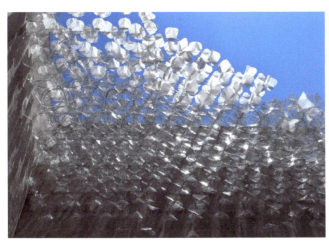

12 Module variation: "compact".

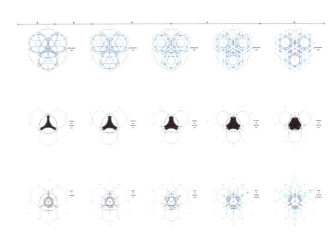

13 Set of five geometric variations between wire and plastic components.

14 Module variation: "leafy".

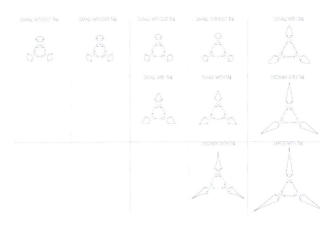

15 Final matrix of 2D-part shapes.

Lumina Pavilion

Michael Leighton Beaman
Beta-field

Melissa Goldman
University of Virginia

Andrew Kudless
California College of the Arts /
Matsys

1   Lumina Pavilion: As-built SW elevation (© Sanjay Suchak 2017).

Pavilion

As an architectural artifact, Lumina is a family of non-planar vaults that play off each other's formal configuration while maintaining a distinct individual quality. They translate a relationship between the ten Pavilions that define the University of Virginia's Academical Village—similar in material and scale, but stylistically different—to represent the various academic pursuits within. The delicate arches, growing in size and arranged around a clearing, frame views of the historic Lawn while rooting themselves into the ground, evoking new growth from this hallowed space; a new way of learning, thinking, and designing for the university's third century.

Process

The pavilion was designed, fabricated, and built by 26 undergraduates and graduate students, instructors Michael Leighton Beaman and Melissa Goldman, and the Fall 2017 Visiting Innovator in Practice, Andrew Kudless, over the course of an intense six-week period. Bringing together students from architecture, landscape architecture, drama, and engineering, Lumina catalyzed interdisciplinarity at the School of Architecture. Kudless conducted two workshops that introduced a number of parametric processes and procedures for defining, articulating, detailing, and communicating formal and structural logics of catenary vaults. Informed by previous work from Beaman, Goldman, and Kudless as well as designers Marc Fornes, Frei Otto and Laurent Delrieu the course developed a

PROJECT DATA

Faculty: Michael Beaman (Beta-
            field & UVa); Melissa
            Goldman (UVa);
            Andrew Kudless
            (Matsys &CCA)
Location: Charlottesville, VA, USA
Date: 2017

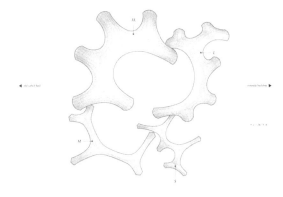

2   Lumina Pavilion: As-built plan (© Michael Leighton Beaman 2018).

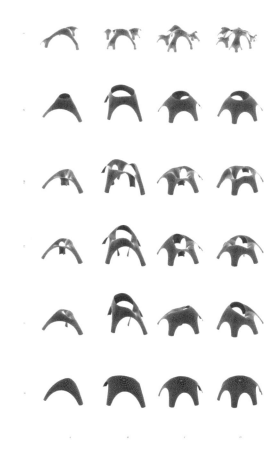

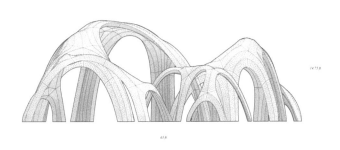

3   Lumina Pavilion: As-built SW elevation. (© Michael Leighton Beaman 2018).

4   Formal Typologies Matrix: *24 of 68* (© Michael Leighton Beaman 2018).

process for creating two-dimensional branched topologies that then transformed into families of vaulted catenaries ranging from monolithic undulating surfaces to delicate spindle-like arches. Using a few key parameters such as height, part area, and joint configuration, we generated four architectural artifacts—Small, Medium, Large, and Extra Large—that became the pavilion.

Production
Lumina is constructed out of 736 unique CNC-routed flat polypropylene ribs, joined using over 20,000 nylon zip ties to form a collection of doubly curved lightweight shell structures. It builds off of many traditions of flat building material assembled into non-planar geometry, and integrates a collaborative, parametric design process. Completely iterated, designed, tested, and organized using a collection of VB modules and native components in Grasshopper, the project allowed students to engage in a rigorous computational-design-to-construction practice, with little or no experience using parametric software

or CNC-fabrication equipment. Within this framework, students were able to develop a series of structures, test their formal and performative qualities, then fabricate mock-ups, test joints, and develop assembly techniques.

Following what was the majority of students' first foray into parametric design for fabrication and CNC routing, the class embarked on a condensed fabrication and installation period. We recognized the immense labor force at all skill levels present in the course and developed a simple, forgiving joint, assembly technique, and construction logic. Flat ribs were assembled in arches, and arches zip tied together to create a truss-like cross-section, giving the shell much of its strength. Due to the inherent strength of the vaulted geometry and the ubiquity of the zip joint holes, we were able to build in redundancies that insured structural performance despite inconsistencies in assembly. Comparing scans of the as-built arches to the digital model revealed where labor decisions, material tolerances, and the structure's settling over time could return and yield

5   Lumina Pavilion: Lighting scheme 2 (© Sanjay Suchak 2017).

Lumina Pavilion Beaman, Goldman, Kudless

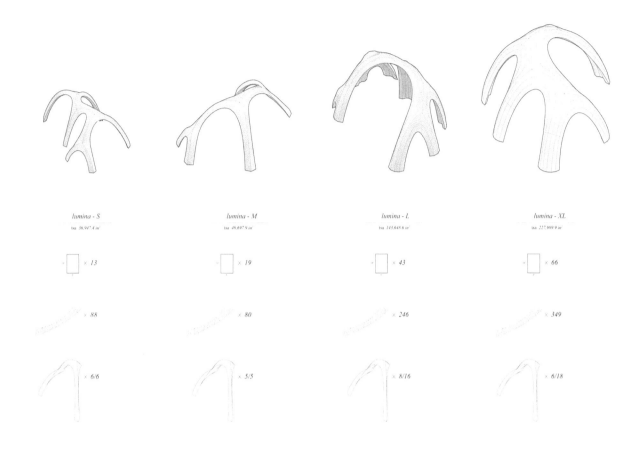

lumina - S   lumina - M   lumina - L   lumina - XL
tsa 36,947.4 in²   tsa 48,697.9 in²   tsa 143,648.6 in² tsa 227,989.9 in²

□ × 13   □ × 19   □ × 43   □ × 66

× 88   × 80   × 246   × 349

× 6/6   × 5/5   × 8/16   × 6/18

6   Lumina Pavilion: SMLXL | Each structure was tested for material consumption and budgeted before production began. The final 4 structures utilized 141 5′ x 10′ x 1/8″ thick polypropylene sheets—with a total constructed surface area of 457,283.8 sq inches. (© Michael Leighton Beaman 2018).

future design parameters to maintain an acceptable long-term degree of fidelity to the original catenary vault.

The process of installation in situ garnered much public interest, creating a discourse around project-based learning and design techniques capitalizing on interdisciplinary strengths. Expertise in lighting design, project management and logistics, 3D modeling and rendering, and experimental fabrication were all critical to the success of the rapid process and allowed students from various departments to utilize their capabilities in the project.

ACKNOWLEDGMENTS
The authors would like to acknowledge the many students, staff and faculty at the University of Virginia's School of Architecture that assisted with fabrication, assembly, and transportation. We would also like to thank the School of Architecture's administration and University of Virginia's Bicentennial Committee for support and funding for this project. Finally, we would like thank volunteers from the University's facilities management, who helped coordinate transportation and installation of this work onto a UNESCO World Heritage site.

Students: Rosvel Brancho- Sanchez, Kimberly Corral, Ziqi Chen, Samuel Feldman, Kyle J Gename, Joshua Gritz, Jack Hatcher, Sam Adams Johnson, Steven Johnson, Sihan Lai, Katie LaRose, Katherine Lipkowitz, Zeyu Liu, Ian MacPherson, Jacob McLaughlin, Veronica Merril, Anna Morrison, Tim Nielsen, Gabriela Rodas, Rosalie Reuss, Zazu Swistel, Michael Tucker, Hao Wang, Chris Weimann, Jinguang Xie, Yi Yang.

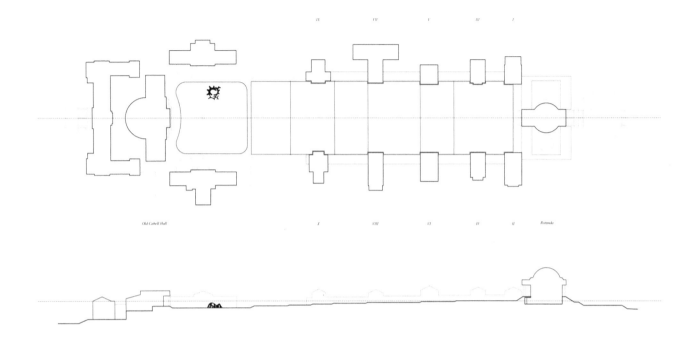

IX   VII   V   III   I

Old Cabell Hall   X   *VIII*   *VI*   *IV*   *II*   *Rotunda*

7   Lumina Pavilion: As-built site plan | The pavilion is sited along the University's original campus lawn, taking up a position within the landscape that extends the order of public pavilions dating back over 200 years. (© Michael Leighton Beaman 2018).

Michael Leighton Beaman is an architectural designer, researcher, and writer. His work focuses on the history, discourse, and speculative future of technology in architecture and landscape architecture, and its implications for design culture, environmental responsibility, and socially conscious design practices. Michael is the founder Beta-field, a speculative design studio; and is a co-founding principal of the design non-profit GA Collaborative, which works with vulnerable and underrepresented communities internationally. Michael currently teaches at the University of Virginia and the Rhode Island School of Design.

Mellissa Goldman is the Fabrication Facilities Manager at the University of Virginia School of Architecture. From crafting new tools and processes to designing and building gigantic moving creatures, her research interests combine exploiting material properties, hacking tools, and working at various scales related to the body. She has taught classes on experimental fabrication, set and puppet design, and design robotics. Last year, her research

group's work on ferro-structures received the Autodesk Emerging Research Award at ACADIA. She graduated with her masters in architecture from Columbia GSAPP and her BA in English from Harvard.

Andrew Kudless is a designer based in San Francisco where he is an Associate Professor at the California College of the Arts. In 2004, he founded Matsys, a design studio exploring the emergent relationships between architecture, engineering, biology, and computation. He holds a Master of Arts in Emergent Technologies and Design from the Architectural Association and a Master of Architecture from Tulane University. The work of Matsys has been exhibited internationally and is in the permanent collections of the San Francisco Museum of Modern Art, the Centre Pompidou in Paris, and the FRAC Centre in Orleans, France.

8   Lumina Pavilion: Aerial photo, sited in UVa's Academical Village (© Sanjay Suchak 2017).

Marching Cubes Made Physical

Jesse Colin Jackson
University of California, Irvine

Luke Stern
Patkau Architects

1   Marching Cubes Assembly #19. Grace Building, NYC, 2017. Detail.

Drawing inspiration from a computer algorithm of the same name, Marching Cubes Made Physical leverages computational design and fabrication to make the virtual world material and tangible. In the 1980s, researchers devised an algorithm for generating computer graphics from medical scan data that featured an underlying language of faceted cubes. Taking Frank Lloyd Wright's Usonian Automatic projects as an initial point of departure, Marching Cubes Made Physical translates this virtual procedure into interactive installations assembled from a modular set of 3D-printed components. By enacting the algorithm in the real world, this project generates dialogue about the ways in which information technologies create the building blocks of contemporary culture.

Project Overview

An algorithm is nothing more than a step-by-step procedure. Conceptual artists have a long-standing engagement with step-by-step procedures as generators of form: per Sol Lewitt, the "idea becomes a machine that makes the art." In this case, the "machine" is an algorithm appropriated from one of the most transformative cultural forces in history: information technology. By inverting the normal application of this machine—from a procedure for converting form into computer-digestible units to a procedure for converting computer-digestible units into form—Marching Cubes Made Physical allows the audience to directly experience, through tangible interaction, the algorithm's procedure and the visual language this procedure embodies. Extended interaction begins to reveal the syntax patterns of this language, and its representational limitations.

PRODUCTION NOTES

Status: in progress
Site Area: variable
Location: multiple
Date: 2016 to present

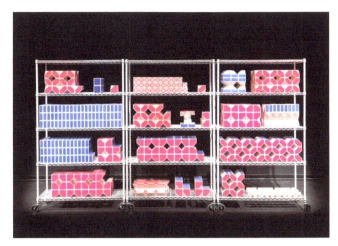

2 Marching Cubes interactive performance. xMPL, Irvine, 2016. Before.

3 Marching Cubes Assembly #7. xMPL, Irvine, 2016. In progress (1 of 2).

4 Marching Cubes Assembly #7. xMPL, Irvine, 2016. In progress (2 of 2).

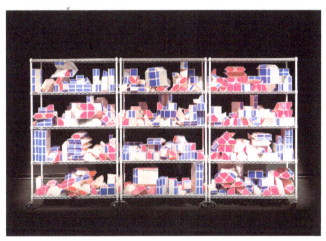

5 Marching Cubes interactive performance. xMPL, Irvine, 2016. After.

Embodying the algorithm in a construction unit—a traditional vehicle for open-ended play and experimentation—places Marching Cubes at our fingertips, extracted from its usual background position within the inner workings of screen-based visualization technologies. Enabling the algorithm in this way requires physical movement on the part of the user, which, released from the error-correcting mechanisms present in a virtual instantiation, permits them to exploit the potential of "glitches" or other unintended consequences. Put another way: while assembly instructions are provided, they need not be followed.

Marching Cubes Made Physical equally embodies the themes and topics of ACADIA 2018. As a contemporary interpretation of a historical procedure, the project recalibrates our interest in computational design towards the long arc of technological advancement, from early computer graphics through parametric methods and additive manufacturing, and finally to a critical interrogation of these technologies' relationship with human labor. Each

installation is high-precision assembly of a low-resolution simulation, reversing the expected relationship between computational accuracy and the limitations of fabrication. The project is a meditation on fidelity, and leverages noise at several frequencies, ranging from the computational deviation between the input reference object and the output aggregation of 3D printed components, to the unanticipated results made possible by communication failure or deliberate subterfuge on the part of participants.

Interactive Performances and Installations
The documentation presented here provides an overview of the expressive possibilities of this project, as demonstrated at venues around the world over the past two years. Irvine, California's Experimental Media Performance Lab (xMPL) hosted the first public demonstration of Marching Cubes Made Physical, during which, over the course of three days, participants were invited to help create nine increasingly complex architectonic assemblies. Next, Pari Nadimi Gallery in Toronto, Canada featured a site-specific refinement of the most sophisticated of these assemblies, along with a

RECALIBRATION ON IMPRECISION AND INFIDELITY

6   Marching Cubes Assembly #17. Pari Nadimi Gallery, Toronto, 2016.

Marching Cubes Made Physical Jackson, Stern

7   Marching Cubes Assembly #19. Grace Building, NYC, 2017.

complete set of units, and video documentation of the xMPL interactive performances. A further architectonic installation was then developed for the lobby of Gordon Bunshaft's Grace Building in New York City.

The most recent major interactive performance, at Patkau Project Space in Vancouver, Canada, began pursuit of a new direction: assemblies derived from 3D models of a human figure. Finally, two smaller-scale events have taken place to date, at Platform 28 for Art & Architecture in Tehran, Iran and at Kulturhuset Stadsteatern in Stockholm, Sweden. Both opportunities presented logistical and financial constraints that precipitated the design of new assemblies that, when collapsed, could be transported by plane as checked baggage.

The algorithm that drives Marching Cubes Made Physical is not new. Its applicability to physical form has been established and explored by our previous work. The tangibility of the construction units, enabled by the universally familiar and culturally primal act of play, has rendered the abstract

idea of the algorithm accessible. This project provides a way in which one of our foundational computational procedures can be touched and manipulated, generating dialogue about the ways in which information technologies create the building blocks of contemporary culture.

8   Marching Cubes: Boris. Patkau Project Space, Vancouver, 2017.

ACKNOWLEDGMENTS

We acknowledge the support of the Canada Council for the Arts, which last year invested $153 million to bring the arts to Canadians throughout the country. We also acknowledge the support of the Hellman Foundation, the University of California, Irvine, Pari Nadimi Gallery, and Patkau Architects.

REFERENCES

Huizinga, Johan. 1970. *Homo Ludens: A Study of the Play-element in Culture*. Boston: Beacon Press.

Lewitt, Sol. 1967. "Paragraphs on Conceptual Art." *Artforum*, June 1967, 79–83.

Lorensen, William E., and Harvey E. Cline. 1987. "Marching Cubes: A High Resolution 3D Surface Construction Algorithm." *ACM SIGGRAPH Computer Graphics* 21 (4): 163–69.

Rokeby, David. 1995. "Transforming Mirrors: Subjectivity and Control in Interactive Media." In *Critical Issues in Electronic Media*, edited by Simon Penny, 133–58. Albany: State University of New York Press.

Wyvill, Geoff, Craig Mcpheeters, and Brian Wyvill. 1986. "Data Structure for Soft Objects." *The Visual Computer* 2 (4): 227–34. doi:10.1007/978-4-431-68036-9_8.

9 Marching Cubes Assembly #28. Platform 28, Tehran, 2017.

10 Marching Cubes: Son of Boris. Kulturhuset Stadsteatern, Stockholm, 2018.

IMAGE CREDITS

Figure 9: © Platform 28 for Art and Architecture, 2017.

Figure 2: © Kulturhuset Stadsteatern, 2018.

All other images by the authors.

Jesse Colin Jackson is a Canadian artist and designer based in Southern California. His creative practice focuses on object- and image-making as alternative modes of architectural production. Jackson is Associate Professor of Electronic Art and Design at the University of California, Irvine, and is represented by Pari Nadimi Gallery in Toronto.

Luke Stern is a senior design researcher at Patkau Architects in Vancouver, Canada. He focuses on the construction of complex surfaces, utilizing large-scale computer assisted fabrication and the novel application of conventional building techniques. He is the project architect for the recently completed Temple of Light in southeast British Columbia.

OCTOPUS PAVILION
soft space / soft structure

Jordan Kanter
Tectonicus / foundCity

Max Gerthel
Max Gerthel Design

1   Local residents occupying the space under the Octopus Pavilion during the daytime (© Max Gerthel, 2016).

soft is FLEXIBLE / ADAPTABLE / RECONFIGURABLE
soft is MOBILE / DISTRIBUTED / SPONTANEOUS
soft is ACCESSIBLE / OPEN / INVITING

This project engages soft systems in the design of an interactive pavilion in Beijing's historic neighborhood of Baitasi. Soft systems encompass an intellectual trajectory that challenges linear, top-down approaches, embracing adaptability, modularity, and performativity (Negroponte 1976; Kwinter 1993; Manaugh 2013).[1] Installed as part of the 2016 Beijing Design Week, this project employs softness as a strategy to negotiate competing notions of public space and foster dialogue on redevelopment in the old city.

Soft Space

Beijing is both hard and soft. It is marked by extensive physical infrastructure—ring roads, megablocks, and monumental architecture—yet it also supports a host of informal, nomadic, spontaneous systems. These include everything from mobile food carts and Weixin payment nodes to the atmospherics of air pollution and data collection. Nowhere is this more evident than in hutong areas such as Baitasi, where complex entanglements of historical, infrastructural, commercial, and social strata overlap with unexpected, often innovative, results. Exhibiting a dearth of formal public *places* (squares, boulevards, etc.), these neighborhoods nevertheless possess vibrant public *space* in a fragmented topology of informal gatherings, itinerant market stalls, and outdoor BBQ stands. The ephemeral

PRODUCTION NOTES

Type:	Interactive Pavilion
Client:	Beijing Design Week / Baitasi Remade
Status:	Completed
Site Area:	135 sq. m
Location:	Beijing, China
Date:	2016

2 Octopus Pavilion during the day (© Max Gerthel, 2016).

3 Octopus Pavilion during an event at night (© Jordan Kanter, 2016).

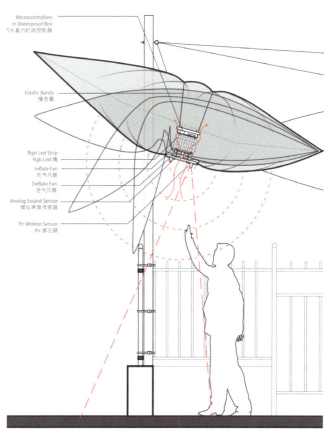

Microcontrollers
In Waterproof Box
5水盒内的微控制器

Elastic Bands
橡皮圈

Rgb Led Strip
Rgb Led 绳
Inflate Fan
充气风扇
Deflate Fan
泄气风扇
Analog Sound Sensor
模拟声音传感器

Pir Motion Sensor
Pir 感应器

4 Module section illustrating system components and soft structure.

publics found in the hutong neighborhood and other inter-
stitial spaces in the city not only represent opportunistic
and at times innovative occupation of a limited spatial
resource, but also foster alternative public spheres that
challenge the dominant modes of spatial politics and public
discourse (Fraser 1993; Farquhar 2009; Nguyen 2017).
Much of the vitality of the hutongs can be traced to the
lived experience of this soft space, yet a lack of concrete
anchoring makes it vulnerable to disruption.[2] Work remains
to provide a degree of spatial formality and durability
without curtailing its improvisational energy.

Soft Structure

The goal of this project was to create an architectural
assemblage that could respond to this soft space and
its need for spatial (in)formality. The octopus, in its
morphology, neurology, and behavior, became a key reference for thinking through structures capable of this kind
of negotiation. Possessing pliable, boneless appendages
with infinite degrees of freedom of movement, octopuses
have evolved unique strategies for mapping and controlling

their body. With two-thirds of their nerve cells distributed
peripherally, and bundled with muscles, sensory receptors,
and pigmentation cells, their mind is quite literally in their
skin (Hochner 2012). This embodied intelligence, coupled
with behaviors such as camouflage, mimicry, and tool-use,
allows octopuses to forge highly specific, improvisational,
soft affiliations with their environment (Godfrey-Smith 2016).

Inspired by the octopus, this project engaged soft structure on the level of organization, behavior, and tectonics.
Employing a pentagon tiling system,[3] the 29 identical,
independently-controlled modules can be arranged in any
number of layouts to conform to a congested site. This
reconfigurability proved useful after damage caused by a
sudden, unseasonable windstorm and allowed the system
to be deployed either as individual cells distributed across
the neighborhood or as a unified body at a single location.
Each module was programmed to react to movement and
sound, cycling through a program of inflation/deflation
and LED color/intensity modulation. Adaptive programming allowed self-calibration to match the activity in the

RECALIBRATION ON IMPRECISION AND INFIDELITY

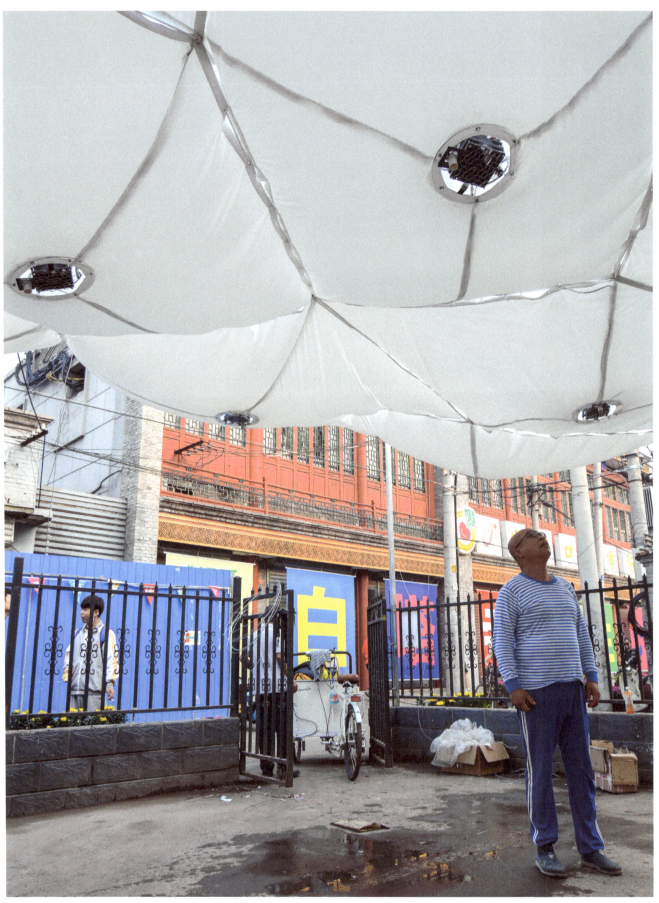

5　A local resident investigating and interacting with the pavilion modules (© Max Gerthel, 2016).

Octopus Pavilion Kanter, Gerthel

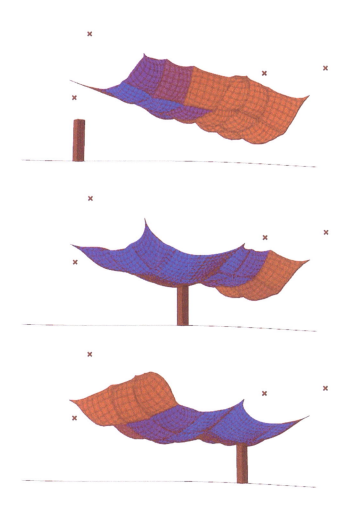

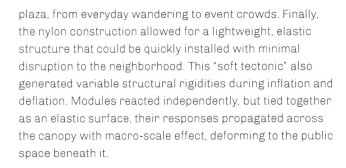

6   Simulation of elastic propagation across the canopy.

7   Octopus Pavilion and nearby White Pagoda Temple (© Max Gerthel, 2016).

plaza, from everyday wandering to event crowds. Finally, the nylon construction allowed for a lightweight, elastic structure that could be quickly installed with minimal disruption to the neighborhood. This "soft tectonic" also generated variable structural rigidities during inflation and deflation. Modules reacted independently, but tied together as an elastic surface, their responses propagated across the canopy with macro-scale effect, deforming to the public space beneath it.

Installed over a two-week period, this project transformed a previously fenced-off plaza in the center of Baitasi's market area into a magnet for activity. Children were quick to grasp the interactive potential of the pavilion. They incorporated it into their play, challenging each other to see who could make more modules light up or inflate. This playfulness brought the plaza to life for people of all ages, while helping to open a dialogue on use, ownership, and design of public space.

ACKNOWLEDGMENTS

Thanks to Beijing Design Week, Baitasi Remade, and the Embassy of Sweden for their support for this project. Thanks to Beatrice Leanza and her staff at Baitasi Remade for their tireless intellectual and logistical support in bringing project to life. Additional thanks to K1ND for their technical support in the development of the pavilion electronics, Casey Kell and his help with the Grasshopper simulations, Professor Sheng Qiang and his students from Beijing Jiaotong University for their help in the final installation, and to Victoria Nguyen and Walter Fischler for their assistance in the research for this article. And a very special thanks to Nicolas Walz and Amanda Schwarz for their extraordinary contribution to the design and implementation of this project, without whom this project would not have been possible.

NOTES

1. Soft systems thinking grew out of cybernetics, emerging computational paradigms, and a critique of top-down planning and management regimes in 1960s and 1970s. It has found new relevancy in contemporary discourse for disciplines from business management to design, particularly in the aftermath of the crises of 2001 and 2008.

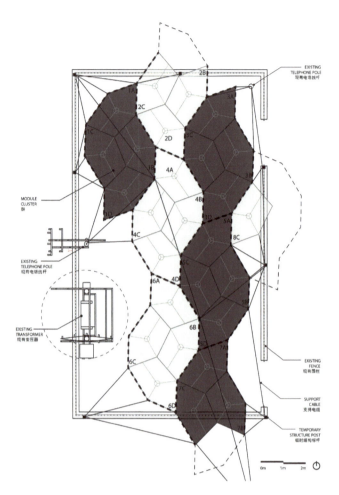

8   Module layout plan illustrating the Kersher-type pentagon tilinig.

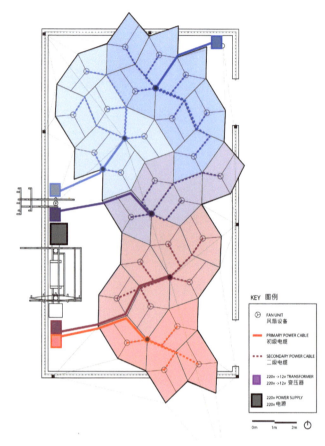

9   Electrical layout plan illustrating the transformer wiring schema.

2. The tenuous nature of these public spaces was dramatically illustrated in the recent "bricking-up" campaign that effected many hutongs throughout Beijing in 2017. City government-initiated sweeps resulted in wholesale demolition of any construction deemed illegal, including a large proportion of the small shops and restaurants located throughout these neighborhoods.

3. The pentagon tiling used in this project was the Kersher Type 8 tiling, one of fifteen tiling solutions that will fill a plane with identical pentagons. This one was chosen for its dynamic, organic composition.

REFERENCES

Farquhar, Judith. 2009. "The Park Pass: Peopling and Civilizing a New Old Beijing." *Public Culture* 21 (3): 551–76.

Fraser, Nancy. 1993. "Rethinking the Public Sphere: A Contribution to the Critique of Actually Existing Democracy." In *The Phantom Public Sphere*, edited by B. Robbins, 1–32. Minneapolis: University of Minnesota Press.

Godfrey-Smith, Peter. 2016. *Other Minds: The Octopus, the Sea, and the Deep Origins of Consciousness*. New York: Farrar, Straus and Giroux.

Hochner, Binyamin. 2012. "An Embodied View of Octopus Neurobiology." *Current Biology* 22 (20): R887–R892.

Kwinter, Sanford. 1993. "Soft Systems." In *Culture Lab*, edited by Brian Boigon, 207–28. New York: Princeton Architectural Press.

Manaugh, Geoff. 2013. "Soft Serve." in *Bracket 2: Goes Soft*, edited by Neeraj Bhatia and Lola Sheppard, 10–16. Barcelona: Actar Publishers.

Negroponte, Nicholas. 1976. *Soft Architecture Machines*.

Nguyen, Victoria. 2017. "Slow Construction: Alternate Temporalities and Tactics in the New Landscape of China's Urban Development." *City* 21 (5): 650–62.

IMAGE CREDITS

All other drawings and images by the authors.

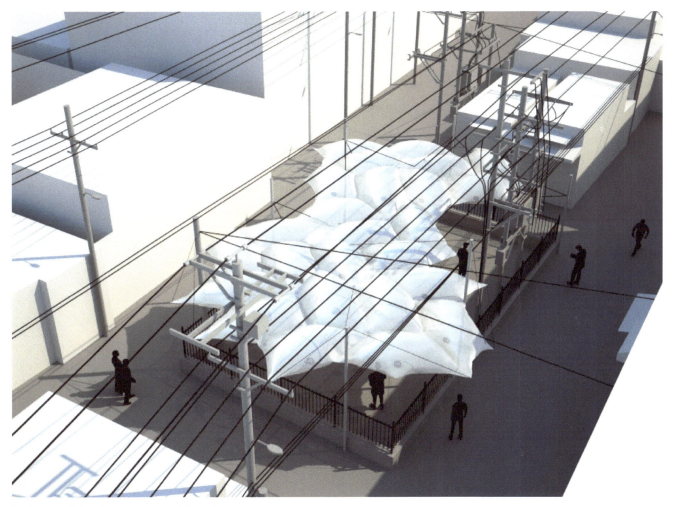

10 A rendered view of the pavilion viewed from above.

Jordan Kanter is an architect and urban researcher based in Los Angeles. He is a founding principal of Tectonicus, a design collaborative focused on highly site specific, critically engaged design work in the city and beyond, as well as foundCity, a research platform dedicated to re-engaging existing urban fabrics and ecological landscapes through design thinking. He has held senior design roles at Michael Maltzan Architects and MAD, and has led the design of a number of high profile cultural, mixed-use, housing, and infrastructure projects throughout the world. He received his undergraduate degree in Biology at MIT, a Masters of Architecture degree at the Southern California Institute of Architecture, and has held teaching appointments at IIT, Tsinghua University, and Tianjin University.

Max Gerthel is an architect, designer and curator working in the fields of art, architecture, and design. Originally from Malmö, Sweden, he graduated from the Royal Danish Academy of Fine Arts School of Architecture in Copenhagen in 2010 and moved to settle in Beijing the same year. He is Program Director of Institute For Provocation, a workspace and research platform for artists and architects based in Beijing. IFP hosts artist residencies, research projects, workshops and public events such as lectures, film screenings and artist talks. Previous experiences include Spatial Practice, MAD Architects and Edouard François. He has also taught at Huazhong University of Science and Technology in Wuhan, Tsinghua University, Academy of Art & Design, and CAFA in Beijing.

Discrete Arrays: The Creek Zipper

Kory Bieg
The University of Texas at Austin

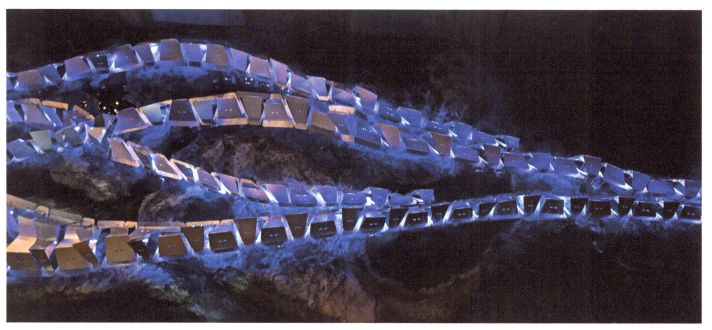

1   The Creek Zipper from above (Kory Bieg, 2017).

Discrete Arrays is a zipper that establishes a new relationship between the synthetic and natural, inflates a two-dimensional graphic into a three-dimensional form, and is an assemblage of exo-related units whose identity oscillates between part and whole. The project can be clearly read as a whole from a distance, but as one approaches, the legibility of each part overwhelms the whole. As the figure of the whole dissipates, the project gains a field-like presence. Discrete Arrays is an installation addressing these multiple overlapping dichotomies that act as design generators and promote a dynamic expression of the project.

The project consists of a number of free-flowing strands that occasionally intersect to form larger strands. The units at these intersections are unique parts in the array that compound the object properties from each strand at one moment, causing a feedback of new properties to ripple back into the individual strands. These units are what Deleuze and Guattari refer to as "operators" (Bennett 2010).

The entire project, each strand, and each unit can be read as whole in and of itself. Breaking a whole into parts allows for the introduction of additional object properties, which increases the qualitative impact of the project and diversifies its capacity to connect to its environment (Harman 2006). The high level of differentiation from unit to unit further promotes the variation of shared qualities as well. For example, reflectivity, light, form, size, and color are properties common to all units, but vary from part to

PRODUCTION NOTES

Architect:	Kory Bieg
Client:	The Waller Creek Conservancy
Status:	Built
Location:	Austin, TX
Date:	2017

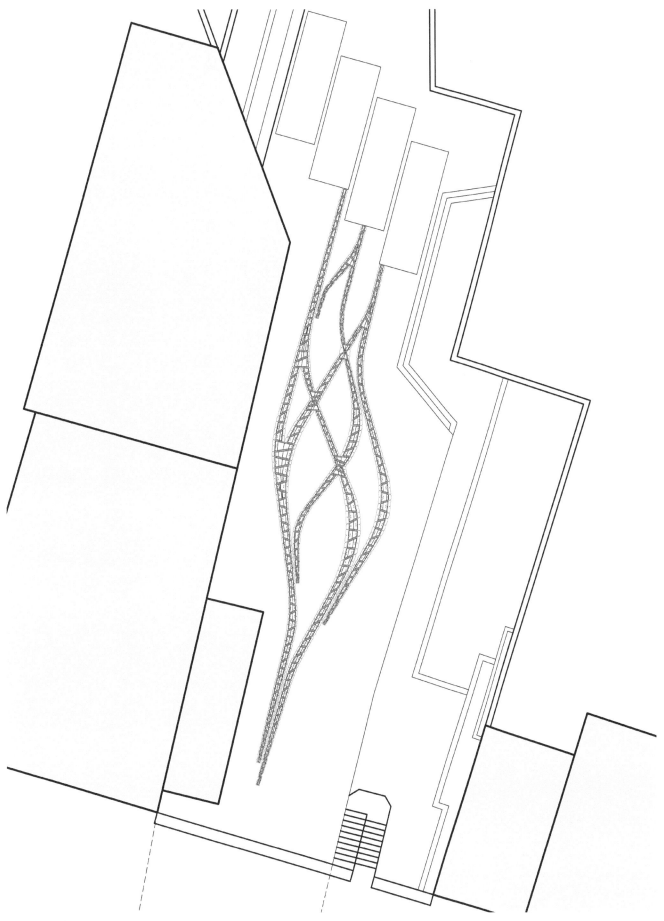

2   Plan drawing.

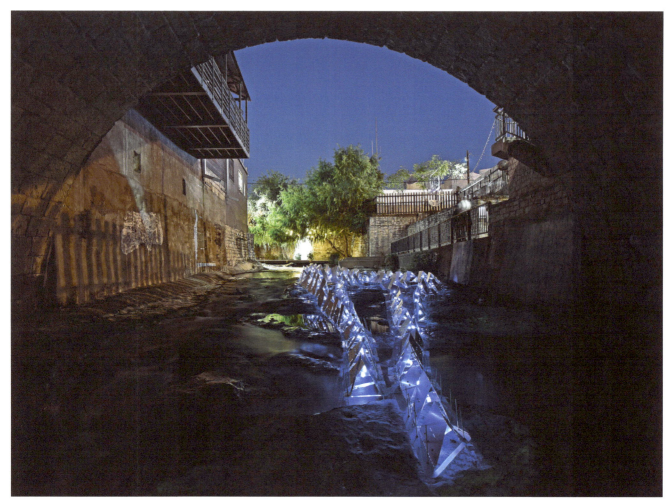

3   The Creek Zipper from water level (Kory Bieg, 2017).

part to fully express a range of effects found in the whole (Bryant 2011).

Since the project is located between 5th and 6th Streets in Austin, Texas, one encounters the project from two vantage points. The first view of the project is from the bridge above. People see the overall form as a two-dimensional graphic overlaid on the creek below. Once they descend the stair and view the project from eye level, the two-dimensional form inflates into a three-dimensional series of highly differentiated units. One experiences the project as both graphic and form. As Robins Evans notes in his book *Translations from Drawing to Building*, "To imply depth within a sold three-dimensional body is to conceive of it as being made up of flat surfaces modulated within a thin layer yet giving the impression of being much deeper. It is to attempt to make virtual space and real space at one and the same time and in the same place...for into patterns of lines stopping and starting we project, by a well understood reflex of over-determination, a deeper space" (1999, 169–70). This deeper space is activated by the creek

over time. Though the water level will stabilize once the Tunnel Project is complete, the level will still rise and drop within acceptable limits. Each unit is raised on adjustable pedestals, so the flat bottom of the unit coincides with the average water level. When the water level is below average, the water will pass below the strands and only be minimally affected by the legs that support the units. When the water level rises above average, the water will interact with the folded geometry of each unit, causing a turbulent flow. The distortion of water as it rises reflects the devastation that used to occur when the creek flooded and makes visible the power of water with even a small change in level.

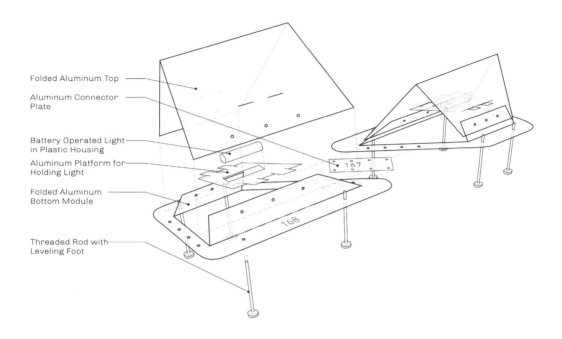

Folded Aluminum Top

Aluminum Connector
Plate

Battery Operated Light
in Plastic Housing

Aluminum Platform for
Holding Light

Folded Aluminum
Bottom Module

Threaded Rod with
Leveling Foot

4 Exploded axonometric of individual unit.

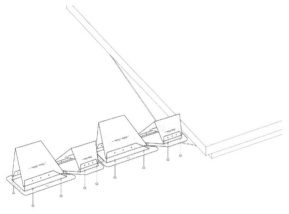

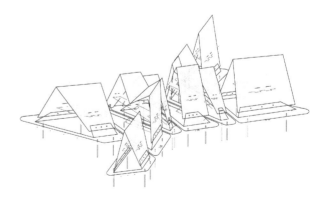

5 Strand at fixed concrete paver.

6 Double strand.

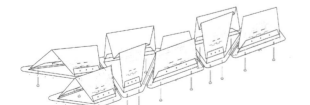

7 Strand at split.

8 Strand at crossing.

RECALIBRATION ON IMPRECISION AND INFIDELITY

9 Strands crossing (Kory Bieg, 2017).

10 Strands splitting (Kory Bieg, 2017).

11 The Creek Zipper detail (Kory Bieg, 2017).

Discrete Arrays: The Creek Zipper Bieg

12 The Creek Zipper at Dusk (Kory Bieg, 2017).

ACKNOWLEDGMENTS

This project was made possible by The Waller Creek Conservancy and The Univeristy of Texas at Austin School of Architecture.

Project Design: Kory Bieg; Design Support: Zach Walters.

Installation and Assembly Team: Raymond Castro, Johan Cheah, Micayla Garza, Christian Pena, Draven Pointer, Tanvi Solanki, Camille Vigil.

REFERENCES

Bennett, Jane. 2010. *Vibrant Matter: A Political Ecology of Things*. Durham, NC: Duke University Press.

Harman, Graham. 2007. *Heidegger Explained: From Phenomenon to Thing*. Chicago: Open Court.

Bryant, Levi R. 2011. *The Democracy of Objects*. Ann Arbor: Open Humanities Press.

Evans, Robin. 1997. *Translations from Drawing to Building*. Cambridge, MA: MIT Press.

IMAGE CREDITS

All drawings and images by the author.

Kory Bieg AIA is an Associate Professor of Architecture at the University of Texas at Austin. He received his Master of Architecture from Columbia University and is a registered architect in the states of California and Texas. Since 2013, he has served as Chair of the TxA Emerging Design + Technology conference and co-Director of TEX-FAB Digital Fabrication Alliance. He has served on the Board of SXSW Eco Place by Design and the Association for Computer Aided Design in Architecture.

In 2005, Kory Bieg founded OTA+, an architecture, design, and research office that specializes in the development and use of current, new, and emerging digital technologies for the design and fabrication of buildings, building components, and experimental installations. OTA+ uses current design software and CNC machine tools to both generate and construct conceptually rigorous and formally unique design proposals.

THICK SKIN: Graphic Tectonics + Digital Fabrication

Viola Ago
Taubman College of Architecture and Urban Planning,
University of Michigan

Hans Tursack
Taubman College of Architecture and Urban Planning,
University of Michigan

1   Thick Skin installed at the A+D Museum (Taiyo Watanabe, 2018, © TaiyoWatanabe).

Thick Skin is an attempt to build a three-dimensional physical sculpture (10´ tall) of a digitally modeled object that was painted with a complex, custom blush using sculpting and animation software. The final physical piece was installed in an urban downtown courtyard where the public was free to view it in the round and interact with it.

As a design exercise, "Thick Skin" explores complex 3D modeling and graphics applications. The project utilizes a 3D-painting process unique to the ZBrush digital sculpting environment (canvas), which integrates Adobe Photoshop's native 2D viewport as a drawing tool. This technique generates an intermediate 2.5D environment. With this ZappLink feature, we were able to dynamically navigate around our primary mesh model (the massing model for our physical installation) in the ZBrush canvas, export specific views of the 3D object to Photoshop, paint on those frozen views of our mesh, and import the painted views back into ZBrush. After importing our Photoshopped view through the ZappLink back to Zbrush, the software seamlessly maps the 2D graphic (applied in the PSD viewport) onto the mesh geometry of the massing model. This process facilitated the precise application of graphics to specific areas of our mesh's three-dimensional surface.

To realize our 3D model (with its ZBrush texture map) as a full-scale sculpture, we employed several digital-modeling and fabrication techniques. The piece is built primarily out of flatbed-printed ¼″ DuPont Corian panels (cladding with printed graphics) and ¼″ aluminum profiles (structure). Each aluminum profile is connected to its neighboring unit

PRODUCTION NOTES

Design: Viola Ago+Hans Tursack
Client: A+D Museum
Location: Arts District, Los Angeles
Date: March - June 2018
Built: FABLab Taubman College

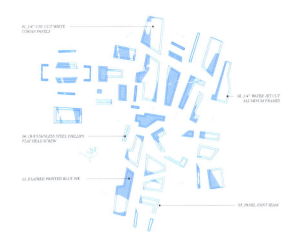

01_1/4" CNC CUT WHITE
CORIAN PANELS

02_1/4" WATER JET CUT
ALUMINUM FRAMES

04_18-8 STAINLESS STEEL PHILLIPS
FLAT HEAD SCREW

05_FLATBED PRINTED BLUE INK

05_PANEL JOINT SEAM

2   Unrolled surface diagram.

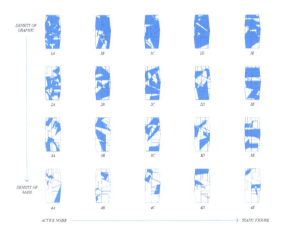

DENSITY OF
GRAPHIC

1A   1B   1C   1D   1E

2A   2B   2C   2D   2E

3A   3B   3C   3D   3E

DENSITY OF
MASS

4A   4B   4C   4D   4E

ACTIVE NOISE   STATIC FIGURE

3   Graphic diagram showing matrix of graphic-mass relationships.

4   Thick Skin installed at the A+D Museum (Taiyo Watanabe, 2018, ©
TaiyoWatanabe).

using a combination of off-the-shelf metal brackets and custom, water-jet connection plates that negotiate contacts at irregular angles. The structure was designed as a kit of parts—with unique profiles, unique connection plates, and standard hardware (brackets, nuts, and bolts)—to facilitate the economic packing, shipping, and construction of the final piece by two unskilled workers over the course of 5 days. The cladding that attaches to the structure is made up of 41 unique CNCed Corian panels. Each panel is flatbed printed with the ZBrush-designed graphic using an Arizona large-format, commercial sign printer.

We wrote Grasshopper definitions to facilitate the translation of "Thick Skin" from an infinitely thin Rhino polysurface to a fully fabricated and built piece. At first, we scripted small definitions for panel thicknesses and edge conditions for the cladding. Then we built multiple standalone definitions for three separate tasks: modeling the structural aluminum frame, placing the standard connection pieces of the McMaster Carr downloaded STEP files (nuts, bolts, brackets), and modeling all of the unique connector plates

that hold the structural frame together. Eventually, we wrote one master definition that linked the parameters between all three of these tasks, accommodated for tolerances, labeled all of the components, and laid them out on cut sheet templates ready for the different machines.

For "Thick Skin," we were interested in using computational tools to generate unique connections made out of planar surfaces (flat material), such that one could use a CNC or a high-powered laser cutter when robotic arms, extruders, and other state-of-the-art machinery may not be available. Our contribution to this year's conference theme and location rests in the mediation, or rather "Recalibration" between architectural design and machine availability. Our desire is to bring attention to computation as a tool to realize/materialize a design, rather than as a standalone, autonomous project.

In conclusion, "Thick Skin" is an exercise in the coordination of a three-dimensionally conceived graphic (made in ZBrush and Photoshop), a geometrically robust massing

RECALIBRATION ON IMPRECISION AND INFIDELITY

5   Thick Skin installed at the A+D Museum (Taiyo Watanabe, 2018, © TaiyoWatanabe).

Thick Skin Ago, Tursack

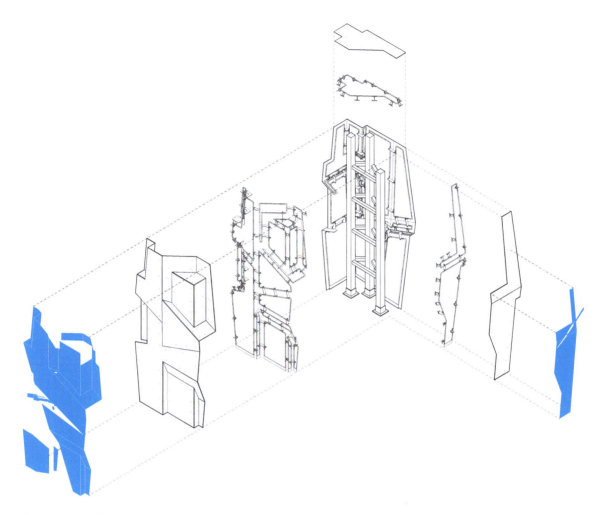

6 Exploded parallel projection assembly diagram.

model (Rhino), and an intricate set of standard and uniquely
fabricated structural components (Grasshopper).

ACKNOWLEDGMENTS

Research and fabrication for this project were executed at
the Taubman College of Architecture and Urban Planning. The
exhibition "Thick Skin" was held at the A+D Museum in downtown
Los Angeles, CA from March to June 2018. We would thank the
University of Michigan, Taubman College, DuPont Corian Solid
Surface, Alro Steel, 3M Materials, and Brilliant Graphics for their
generous support.

Project team: Colleen Fellows, Lisa Kuhn, Linda Lee, Kyle Reich,
Kimball Kaiser

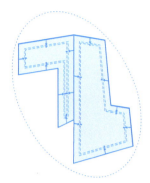

_01 DETERMINE FRAME FROM PANEL PROFILE

_02 OFFSET FOR FRAME WIDTH

_03 PULL FRAME FROM PANEL TO ACCOMMODATE HARDWARE

_04 FILLET FRAME CORNERS

_05 OFFSET FRAME FOR MATERIAL THICKNESS

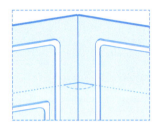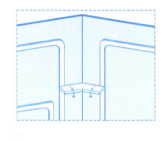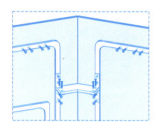

_06 DETERMINE INTERIOR ANGLE BETWEEN PANELS

_07 OFFSET FOR CONNECTION PLATE WIDTH AND MATERIAL THICKNESS

_08 ADD HOLES AND ADDITIONAL HARDWARE

7   Grasshopper was used to generate aluminum–Corian connections and structural system.

Viola Ago is an architectural designer, educator, and practitioner. She is currently serving as the Christos Yessios Visiting Professor at the Ohio State University's Knowlton School of Architecture, and as a lecturer at the Harvard University Graduate School of Design. She was the 2016-2017 William Muschenheim Design Fellow at the Taubman College of Architecture and Urban Planning, University of Michigan. Viola earned her Master of Architecture degree from the Southern California Institute of Architecture in Los Angeles, and a Bachelor of Architectural Science from Ryerson University in Toronto. She has previously taught at Taubman College and the Southern California Institute of Architecture in the graduate and undergraduate programs. Prior to joining Taubman in 2016, she worked as a lead designer in the Advanced Technology Team at Morphosis Architects and was involved in international design and construction projects.

Hans Tursack is a designer and artist from Philadelphia, Pennsylvania. He received a BFA in studio art from the Cooper Union School of Art, and an M.Arch from the Princeton University School of Architecture where he was the recipient of the

Underwood Thesis Prize. He recently received the Willard A. Oberdick teaching/design fellowship from the University of Michigan's Taubman College of Architecture where he is currently a lecturer. This fall he will serve as the 2018-2019 Pietro Belluschi Research Fellow at the MIT School of Architecture + Planning.

8   Thick Skin in construction at the A+D Museum, Los Angeles.

9   Detail of water-jet aluminum structure.

Stock Wall

Jason S. Johnson
Laboratory for Integrative
Design, University of Calgary

Guy Gardner
Laboratory for Integrative
Design, University of Calgary

1   Stock Wall permanent installation. Calgary, AB (Jaime Hyatt, 2017).

The Stock Wall is part of an ongoing body of research into public art as a vehicle for testing image-based protocols for disrupting singular readings and narratives of cultural artifacts. The piece was commissioned by McKinley Burkart and Solium and installed in the reception area of the financial services firm. The constraints for the project included a limited depth of protrusion from the wall and minimal interference with construction on site. The reception area itself was limited in depth, with a column that did not allow for a full frontal view of the piece. The initial proposals from the client requested that we include images that reflect the region's iconic landscapes, characters, and financial drivers.

Conceptual Approach

In response to the brief, the project team developed a series of strategies for combining sets of data related to the economy of Western Canada and images that are often used as proxies for economic drivers in the region (Figure 2). The financial data collected relative to stock and commodity prices was used to blur/disrupt the fidelity of the image. This process of defamiliarization was simulated on a number of images in an attempt to test the capacity of the procedure to induce multiple readings of images based on the amount of disruption introduced through the processes of manipulating the angles of the colored dowels that made up the pixelated image. After each iteration people unfamiliar with the project were asked to identify the image. Preference was given to images that produced the most variable responses. Conversations with the client did not discuss the multiple readings possible, but rather focused on the material effects of the piece in the space and

PRODUCTION NOTES

Laboratory for Integrative Design
Designers: Jason S. Johnson
          Guy Gardner
Production: Kim Tse
          JP Hammill
          Hayden Pattullo
Architect: McKinley Burkart
Client: Solium
Status: Built
Location: Calgary, Canada
Date: 2017

2   Image study iterations.

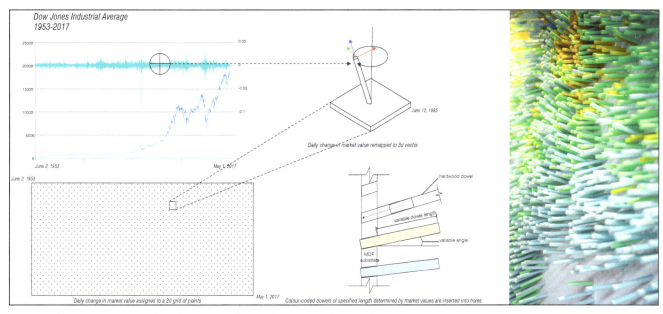

3   Protocol for the introduction of financial data in the image field. Detail (Hayden Pattullo, 2017).

the artifact's role as a focal point of the space.

Processes and Tools

The client's interest in the Laboratory for Integrative Design was in part based on the potential to use robots in the fabrication of the piece and an interest in using colored dowels as a medium. As such, all the computational processes developed for the project needed to be developed in acknowledgement of the tools and materials that would be used for its production. This productively limited the number of variables for manipulating the image to dowel density, dowel length/colour, and dowel angle. The density variable is related to the tonal values of the original image, and the colour, length, and angle variables are associated with the performance of financial markets through time, remapped to the two-dimensional grid (Figure 3). The

values were translated into vectors, which informed the angle and length of dowels inserted into the grid. The grid points were assigned colour values and culled using an overlaid abstracted image. Outputs from the computational processes included robotic motion paths, shop drawings, and material cut lists. The surface grid of vectors was panelized, and eight discrete robotic routines for milling and colour-coding were exported, along with material quantity and cut lists for the different lengths and colours of dowels.

Vectors from the parametric model were translated into RAPID Code for an ABB industrial robot. A spindle mounted to the robot arm milled holes in MDF panels at the angles and depths that corresponded to the translations of the financial data. In order to reduce the time needed to match

4   Stock Wall after installation (Jason Johnson, 2017).

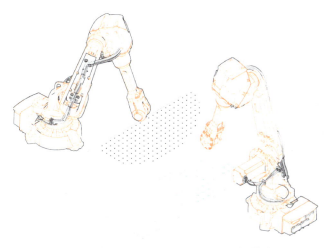

5 Hole patterns broken up into individual patterns and milled.

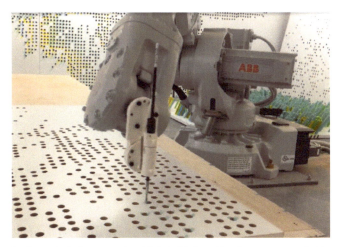

6 Second robotic arm protocol "labeled" holes with colour corresponding to dowel colours.

7 Dowels inserted into panels, final touch-ups before installation.

the three colours of dowels with the corresponding openings, the robotic arms were fitted with paintbrush holders to mark all the holes with the colours that matched the appropriate dowel. This allowed for assembly by individuals unfamiliar with the project.

Disassociating Narratives

The final work is installed in a space that does not allow for a fully frontal view of the piece. This combined with the abstracted coloration, variable depths and angles, shadow casting, and density of parts leads to a wide range of readings of the piece by visitors to the space. We have begun the process of cataloging these readings and their relationships to the position of the viewers in the space. Initial respondents have identified the piece as everything from a form of cartography to a wide range of biological entities. This project and concurrent projects within the lab of this type attempt to diversify the subjects and readings of artifacts produced for the public sphere.

8 Installation of prefinished panels on site (Hayden Pattullo, 2017).

RECALIBRATION ON IMPRECISION AND INFIDELITY

9   Stock Wall at Solium offices (© Jaime Hyatt, 2017).

ACKNOWLEDGMENTS

This project was partially funded by an Insight Grant from the Social Sciences and Humanities Research Council (SSHRC) of Canada and developed in the Laboratory for Integrative Design (www.integrativedesign.org) at the University of Calgary. Special thanks to Liyan Wong, Ashlen Thomson, and Emma Moss of McKinley Burkart for their support in this project.

IMAGE CREDITS

Figures 1, 9 and 10: © Jaime Hyatt, 2017.

Figures 3, 8: © Hayden Pattullo, 2017

All other drawings and images by the authors.

Jason S. Johnson has practiced and taught architecture in North and South America and Europe. He is a founding partner of the Laboratory for Integrative Design at the University of Calgary and has exhibited design work related to research in the areas of responsive architecture, generative design, digital fabrication, and integrated techniques. Mr. Johnson maintains a design research practice called Minus Architecture Studio in Calgary, where he lives with his wife and three sons.

Guy Gardner trained as an architect and is currently completing a Masters of Environmental Design thesis exploring the inter-sections of art and architecture through the lens of digital craft. Guy completed a Bachelor of Fine Arts in sculpture at the Alberta College of Art and Design, and is a journeyman welder. Guy is a project leader and research assistant in the Laboratory for Integrative Design, where he has collaborated on a variety of public and community art projects in Calgary, both as a designer and a fabricator.

10 Installation on site behind reception desk (© Jaime Hyatt, 2017).

RECALIBRATION ON IMPRECISION AND INFIDELITY

Negotiating Design for On Site Robotics

Alexandre Dubor
IAAC

Edouard Cabay
IAAC

Jean-Baptiste Izard
Tecnalia

Aldo Sollazzo
IAAC / Noumena

Areti Markopoulou
IAAC

1   Resulting construction after removal of the cable robot (© Joan Guillamat).

On Site Robotics is a collaborative project that demonstrates the potentials of additive manufacturing technology and robotics in the production of sustainable low-cost buildings that can be fabricated on site with 100% natural materials. Combining technological advances in robotics (cable robot and drones), natural materials, and computational design, the project demonstrates the possibilities of bringing automation to the construction site, allowing for the production of high-performance buildings and monitoring them in real time during construction.

Soil-based material has been used for millennia and has numerous qualities for construction: it is available all over the world, is cheap to excavate, can be used without any major processing energy, possesses performative properties for hygrothermal regulation and air quality, and can be fully recyclable. Nevertheless, poor structural properties and a labour intensive process requiring skilled craftsmanship are some of the reasons for its decline within contemporary architecture, having being replaced by other materials such as concrete. Given the potential of this natural material to reduce the ecological impact of the building industry, research has been driven to explore technological advances in material science and robotics to reintroduce this ancestral material into contemporary architecture. This team has developed a custom material mix and an extrusion system capable of achieving 3D printing of adobe that is three times stronger than traditional earth construction, using only organic additives.

PRODUCTION NOTES

Architect:	IAAC
Client:	BB Construmat
Status:	Demolished / Recycled
Site Area:	500 sq. ft.
Location:	Barcelona, Spain
Date:	2017

2 Overview of the "On site Robotics" installation at the construction fair (© Joan Guillamat).

3 Ongoing process of printing while other craftsmen assemble the prefabricated columns (4 pieces) (© Federica Ciccone).

4 Roof assembly using the cable robots as precise crane (© Joan Guillamat).

Using a material that can be found on location, consequent effort has been developed to deploy robotic technology on site. Cable robotics offer numerous advantages in this aspect: they have a very large build space, are well suited for heavy payloads, are easily relocalizable from one site of operation to another, and have sufficient precision for 3D printing. The project presented here succeeded in demonstrating the feasibility of assembling the cable robot, printing the building (8,900 m of toolpath), placing the roof element, and disassembling the robot within only 15 days. This specific installation of the robot was capable of printing on an area of 6.6 x 4.4 x 3.5 m, but could be easily expanded to any dimension given the right support structure.

Custom drone scanning and human–machine interaction processes have been developed and used in this project to ensure good workflow and quality while working with such a sensitive material as adobe. Combining craftsmanship and digital analysis, the fabrication process has constantly been adapted to fit the changes of material in reaction to the environment.

A computational design strategy has been developed to consider machine and material challenges in order to minimize material use and maximize printing efficiency. Curvilinear shapes were prefered to sharp angles to avoid strong acceleration in the cable robot, while geometries were designed to absorb material shrinkage by deformation. Such design constraints were counterbalanced by new design opportunities raised by the 3D-printing process, allowing freeform shapes as well as new textures and performative infills. The final design chosen in this project exhibited a 7 x 2 m wall printed in situ, four prefabricated 2 m tall columns, and a 20 m² prefabricated wooden roof. The wall is 40 cm thick and includes two internal layers (three cavities). Overall the wall weighs only one ton, as 75% of it consists of air, but it still support itself and the wooden roof thanks to an efficient material distribution.

The project On Site Robotics has successfully deployed a contour-crafting cable robot with a drone monetization system in an international construction fair over 15 days, and erected a 20 m² construction using 100% natural

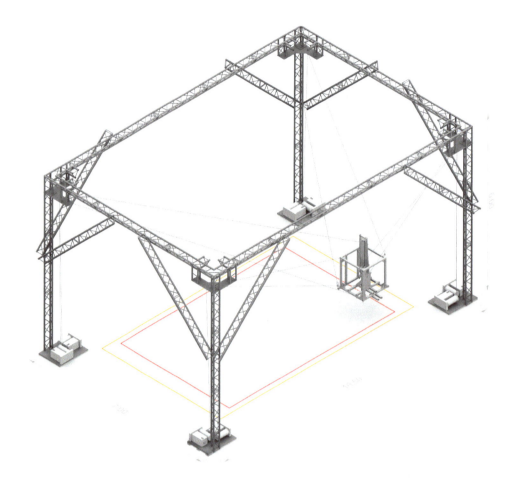

5   Overview of the cable robot assembly (© IAAC).

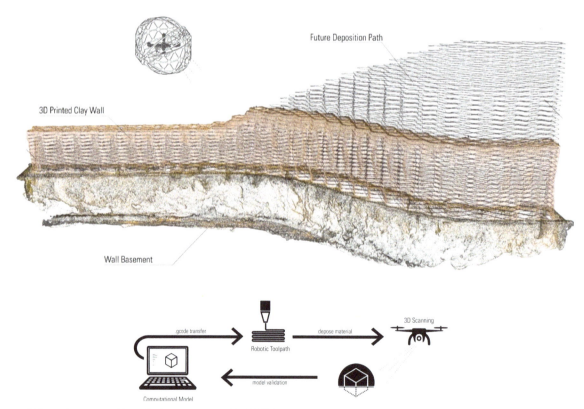

Future Deposition Path

3D Printed Clay Wall

Wall Basement

gcode transfer

Robotic Toolpath

depose material

3D Scanning

Computational Model

model validation

6   3D-scanned information extracted from the drone cameras (© NOUMENA).

Negotiating design for On Site Robotics Dubor, Cabay, Izard, Sollazzo, Markopoulou

7   Human–machine interface used by craftman to control the printing process on site (© Joan Guillamat).

8   Live monitoring of the adobe drying process using custom-built drone with thermal camera(©Joan Guillamat).

9   First days of 3D printing with enhanced ventilation system to control and accelerate the curing time of adobe (© Joan Guillamat).

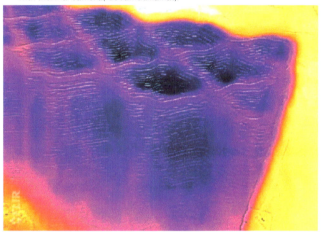

10 Thermal imaging of the printed wall extracted from the drone's camera. Darker area of the image exhibit the cold area of the adobe not yet fully cured (hence evaporating water and cooling down).

material. In this project, machine and material challenges have been resolved thanks to an adaptive computational design strategy constantly updated by 3D-scanned data. On the other hand, adapted human–machine interfaces allowed skilled technicians and craftsmen to calibrate (or adapt) their production settings and technical and design solutions according to a real-time analysis feed.

ACKNOWLEDGMENTS

"OnSite Robotics" is a collaborative project between Institute for Advanced Architecture of Catalonia (IAAC) and TECNALIA

IAAC team (Concept, Coordination, Design, Extrusion, Material & Sensors): Areti Markopoulou, Aldo Sollazzo, Alexandre Dubor, Edouard Cabay, Raimund Krenmueller, Ji Won Jun, Tanuj Thomas, Kunal Chadha, Sofoklis Giannakopoulos.

TECNALIA Robotic Team (Cable Robot) : Mariola Rodríguez, Jean-Baptiste Izard, Pierre-Elie Herve, Valérie Auffray, David Culla, Jose Gorrotxategi.

TECNALIA Construction Division team: Mikel Barrado, Idurre Fernandez, Juan José Gaitero, Elena Morales, Iñigo Calderón, Amaia Aramburu.

NOUMENA Team (Drone development, Data collection) : Starsky Lara, Chirag Rangholia, Daniele Ingrassia (Fab Lab Kamp Lintfort), Marco Sanalitro, Eugenio Bettucchi, Andrea Melis, Adrien Rigobello

Other partners: LIRMM (Robot research center), Luciano Carrizza (Technical adviser), Joaquim Melchor - Art Cont (Material expert), Lenze (Automation), Wam (Solid process), NanoSystem (Material nanotechnology), Nicolas Weyrich (Video animation) and Joan Guillamat (Video & Photographic documentation)

REFERENCES

Bosscher, P., R. L. Williams II, L. S. Bryson, and D. Castro-Lacouture. 2007. "Cable-Suspended Robotic Contour Crafting System." *Automation in Construction* 17 (1): 45–55.

Brell-Cokcan, Sigrid, and Johannes Braumann. (eds.). 2012. *Rob|Arch Robotic Fabrication in Architecture, Art, and Design*. Vienna: Springer-Verlag.

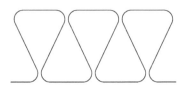

periodic & continuous

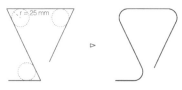

rounded edge
(min. fillet radius = 25 mm)

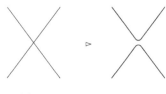

avoid
self-intersection

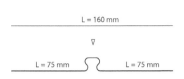

avoid straight line
length > 160 mm

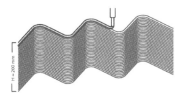

max 200 mm height / day
of printing for drying & stability

**PRINTING / DESIGN
LIMITATIONS**

11 Some of the design limitation extracted from material and machine challenges (© IAAC).

Dubor, Alexandre, and Edouard Cabay. 2017. "Energy Efficient Design for 3D Printed Earth Architecture." In *Humanizing Digital Reality: Digital Modeling Symposium Paris 2017*, edited by Achim Menges, 69–76. Singapore: Springer.

Gianakopoulous S. "Pylos." IAAC. http://pylos.iaac.net/

Gramazio Fabio, Matthias Kohler, and Jan Willmann. 2014. *The Robotic Touch*. Zürich: Park Books Architectural Press.

Kwon H.. 2002. "Experimentation And Analysis Of Contour Crafting (cc) Process Using Uncured Ceramic Materials." Ph.D. diss., University of Southern California.

Lagüela, S., H. González-Jorge, J. Armesto, and P. Arias. 2011. "Calibration and Verification of Thermographic Cameras for Geometric Measurements." *Infrared Physics and Technology* 54 (2): 92–99.

Minke, Gernot. 2006. *Building with Earth: Design and Technology of a Sustainable Architecture*. Germany: Birkhäuser.

IMAGE CREDITS

Figures 1, 2, 4, 7–9: © IAAC, by Joan Guillamat, 2017

Figure 3: © IAAC, by Federica Ciccone, 2017

Figures 11–12: © IAAC, by Ji Won Jun, 2017

All other drawings and images by the authors.

Alexandre Dubor is an architect and an expert in digital and robotic fabrication currently working at IAAC as researcher, teacher, and project manager in R+D. He studied architecture and engineering (M.Arch. ENSAVT / ENPC, M.Arch. IAAC) and has previously worked at Studio Libeskind, Atenastudio, iDonati, AREP, and Appareil. He's a multidisciplinary designer exploring the potential raised by digital tools and new materials for the improvement of the built environment. He is now leading the Open Thesis Fabrication program as well as the Master in Robotic and Advanced Construction at IAAC.

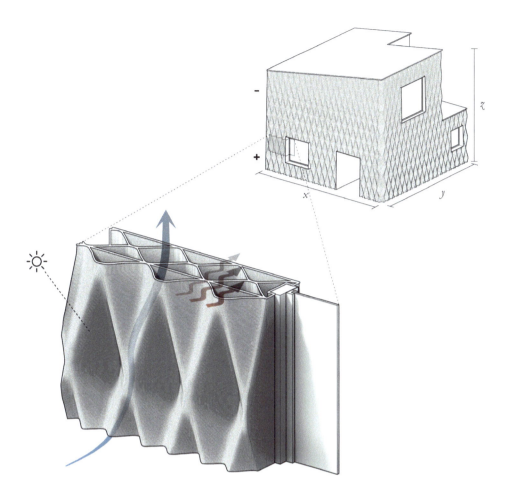

12 Design possibilities with 3D printing (© IAAC).

Edouard Cabay is an architect and educator. He founded and currently directs Appareil, an experimental architectural office in Barcelona. He teaches, as senior faculty, at the Institute for Advanced Architecture of Catalonia, where he also codirects the Open Thesis Fabrication program. He has taught experimental design studios at the Architectural Association School of Architecture in London, at the École Speciale d'Architecture in Paris and at the École Polytechnique Fédérale de Lausanne.

Jean Baptist Izard holds a PhD in engineering for robotics, and has been involved in industry-specialized robotics research in Tecnalia France since 2010. He has contributed to the design of several high-level robot prototypes since then. His profile combines research excellence and a practical sense of application for robotics in industry. He is now a lead researcher in cable-driven parallel robots, focusing on applying this technology to many fields where precise and complete control of heavy loads along large workspaces are required, including the construction industry.

Aldo Sollazzo is an expert in computational design and digital fabrication. He is the director of Noumena and faculty at Design by Data Master in Paris. At IAAC, he is the director of the Master in Robotics and Advanced Construction and the Global Summer School.

Areti Markopoulou is a Greek architect, researcher, and educator working at the intersection between architecture and digital technologies. She is the Academic Director at IAAC in Barcelona, where she also leads the Advanced Architecture Group, a multidisciplinary research group exploring how design and science can positively impact and transform the present and future of our built spaces, the way we live and interact. Her research and practice seeks to redefine architecture as a performative "body," beyond traditional notions of static materiality, rigid forms, or standardized manufacturing.

CORBEL CABIN
3D-Printed Concrete Building

Leslie Lok
Cornell University

Sasa Zivkovic
Cornell University

1   Located at a remote site, the concrete structure is characterized by three programmatic areas: a table, a storage seat element, and a 20-foot-tall fireplace. The building's wood skin envelope is currently under construction.

From Tool to Construction Process to Building

Corbel Cabin recalibrates expectations around concrete 3D printing and explores the architectural opportunities of digital–analogue construction hybrids. Adding to current discourse in concrete 3D printing, the project develops a ground-up methodology from tool to construction process to building, which involves explorations of large-scale fabrication equipment design, software adaptation, material experimentation, construction methodology development, implementation of tolerances, and logistics of on-site construction.

Corbel Cabin is a building case study at full scale that questions common notions of "high-tech" and "low-tech" techniques in building practices. Utilized construction methodologies mediate between the precise control of digital tools, the volatility of material behavior in concrete, and the idiosyncratic layered printing process. The cabin has a footprint of 10 x 10 feet and lifts off the ground on 3D-printed legs that adjust to the terrain. Architectural manifestations of corbelling are explored throughout the structure by geometrically manipulating 3D-printed sacrificial concrete formwork modules.

Rethinking the Tool: Modest Digital Machines and Human–Analog Feedback

A large-scale open-source 3-axis gantry 3D printer named Daedalus (Zivkovic and Battaglia 2017) was designed and fabricated at the Cornell Robotic Construction Laboratory (RCL). Based on smaller scale open-source machines, such as the RepRap and the Prusa Mendel 3D printers, the 8 x 8 x 16 foot lightweight steel frame gantry uses adapted

2 Concrete extrusion process and gravel support material.

3 The Daedalus 3D-printing platform.

4 Top view of the print bed; gravel as temporary support for cantilevers.

Marlin firmware to run Silkworm-generated g-code from Grasshopper.

Utilizing a gravity-fed hopper-auger nozzle system, the concrete mixture was designed to work with readily available off-the-shelf materials and admixtures. Methodologically, the printing process follows a well-established line of precedents in concrete 3D printing (Khoshnevis 2004; Bos et al. 2016; Gosselin et al. 2016). While the highly economical Daedalus fabrication platform offers a certain degree of automation, the machine heavily relies on a set of human helpers to mix concrete, apply gravel, and adjust flow parameters during the printing process. Rather than automating the full system, Daedalus embraces a "collaboration" between analog humans and digital machines.

Rethinking the Fabrication Process through Material Properties: Layered Gravel-Corbel Assemblies
In horizontal layer concrete 3D printing, geometric surface complexity and sectional transformation are achieved

through corbelling—an incremental offset of toolpath trajectories.

To enable steep cantilevers of up to 60 degrees for printed geometries, a reusable support material method was developed using 10 mm top-size gravel to provide necessary structural support during the concrete printing process. The 3D-printed components function as sacrificial zero-waste formwork for the main structural system: a cast-in-place concrete structure with custom rebar cages. As the construction site is remote, the printed formwork was designed in small sectional modules to be transported and assembled manually without the use of any heavy machinery.

Throughout the project, the imprecisions and volatility of the concrete material properties inform joinery details and assembly strategy tolerances. Both the design and manual on-site assembly leverage deviation in tolerance to articulate reveal details.

5　The resulting structure is a play on machine precision in contrast with material imperfection and subsequent tolerance deviations during fabrication.

　　　　　Corbel Cabin Lok, Zivkovic

6   Interior of the 3D-printed concrete leg with inserted rebar cages.

7   Underside of the cabin showing corbelled 3D-printed concrete legs.

8   Assembly of concrete legs.

9   Chimney assembly using temporary scaffolding.

Techno-Archaic Architectures: Oscillations Between Low-tech and High-tech

The cabin's architectural qualities lie in the reciprocal relationships that emerge from the oscillation between digital and analog processes of construction. The structure is a play on machine precision in contrast with material imperfection and subsequent tolerance deviations during fabrication. The concrete has texture, and is alive and liquid. Similar to board form concrete casting, local conditions during the construction process are inextricably engrained in the printed structure.

Corbel Cabin is a techno-archaic, ruin-esque, massive-primitive, and nearly anachronistic structure, which emerges from the recalibration and combination of machine-, material-, and people-informed construction processes. Contributing to disciplinary self-reflection by developing a comprehensive and ground-up methodology *from* tool to construction process to building, Corbel Cabin suggests alternate modes of design research at full scale.

ACKNOWLEDGMENTS

For this project, *HANNAH* and the *Cornell Robotic Construction Laboratory (RCL)* received generous support from: AAP College of Architecture, Art, and Planning, the AAP Department of Architecture at Cornell University, HY-Flex Corporation, and the David R. Atkinson Center for a Sustainable Future at Cornell University. Thank you to the research sponsors and all the academic student researchers at the Cornell Robotic Construction Laboratory (RCL).

REFERENCES

Bos, Freek, Rob Wolfs, Zeeshan Ahmed, and Theo Salet. 2016. "Additive Manufacturing of Concrete in Construction: Potentials and Challenges of 3D Concrete Printing." *Virtual and Physical Prototyping* 11 (3): 209–25.

Gosselin, Clément, Romain Duballet, Ph. Roux, Nadja Gaudillière, Justin Dirrenberger, and Ph. Morel. 2016. "Large-Scale 3D Printing of Ultra-High Performance Concrete: A New Processing Route for Architects and Builders." *Materials & Design* 100: 102–09.

10 The g-code and print path generate the pattern of the 3D-printed floor slabs (Floornament).

11 The printed formwork was designed in small sectional modules to be transported and assembled manually without the use of any heavy machinery.

Corbel Cabin Lok, Zivkovic

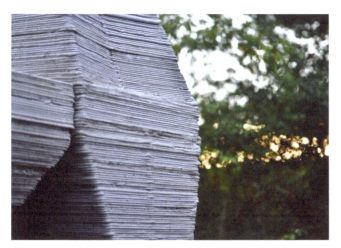

12 Reveal and joinery detail between components.

13 Assembly of concrete legs.

14 View of completed concrete structure.

15 "Low-tech" pile foundation construction method.

Khoshnevis, Behrokh. 2004. "Automated Construction by Contour Crafting: Related Robotics and Information Technologies." *Automation in Construction* 13 (1): 5–19.

Zivkovic, Sasa, and Christopher Battaglia. 2017. "Open Source Factory: Democratizing Large-Scale Fabrication Systems." In *Disciplines & Disruption: Proceedings of the 37th Annual Conference of the Association for Computer Aided Design in Architecture*, edited by Takehiko Nagakura, Skylar Tibbits, Mariana Ibanez, and Caitlin Mueller, 660–69. Cambridge, MA: ACADIA.

IMAGE CREDITS

Leslie Lok is assistant professor and B.Arch coordinator at Cornell University, where she teaches design studios and seminars with a focus on representation and urbanism. Lok is a co-principal at HANNAH, an experimental design practice for built and speculative projects across numerous scales. Hannah's work focuses on contemporary building practices and utilizes novel material applications and innovative construction methods to address subjects of architecture and urbanism. Allied with computational technology, Lok's research explores the intersection of housing, urbanization, and mass-customized construction methods at multiple scales.

Sasa Zivkovic is an assistant professor at Cornell University, where he directs the Robotic Construction Laboratory (RCL), an interdisciplinary research group investigating advanced materials and novel construction technology. Zivkovic is a co-principal of HANNAH, an architectural practice advancing traditional building construction techniques by implementing new technologies and processes of making to address subjects of construction, rapid urbanization, and mass customized housing design. In close collaboration with the high-tech building industry, HANNAH and RCL explore the implementation of construction techniques such as additive concrete manufacturing and robotic wood construction.

Ceramic Constellation Pavilion

Christian J. Lange
The University of Hong Kong

Donn Holohan
The University of Hong Kong

Holger Kehne
The University of Hong Kong

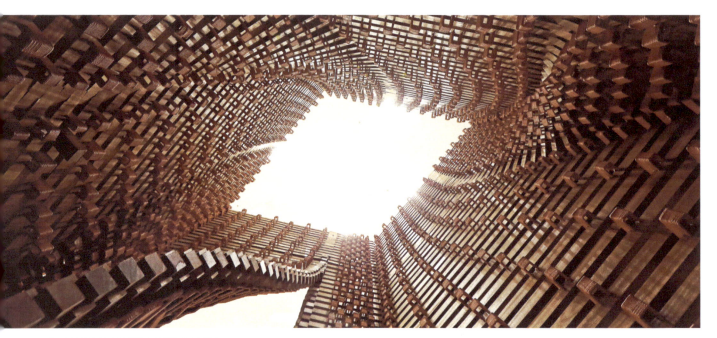

1 Interior perspective, worms-eye view.

Spatial Shifts through Robotically Fabricated Terracotta Bricks

The essential ingredient of ceramics is clay, a material that can be found in abundance throughout the lithosphere. Accessible, versatile, and easily shaped into a wide variety of forms, it offers both robustness and longevity once fired. One of the oldest and yet most enduring construction materials, the fired clay brick or tile has a particular and significant cultural tradition in China. The Iron Pagoda in Kaifeng City, Henan province (built in 1049), exemplifies this. Featuring more than fifty different types of brick specials on its exterior façade, the structure demonstrates the expressive, decorative, and performative potentials of its material system. However, with few exceptions in contemporary Chinese architecture, the materials' remaining territory in the building industry is diminished and has become limited to the use of homogeneous façade tiles.

The decline of this building culture can be seen as a product of China's rapid industrialization, the development of cheap, prefabricated, concrete and steel alternatives, and the high labor costs associated with traditional crafts. However, with advances in robotics and parametric digital design technologies, it has become possible to develop individualized construction and material systems at efficiencies close to those of more generic and standardized production lines. Integration of these new systems with traditional material systems offers a means by which to combine the best features of the traditional system with the economy of effort and labour delivered by modern digital processes.

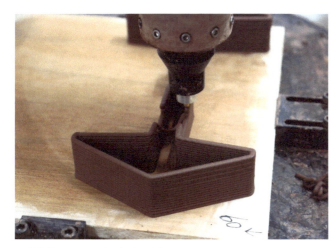

2 Printing process of a single brick.

4 DIW process with linear ram extruder attached to ABB 6700.

3 Printed bricks set for drying.

This project focuses on the rapidly developing technology of 3D printing, in tandem with an industry-standard industrial robotics platform. Traditionally, 3D printing has been utilized in small-scale manufacturing and rapid prototyping. Latterly however, many professionals in the industry are pushing for the development of large-scale printers capable of manufacturing entire houses, such as Enrico Dini with his D-Shape printer setup.

There are, however, limits to the application of this approach. Confronted with remote or difficult site conditions, lack of available expertise, or necessary technical support, the fabrication methodology could become restricted or impractical. The traditional brick module represents an alternative—lightweight and transportable, both the individual unit and the global form can be specifically designed to adapt to site conditions or user requirements. Further, embedded intelligence in the form of interlocking joints and graphic devices can overcome the complexities of constructing highly site specific, articulated structural or façade systems. Recent work by Ronald Rael

and Virginia San Fratello has demonstrated the opportunities presented by the non-standard module, illustrated in "Cabin of Curiosities" and "Bloom" (2017). Rather than focusing on novel materials, this research seeks to embrace an existing industrial base and material supply chain and to develop a system that can respond to its inherent variability (Lange, Holohan, and Kehne 2018).

The "Ceramic Constellation Pavilion" is part of a continuous research project that seeks to understand the potentials of new technologies to revive and optimize traditional material systems for architectural production today.

In this specific iteration, the research team explored the use of standard terracotta clay to produce brick specials. In a context that has been largely shaped by standardization and mass production, the project seeks to overcome the constraints of today's architectural production through the introduction of a structure made entirely of non-standard components.

RECALIBRATION ON IMPRECISION AND INFIDELITY

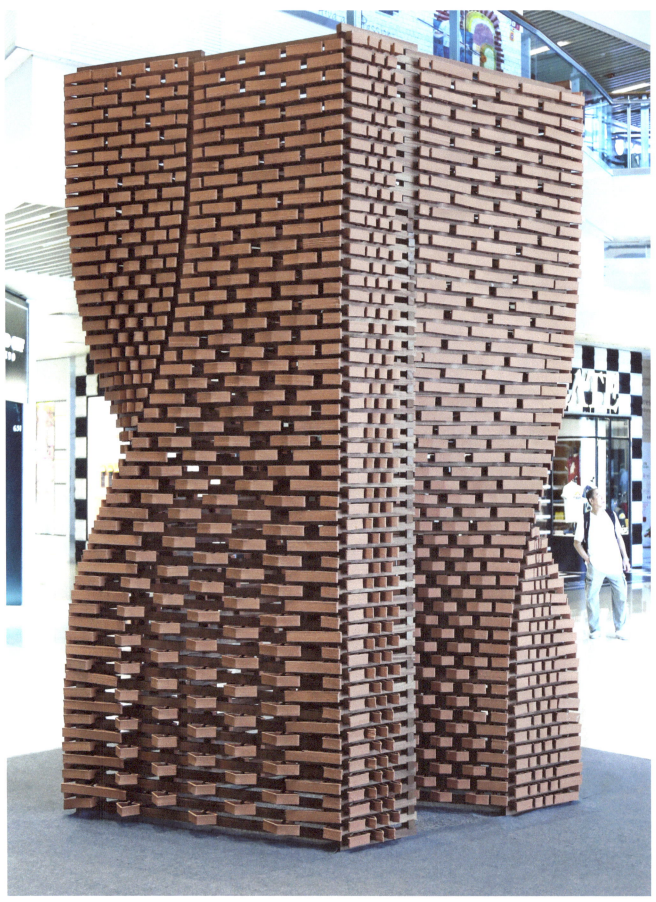

5   Pavilion in exhibition space.

Ceramic Constellation Pavilion Lange, Holohan, Kehne

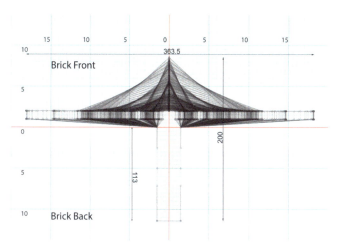

6   Superimposed outline of all bricks, top view.

7   Connection detail of special bricks with timber section.

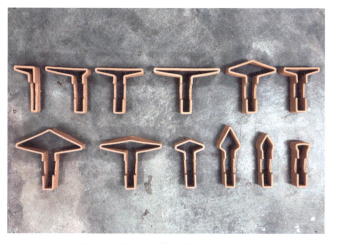

8   Random selection of continuous differentiated brick types.

9   Assembly process.

For the project, the team developed a specific design, manufacturing, and assembly methodology, which was based on a generative parametric design approach, while the manufacturing process involved 3D robotic clay printing in conjunction with CNC milling. Departing from traditional brick bonds, the 3.8 m tall project articulates a load-bearing composite structure, where each of the nearly 2,000 robotically printed terracotta bricks is unique and different, enabling varying degrees of transparency, morphological shifts, and new experiences. Around 700 kg of raw terracotta clay was printed over a period of 3 weeks into individual bricks that were then fired at 1,025° C. Over a period of six days, all components were assembled into three larger units, each weighing around 350 kg. These were then transported to the construction site and assembled with a crane.

The scale and antiquated nature of the brick industrial complex offers a significant opportunity for growth and redevelopment. The outlined project attempts to reconcile this imprecise material process with an innovative digital design approach and a robotic workflow, and to refocus attention on the advantages of one of the oldest material systems we have in architecture.

ACKNOWLEDGMENTS

The research project has been significantly supported by a donation from Sino Group. The design team for the Ceramic Constellation Pavilion consisted of Christian J. Lange, Donn Holohan, and Holger Kehne. The authors would like to thank the following students of the Department of Architecture at The University of Hong, who assisted in various aspects throughout the research: Tony Lau, Anthony Hu, Teego Ma Jun Yin, Ernest Hung Chi Lok, Chau Chi Wang, Ren Depei, Mono Tung, He Qiye, Henry Ho Yu Hong.

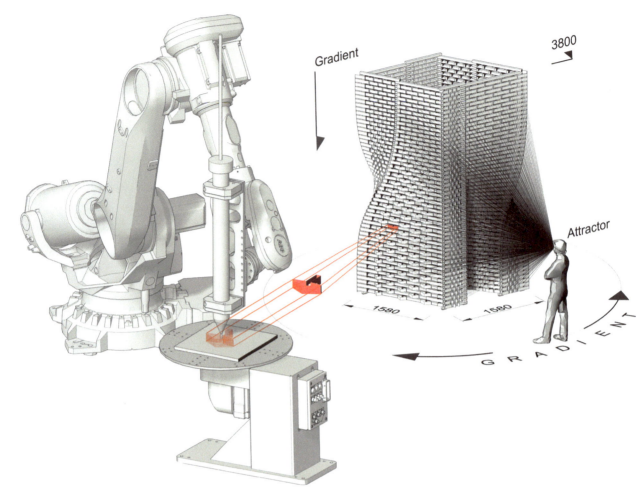

10 Concept diagram of production showing attractor influence for continuous brick differentiation .

REFERENCES

Dini, Enrico. 2013. Method and device for building automatically conglomerate structures CA 2602071 A1. US Patents. Retrieved 11 November 2013.

Lange, Christian, Donn Holohan, and Holger Kehne. 2018. In *Robotic Fabrication in Architecture, Art and Design*, edited by J. Willman, P. Block, M. Hutter, K. Byrne, and T. Schork. Cham, Switzerland: Springer.

Rael, Ronald, and Virginia San Fratello. 2017. "Clay Bodies: Crafting the Future with 3D Printing." *Architectural Design* 87 (6): 92–97.

———. 2018. *Printing Architecture*. New York: Princeton Architectural Press.

IMAGE CREDITS

Figures 1–9, 11 and 12: © Christian J. Lange, 2017

All other drawings and images by the authors.

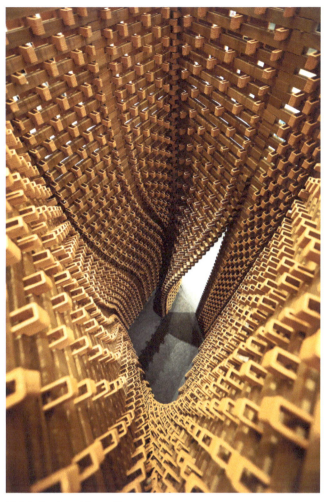

11 Exterior of pavilion, transitional brick pattern.

12 Interior view of the pavilion.

Christian J. Lange is a founding partner of Rocker-Lange Architects, a research and design practice based in Hong Kong and Boston. He is a registered German architect and Senior Lecturer in the Department of Architecture at the University of Hong Kong, where he teaches architectural design and classes in advanced digital modeling and robotics. A strong emphasis in his work is the implementation of computation and novel fabrication methods in the design and construction process. His work and research has been published internationally and featured in over 30 exhibits, including the Venice Biennale and the Hong Kong & Shenzhen Bi-city Biennale.

Donn Holohan is a designer and educator based in Hong Kong and Ireland. His work is primarily based on the potentials of emerging technology—not only as it relates to the practice of architecture, but also to the question of social and environmental sustainability. A founding partner of the multidisciplinary design studio Superposition, he is also currently working as Assistant Lecturer at the University of Hong Kong, where his teaching focuses on empowering designers to effectively engage with emerging

technologies through an increased understanding of both material and technical aspects of design.

Holger Kehne co-founded the experimental practice Plasma Studio 1999 in London after studying architecture in Germany and the UK, winning numerous accolades such as BD/ Corus' Young Architect of the Year Award and Architectural Record's Design Vanguard while completing a wide range of buildings, interiors and urban projects in Europe and China. He aims at engaging practice and academic research in unison, from 2002 to 2010 at the Architectural Association and since 2011 the University of Hong Kong. His research is context and material driven, exploring systemic relationships across scales, types, and registers.

RECALIBRATION ON IMPRECISION AND INFIDELITY

ACADIA 2018
MEXICO CITY CREDITS

RECALIBRATION ON IMPRECISION AND INFIDELITY

ACADIA
ORGANIZATION

The Association for Computer Aided Design in Architecture (ACADIA) is an international network of digital design researchers and professionals that facilitates critical investigations into the role of computation in architecture, planning, and building science, encouraging innovation in design creativity, sustainability and education.

ACADIA was founded in 1981 by some of the pioneers in the field of design computation including Bill Mitchell, Chuck Eastman, and Chris Yessios. Since then, ACADIA has hosted over 30 conferences across North America and has grown into a strong network of academics and professionals in the design computation field.

Incorporated in the state of Delaware as a not-for-profit corporation, ACADIA is an all-volunteer organization governed by elected officers, an elected Board of Directors, and appointed ex-officio officers.

PRESIDENT
Kathy Velikov _ *University of Michigan*
pres@acadia.org

VICE-PRESIDENT
Jason Kelly Johnson _ *California College of the Arts*
vp@acadia.org

SECRETARY
Mara Marcu _ *University of Cincinnati*
secretary@acadia.org

VICE-SECRETARY
Marcella Del Signore _ *New York Institute of Technology*

TREASURER
Mike Christenson _ *North Dakota State University*
treasurer@acadia.org

VICE-TREASURER
Jason Kelly Johnson _ *California College of the Arts*

MEMBERSHIP OFFICER
Phillip Anzalone _ *New York City College of Technology*
membership@acadia.org

TECHNOLOGY OFFICER
Andrew Kudless _ *California College of the Arts*
webmaster@acadia.org

DEVELOPMENT OFFICER
Alvin Huang _ *University of Southern California*
development@acadia.org

COMMUNICATION OFFICER
Adam Marcus _ *California College of the Arts*
communications@acadia.org

BOARD OF DIRECTORS
2017 (Term: Jan 2018 - Dec 2018)

Behnaz Farahi
Adam Marcus
Gilles Retsin
Jane Scott
Skylar Tibbits
Phillip Anzalone
Dana Cupkova
Mara Marcu
Jose Sanchez
Lauren Vasey
Manuel Jimenez Garcia *(alternate)*
Christoph Klemmt *(alternate)*
Gernot Riether *(alternate)*
Mike Christenson *(alternate)*
Marcella Del Signore *(alternate)*
Andrew John Wit *(alternate)*

CONFERENCE
MANAGEMENT

CONFERENCE CHAIRS

Pablo Kobayashi _ *Adjunct Professor, Department of Architecture, Urbanism and Civil Engineering, Universidad Iberoamericana / Principal, Protocolos*

Brian Slocum _ *Adjunct Professor, Department of Architecture, Urbanism and Civil Engineering, Universidad Iberoamericana / Principal, Diverse Projects*

TECHNICAL CHAIRS

Phillip Anzalone _ *Associate Professor of Architectural Technology, New York City College of Technology / Principal, aa64*

Marcella Del Signore _ *Associate Professor, School of Architecture & Design, New York Institute of Technology*

Andrew John Wit _ *Assistant Professor, Tyler School of Art, Temple University / Co-Founder, WITO**

WORKSHOPS CHAIRS

Jorge Ramírez _ *Founder, DNNV Media / Director, ANEMONAL*

Marcela Delgado _ *Associate Professor, Facultad de Arquitectura, Universidad Nacional Autónoma de México*

EXHIBITION CHAIRS

Pablo Iriarte _ *Computational Design, New York*

Irma Soler _ *Assistant Professor, Department of Architecture, Urbanism and Civil Engineering, Universidad Iberoamericana*

SPECIAL ADVISOR

José Luis Gutiérrez Brezmes _ *Director, Department of Architecture, Urbanism and Civil Engineering, Universidad Iberoamericana*

CONFERENCE ADVISOR

Jordan Geiger

EVENTS COORDINATOR

Alberto Vivar _ *Industrial Designer*

CONFERENCE ADMINISTRATIVE SUPPORT

Mirna De Paz _ *Department of Architecture, Urbanism and Civil Engineering, Universidad Iberoamericana*

Hilda Montalvo _ *Department of Architecture, Urbanism and Civil Engineering, Universidad Iberoamericana*

HOTEL LIAISONS

Israel García
Montserrat Martínez

WEBSITE

Phillip Anzalone
Raymundo Aramburu

COPY EDITING FOR PUBLICATION

Pascal Massinon
Mary O'Malley

GRAPHIC IDENTITY

Emilio Pérez

LAYOUT + DESIGN

Marcella Del Signore
Andrew John Wit

PUBLICATION EDITOR

Phillip Anzalone
Marcella Del Signore
Andrew John Wit

TRANSLATIONS

Gabriela Lee _ *Professor, Department of Architecture, Urbanism and Civil Engineering, Universidad Iberoamericana*
Brian Slocum
Pablo Kobayashi

UNIVERSIDAD IBEROAMERICANA (CONFERENCE ACADEMIC HOST)

Mtro. David Fernández Dávalos _ *S. J., Rector*

Mtro. José Antonio Morfín Rojas _ *Director de la División de Ciencia, Arte y Tecnología*

Mtra. Araceli Téllez Trejo _ *Directora General del Medio Universitario*

Mtro. Jorge Meza Aguilar _ *Director General de Vinculación Universitaria*

C. P. Leopoldo Navarro Flores _ *Director General Administrativo*

Mtro. José Luis Gutiérrez Brezmes _ *Director, Departamento de Arquitectura, Urbanismo e Ingeniería Civil*

Dra. Gabriela Estrada Díaz _ *Coordinadora, Departamento de Arquitectura, Urbanismo e Ingeniería Civil*

UNIVERSIDAD NACIONAL AUTÓNOMA DE MÉXICO (WORKSHOPS HOST)
Dr. Enrique Graue Wiechers _ *Rector*

Dr. Leonardo Lomelí Vanegas _ *Secretario General*

Ing. Leopoldo Silva Gutiérrez _ *Secretario Administrativo*

Dr. Alberto Ken Oyama Nakagawa _ *Secretario de Desarrollo Institucional*

Mtro. Javier de la Fuente Hernández _ *Secretario de Atención a la Comunidad Universitaria*

Dra. Mónica González Contró _ *Abogada General*

Mtro. Marcos Mazari Hiriart _ *Director de la Facultad de Arquitectura / Presidente Consejo Consultivo MUCA*

CONFERENCE STUDENT VOLUNTEERS, UNIVERSIDAD IBEROAMERICANA
Paulette Adamo _ *Coordinator*
Paolo Sarra _ *Coordinator*
Lucía Ortega _ *Coordinator*
Adrián Abarca
Gesche Capin
Juan José Corona
Emilio Hoppenstedt
Camila Martínez

Regina Moch
Daniel Morgenstern
Humberto Sánchez

WORKSHOPS VOLUNTEERS, UNIVERSIDAD NACIONAL AUTÓNOMA DE MÉXICO
Dr. Ronan Bolaños _ Associate Professor, Facultad de Arquitectura, Universidad Nacional Autónoma de México
Carlos Ruz
Erik Molina
Victor Pineda
Gabriela Manzano
Isaac Medina
Santiago García

RECALIBRATION ON IMPRECISION AND INFIDELITY

PEER REVIEW
COMMITTEE

Henri Achten _ *Czech Technical University in Prague*
Sean Ahlquist _ *The University of Michigan*
Viola Ago _ *University of Michigan*
Chandler Ahrens _ *Washington University in St. Louis*
Rima Ajlouni _ *University of Utah*
Masoud Akbarzadeh _ *The University of Pennsylvania*
Aysegul Akcay Kavakoglu _ *Istanbul Kemerburgaz University*
Sema Alaçam _ *Istanbul Technical University*
Suleiman Alhadidi _ *The University of New South Wales*
Iman Ansari _ *University of Nevada, Las Vegas*
Anna Anton _ *ETH Zurich*
Phillip Anzalone _ *aa64, NYC College of Technology*
German Aparicio _ *Gehry Technologies*
Imdat As _ *The University of Hartford*
Peter Atwood _ *Boston Architectural College*
Phil Ayres _ *CITA / KADK*
Joshua Bard _ *Carnegie Mellon University*
Stephanie Bayard _ *Pratt Institute*
David Benjamin _ *Columbia University*
Chris Beorkrem _ *The University of North Carolina at Charlotte*
Kory Bieg _ *The University of Texas*
Johannes Braumann _ *Robots in Architecture*
Danelle Briscoe _ *The University of Texas*
Mario Carpo _ *Bartlett UCL*
Alejandro M. Castellanos _ *Pontifical Catholic University of Puerto Rico*
Goncalo Castro Henriques _ *Federal University of Rio de Janeiro*
Panagiotis Chatzitsakyris _ *UNStudio*
Mike Christenson _ *North Dakota State University*
Joseph Choma _ *Clemson University*
Angelos Chronis _ *Institute of Advanced Architecture of Catalonia*
Brandon Clifford _ *Massachusetts Institute of Technology*
Kristof Crolla _ *Chinese University of Hong Kong*
Jason Crow _ *Louisiana State University*
Dana Cupkova _ *Carnegie Mellon University*
Pierre Cutellic _ *CAAD ITA D-ARCH ETHz*
Mahesh Daas _ *University of Kansas*
Martyn Dade-Robertson _ *Newcastle University*
Daniel Davis _ *WeWork*
Martina Decker _ *New Jersey Institute of Technology*
Matias del Campo _ *University of Michigan*
Marcela Delgado _ *Universidad Nacional Autónoma de México*

Marcella Del Signore _ *New York Institute of Technology*
Antonino Di Raimo _ *University of Portsmouth*
Nancy Diniz _ *Rensselaer Polytechnic Institute*
Mark Donohue _ *California College of the Arts*
Jefferson Ellinger _ *The University of North Carolina at Charlotte*
Emre Erkal _ *Harvard University*
Alberto T. Estévez _ *iBAG/ESARQ - UIC Barcelona*
Behnaz Farahi _ *University of Southern California*
Thom Faulders _ *California College of the Arts*
Wendy Fok _ *Parsons School of Design*
Michael Fox _ *Cal Poly Pomona*
Pia Fricker _ *ETH Zurich, Aalto University*
Madeline Gannon _ *Carnegie Mellon University*
Manuel Jimenez Garcia _ *UCL The Bartlett School of Architecture*
Jordan Geiger _ *University at Buffalo*
David Gerber _ *University of Southern California*
Marcelyn Gow _ *Southern California Institute of Architecture*
Kimo Griggs _ *University of Washington*
Yasha Grobman _ *Technion - Israel Institute of Technology*
Derya Gulec Ozer _ *Yildiz Technical University*
Onur Gun _ *New Balance Athletics Inc.*
Erik Herrmann _ *Ohio State University*
Justine Holzman _ *University of Toronto*
Alvin Huang _ *University of Southern California*
Michael Jefferson _ *University of Michigan*
Jason Scott Johnson _ *University of Calgary*
Nathaniel Jones _ *Arup*
Sawako Kaijima _ *Harvard University*
Gabriel Kaprielian _ *Temple University*
Neil Katz _ *Skidmore, Owings & Merrill LLP*
Edward Keller _ *Parsons School of Design*
James Kerestes _ *Ball State University*
Ted Kesik _ *University of Toronto*
Sumbul Khan _ *Singapore University of Technology and Design*
Axel Kilian _ *Princeton University*
Jihun Kim _ *CUNY - NYC College of Technology*
Christoph Klemmt _ *University of Cincinnati*
Pablo Kobayashi _ *Universidad Iberoamericana*
Tuba Kocaturk _ *Deakin University*
Reinhard Koenig _ *Bauhaus-University Weimar*
Branko Kolarevic _ *University of Calgary*
Axel Körner _ *University of Stuttgart*
Sotirios Kotsopoulos _ *National Technical University of Greece*

RECALIBRATION ON IMPRECISION AND INFIDELITY

Kihong Ku _ *Jefferson*

Andrew Kudless _ *California College of the Arts*

Carla Leitao _ *Rensselaer Polytechnic Institute*

Brian Lilley _ *Dalhousie University*

Pablo Lorenzo-Eiroa _ *The Cooper Union*

Russell Loveridge _ *ETH Zurich*

Gregory Luhan _ *University of Kentucky*

Ryan Manning _ *University of Texas at Arlington*

Sandra Manninger _ *University of Michigan*

Mara Marcu _ *University of Cincinnati*

Adam Marcus _ *California College of the Arts*

Bob Martins _ *TU Wien*

Duane McLemore _ *Woodbury University*

Alexis Meier _ *Insa de Strasbourg*

Frank Melendez _ *City College of New York*

Annalisa Meyboom _ *University of British Columbia*

Nathan Miller _ *Proving Ground LLC*

Sina Mostafavi _ *TU Delft*

Volker Mueller _ *Bentley Systems, Incorporated*

Taro Narahara _ *New Jersey Institute of Technology*

Andrei Nejur _ *University of Pennsylvania*

Tsz Yan Ng _ *University of Michigan*

Ted Ngai _ *Pratt Institute*

Marta Anna _ *Nowak UCLA*

Betul Orbey _ *Dogus University*

Guvenc Ozel _ *UCLA*

Marialuisa Palumbo _ *inarch*

Dimitris Papanikolaou _ *University of North Carolina–Charlotte*

Ju Hong Park _ *University of Miami*

Vera Parlac _ *University of Calgary*

Andy Payne _ *Autodesk*

Maria Rita Perbellini _ *New York Institute of Technology*

Santiago Perez _ *University of Nebraska–Lincoln*

Brady Peters _ *University of Toronto*

Chris Perry _ *Rensselaer Polytechnic Institute*

Nick Pisca _ *0001D LLC*

Christian Pongratz _ *New York Institute of Technology*

Ebrahim Poustinchi _ *Kent State University*

Marshall Prado _ *University of Tennessee*

Clemens Preisinger _ *University of Applied Arts Vienna*

Brian Price _ *California College of the Arts*

Maya Przybylski _ *University of Waterloo*

Nicholas Puckett _ *OCAD University*

Gilles Retsin _ *UCL The Bartlett School of Architecture*

Gernot Riether _ *New Jersey Institute of Technology*

Siobhan Rockcastle _ *EPFL*

Jose Sanchez _ *University of Southern California*

Simon Schleicher _ *University of California, Berkeley*

Marc Aurel Schnabel _ *Victoria University of Wellington*

Mathew Schwartz _ *New Jersey Institute of Technology*

Jane Scott _ *The University of Leeds*

Bob Sheil _ *UCL The Bartlett School of Architecture*

Brian Slocum _ *Universidad Iberoamericana*

Aldo Sollazzo _ *IAAC*

José Pedro Sousa _ *University of Porto*

Bjorn Sparrman _ *Massachusetts Institute of Technology*

David Stasiuk _ *Proving Ground*

Satoru Sugihara _ *Southern California Institute of Architecture*

Martin Tamke _ *The Royal Danish Academy of Fine Arts*

Joshua Taron _ *University of Calgary*

Oliver Tessmann _ *TU Darmstadt*

Geoff Thun _ *University of Michigan*

Skylar Tibbits _ *Massachusetts Institute of Technology*

Matthew Trimble _ *American University of Sharjah*

Carmen Trudell _ *Cal Poly San Luis Obispo*

Richard Tursky _ *Ball State University*

Graziano M. Valenti _ *Sapienza Università di Roma*

Lauren Vasey _ *University of Stuttgart*

Kathy Velikov _ *University of Michigan*

Joshua Vermillion _ *University of Nevada, Las Vegas*

Emily White _ *Cal Poly San Luis Obispo*

Aaron Willette _ *WeWork*

Andrew John Wit _ *Temple University + wito**

Robert Woodbury _ *Simon Fraser University*

Maria Yablonina _ *University of Stuttgart*

Shai Yeshayahu _ *University of Nevada, Las Vegas*

Christine Yogiaman _ *SUTD*

Lei Yu _ *Tsinghua University*

Machi Zawidzki _ *Polish Academy of Sciences*

RECALIBRATION ON IMPRECISION AND INFIDELITY

SPONSORS *2018*

Zaha Hadid Architects

RECALIBRATION
O   N IMPR   ECISION
AND IN   FID ELITY

Projects Catalog of the 38th Annual Conference of the Association
for Computer Aided Design in Architecture

UNIVERSIDAD IBEROAMERICANA, MEXICO CITY

Editors
Phillip Anzalone, Marcella Del Signore + Andrew John Wit

acadia   IBERO

www.ingramcontent.com/pod-product-compliance
Lightning Source LLC
Chambersburg PA
CBHW041426050326
40689CB00003B/678